LOVE BITES

JULIE SINGLETON

LOVE BITES
First published in Australia by Julie Singleton 2018
www.juliesingleton.com

Copyright © Julie Singleton 2018
All Rights Reserved

ISBN: 978-0-6484105-0-8 (pbk)
ISBN: 978-0-6484105-1-5 (ebk)
Prepublication Data Service details available
from The National Library of Australia

Book cover design by James, GoOnWrite.com © 2018

Typesetting and design by Publicious Book Publishing
Published in collaboration with Publicious Book Publishing
www.publicious.com.au

To Catherine Hale for her unconditional
support and encouragement.

Prologue

1983

Apparently, Sarah was a very lucky girl. Her parents had died in a car accident and she was just taken away from what was left of her family, just her brother and her grandmother, but she knew she was expected to be grateful. Her lucky break was that she had won a scholarship to attend an elite private girl's boarding school. Supposedly, this was something that someone like Sarah should show her appreciation for, not hide under her bed so they could not find her.

Sarah could hear her grandmother calling out her name in a combination of her broken English with her Chinese accent. She was walking around the house shouting "Sala" because she just could not pronounce the "r". This always brought a smile to Sarah's face.

Her brother came into her room. He knew her hiding spot as well as she did. Instead of yelling at Sarah, like he usually did, he knelt and tilted his head under the bed.

"You are upsetting Grandma, Sarah," he whispered. "They have convinced her you should go there, so you should at least try it. If you don't like it there, then I promise I will help you to run away and come back." Sarah crawled out from under the bed and for the first time in a long time, she saw the sincerity in her brother's eyes. "I will miss you," he said, "but Grandma will miss you more. They told us you could call home every Friday night and come home in the school holidays. The first holiday is at Easter which is not far away."

Her grandmother walked into the room and when Sarah saw her, relief flashed across her face like a pop-up ad on the Internet. "The lady is here to take you to school. I miss you already, but you know your father wanted this for you. You are a lucky girl to get this chance. Remember that I am always with you Sarah, no matter where you are." She looked into Sarah's eyes. "Sometimes, when you love someone you have to let them go. I am sorry our time has come earlier than we were ready for." She held out her hand, which Sarah took, and they walked to the front door with her suitcase. Sarah let go of her grandmother's hand and walked to the lady. The lady guided her out of the house and into a waiting car.

Sarah

Chapter 1

1983

Sarah waited for her parents to come home every night. For a child, she worried far too much about her parents and about everyone else, but then as her grandmother kept telling her, she was "a good girl." Although they now lived in Australia, her grandmother, who had the daily care of her and her brother while her parents worked, was Chinese. Both her grandmother and her mother, who was also Chinese, instilled in Sarah their traditional beliefs of the role of a good Chinese girl.

Her grandmother often talked to Sarah and her brother about her life in Hong Kong. She had told them stories about her life there, describing how different her life was to theirs and how lucky they were to be living in Australia. Her grandfather had died before Sarah was born, so she had never met him.

Sarah's family moved to Australia from Hong Kong after her father's term in the military had ended. It had always been her parents' intention to do so, believing that Australia would provide better opportunities. Her grandmother had come with them to help her parents while they established themselves. She did not speak a word of English when she arrived, and her mother spoke English with a heavy Chinese accent, which her father affectionately described as "Chinglish".

Every night after dinner, Sarah would sit staring out of the lounge room window, propped up against the back of the lounge. Her dark lashed violet eyes would widen with hope when car lights loomed past the house, breaking the darkness and stillness of the evening.

Sarah loved the night sky. She thought it was beautiful, dark, with it's basketful of stars sparkling above her. Sarah could not explain her anxiety about her parents' safety, but for an unknown reason since arriving in Australia, she could not go to sleep until her parents had come home.

If it was a lucky day, they would come home early enough so that she could talk to them before she went to bed. There were not many lucky days anymore. After eating dinner, which her grandmother had prepared for them, and then doing her home- work, she would sit in the lounge room and wait until she heard her parents' car pull into the driveway.

Her parents worked seven days a week as they had arrived with no employment or qualifications. It was difficult, as her father's experience in the military was of no use in the work- force. He took a position to work for free for three months to finally get in the door of a real estate agency and her mother worked as a cleaner. Sarah held on to and treasured the rare and special days when her parents came home before bedtime and had dinner with them. Sometimes on a Friday, if her father got to come home from work early, he would let her sit on his knee in the lounge room while they watched the news and just talked. She knew when she was with her father that she could talk about anything and be her brother's equal. It was different with her mother and grandmother, and her father knew it. Sarah knew never to bring it up.

And so, that night in 1984, Sarah maintained her nightly vigil, patiently waiting, her anxiety only to be quelled by the sound of tyres on the gravel driveway. That sound did not arrive until early the next morning, and it was not her parents who arrived at her home.

Sarah

Chapter 2

It was Sunday afternoon and, as usual, Sarah was at her office. She had just finished drafting emails to two of her most demanding clients, updating them on their respective matters. One of the emails was to a repeat client, Phillip Thompson, who preferred to be called "Phil". He had first retained Sarah as his divorce lawyer ten years ago. One of his secretary's jobs was to alert Sarah when the statutory time limit for his current girlfriend was approaching the limit for defacto status, giving the girlfriend standing to make a family law claim against him, so that Sarah could intervene. These emails were always difficult to word diplomatically, and the trick was always to make these powerful and successful men feel that they were in control, not Sarah.

It was a beautiful September evening and Sarah looked out the window to the turquoise water on the harbour spangled with sail boats and ferries. The view always had a calming influence on her while she reflected on her clients' turbulent lives.

One of the cases she had coming up for hearing in the Family Court had been one of the most unpredictable cases in her career. Both her client and her client's ex-husband were wonderful parents but, due to a family tragedy where their son had died after a snow skiing accident, they hated each other. This placed the judge in a very difficult position as joint parenting was obviously not an option. There was no alternative for the judge but to award the children to one parent and alternate weekends to the other. It was one of the few cases where Sarah could not predict the judge's preference for primary carer of the children, but whoever it was to be awarded to, Sarah knew the other parent would be devastated. She felt guilty that she did not want it to be her client, as her client's former husband was a lovely man and a wonderful father.

Sarah's new offices were what she had coveted since she started work as a junior lawyer, twenty years earlier. She was relieved that the days of wood-paneled walls and bookshelves were gone and so the look in her office was slick and streamlined, with leather and chrome furniture, polished marble floors and white, stone-washed walls displaying beautifully lit, over-sized paintings by famous Australian artists. Of course, there were also the magnificent floral arrangements, which arrived every Monday morning and were the size of small forests. Sarah felt the flowers softened the coldness of being in an office building.

The reception area was large, open and impressive. Sarah's own office could be reached through the main reception area but also through her own exclusive access. Sarah had carefully designed her office to include everything she had ever wanted, her own conference room, lounge area with wine fridge, walk-in wardrobe area and her own bathroom complete with a shower. Her office wardrobe held two Armani business suits, a cocktail dress, evening dress and even jeans and tops to cater for any occasion that arose.

The sound of the alarm on her mobile phone jolted Sarah back to reality. Looking at the time, she saw it was now 6pm, leaving her only an hour before she was due home. She walked over to her office fridge and poured herself a glass of wine. Regaining her focus, Sarah returned to her computer screen. As she was finishing the email, Sarah heard from outside snatches of the somnolent layers of the city's Sunday switching off, the distant murmurs of late night diners and the slowing frequency of tyres on bitumen.

Having completed her emails and advices, Sarah logged onto the office internal system to oversee all the current cases in the office. She kept a close eye on all her employed solicitors and the cases she had them working on. She would usually not leave the office on Sunday night until she satisfied herself that the week ahead would run smoothly for the entire office and their clients. After checking all the matters, luckily all was in order for her to go home, as she had promised her daughter Chloe, for dinner at 7 pm tonight.

Geoffrey

Chapter 3

Geoffrey Pemberton was a forty-two-year-old trust fund baby, who had unsurprisingly recently separated from his wife. He arrived at the restaurant in his chauffeured limousine and was shown to his regular table. As one of the restaurant's best customers, Geoffrey was always treated as a VIP. His girlfriend, Amber, would without fail arrive at least thirty minutes late, which always annoyed him.

The waiter came up to the table. "The usual, Geoffrey?"

Geoffrey nodded with a smile, while slinging the waiter a large cash tip. The chilled bottle of French Chablis arrived swiftly thereafter, complete with ice bucket.

Geoffrey knew Amber was going to bring something up today. He had known it as soon as he heard that tone in her voice on the phone this morning. Since they had been together, Amber had gone from barmaid to a life of luxury. He knew from experience though that the gratitude did not last long. He had often lamented to his mates that women quickly grew used to the good things in life and then stopped being grateful. Instead, they just started to expect them.

Geoffrey thought his wife Katrina was the answer to his problems when he married her. His major problem was that he could not be satisfied with just one woman in his life and this got him into trouble time and time again. With Katrina though, because she was so loyal and trusting, he was able to fool around. Foolishly, he thought this would allow him the best of both worlds. He justified his behaviour to himself by believing that if he had the money to keep the party girls entertained and the wife happy, both very generously, he was justified in his lifestyle.

At the start of his relationship with Katrina, when she never asked where he was going or when he was coming back from his business trips, he had thought she was the perfect woman for him. Either she was smart in giving him his freedom or just plain stupid, but whichever, she seemed perfect. Predictably for Geoffrey, after a few years he realised she was not only plain stupid but also plain fucking boring. Initially, he had been attracted to her innocence and complete trust of him, but now, apart from the boredom, the freedom just made it easier for him to have flings and affairs.

It had dawned on him that part of the best sex of his former marriages was after he had fought with his wives. But with Katrina he never fought. He thought he wanted a peaceful life and realised now that was the worst angle possible for him. His favourite saying was, "Marriage means till death do us part; so I prefer divorce."

Amber strolled into the restaurant thirty-five minutes late, just as Geoffrey was being poured his third glass of wine. She sat down and Geoffrey could tell by her body language and by what she was wearing, that she was poised to lecture him on what she needed or wanted next.

"Okay Amber, what do you want now? I can tell that you are here on a mission. So what is it?"

Amber looked offended. "You know what Geoffrey? You are always on the attack!"

"Amber, you have that look on your face. You're dressed like you would fuck me on top of this table and you walked in like you wanted to hit someone. I know when you want something, so what the fuck is it this time?"

Amber looked shocked that Geoffrey had even noticed how she was dressed, let alone the look on her face or how she walked. "I love you and I just want what is normal for any woman. You have been separated for six months now and you've not started a settlement with her. I want you to finalise it with her and get a divorce. You said you would marry me but how can you if you won't divorce her?"

"Can't this wait?" he asked her. "I will get a settlement done, but I don't need to push it just now."

Amber quickly realised she needed to put on her charm if she were to get her way with Geoffrey. She changed tone and in a concerned voice said to him, "I've found you the best lawyer in town, honey. You know you deserve the best. I was only able to get you in to see her this week because of a cancellation, otherwise the wait is over a month. I know she is the best divorce lawyer around because she acted for my ex-husband and she wiped the floor with me, even though I was told I had the best lawyer in Sydney. She made him look like a complete beginner. She will get Katrina in line and we might even get the kids with this lawyer. She took my kids away from me and now you can retain her to get your kids for us. You know what they say; don't get mad, get even!"

Geoffrey started laughing at Amber as he said, "You want custody of my kids? What the hell? You don't like kids. I thought we agreed that life sucks living in a childcare centre. That's why I left Katrina. I don't want to live in a childcare centre anymore!" "We don't want the kids stupid! But if we get custody, she will get less of your money. Then having beaten her down financially, we give the kids back or at the very least, if we scare her about losing the kids she may agree to take less money anyway. The poor stupid bitch will be so grateful she gets to keep them that she won't fight any more and you'll get them when you want. No more of this trying to compromise with the bitch and go to mediation and counselling in the best interests of the children crap."

Geoffrey stared at Amber intently while a smile started to spread across his face. He reached over and grabbed Amber's head in his right hand weaving her hair tightly in his fingers and pulling her towards him as he kissed her passionately. "I remember why I love you, you are a fucking evil bitch!"

Geoffrey knew Amber stirred up desires in him that he thought had gone long ago. She was so damaged that she was evil. Amber would do anything to keep him because she had rat cunning. She was as slippery as a rattle snake and as tough as an old football. She made him feel alive and even excited when she was like this. He had not felt like this for a long time. It would not last - he knew that it never did. But he knew that to keep girls like Amber hooked, a guy had to tell lies about a relationship and marriage. It would work until it stopped working, and then he would move on.

Amber looked very pleased with herself and knew she would be able to close the deal with Geoffrey. She would have her Prince Charming and live happily ever after, with no more worries. She put her hand on Geoffrey's leg and started to move her hand knowingly up and down his inner thigh, finally resting it in the middle of his lap. She felt his reaction as he smiled and looked into her eyes.

"But don't forget, Amber." Geoffrey lifted her hand briefly. "I haven't been divorced before without learning a thing or two. I know what to do and I know how to get her out of the house. I know how to get Katrina to settle and it will cost less in legal fees than your plan. Just trust me."

"I do trust you, Geoffrey, but see this lawyer for the appointment. Even if you think you have the plan sorted you should go and see her, so your wife can't use her. Let me tell you, she is a nightmare to have against you. My ex smirked the whole time we were in court, while she smashed me and my legal team against the wall."

"Well, if she's that good, I should make sure Katrina doesn't use her. I 've yet to meet a male lawyer that I think has balls, let alone a woman. They all talk the talk, but when it comes to the crunch they never deliver. I've negotiated, or rather maneuvered and then negotiated, all my deals and just used the lawyer as a front to do the paperwork that accountants and lawyers insist on." Amber laughed as she replied, "She's as tough as steel Geoffrey. At first glance she looks stunningly beautiful, but then when she gets closer she is the ice maiden; dark, tough and cold. Very quickly the mood in the room changes, the air turns to ice and you feel the knives she is throwing start to pierce you."

"I'm starting to get turned on by what you are saying about this lawyer. Sexy and tough is a rare combination in a woman, let alone a female lawyer." There was nothing that turned Geoffrey on more than an intelligent woman. The only problem was, he thought, intelligent women were usually plain and boring or just as ugly as all fuck. The idea of getting turned on by a woman with a brain and a hot body was starting to consume him.

Jealous, Amber hit Geoffrey on the arm. "She is going to be your lawyer and that's all! Don't even think about looking at her in any other way." Without thinking, Amber added, "And you know what? I can't imagine you would interest her at all. She is worth millions and she's a celebrity."

When Amber saw the thunderous look on Geoffrey's face, she knew she had gone too far. He glared at her and she felt as though shards of glass were piercing her. He snarled, "Don't you fucking think anyone would be interested in me if they had a dollar and were a celebrity too? You think I can't get a woman like that? You are a fucking idiot, Amber. I can get anyone I want and always do. Usually women who are rich or well-known bore the fuck out of me. If this woman is half as interesting as you say she is, I may decide to go for her and if I do then I will, and nothing you can say will have any influence over that. You need to start really understanding our relationship, Amber. You do what you are told and what I want, and everything will be fine. If you think you can make decisions or do my thinking for me, you will quickly regret it."

Amber froze and fought the urge to burst into tears. She knew that crying would irritate him more. She was seeing a side of Geoffrey that scared her and she believed him when he told her that she had no choice but to put up with whatever he wanted.

Geoffrey swiftly pulled her towards him and kissed her roughly. He bit her lip so hard that when he pulled away, Amber felt blood welling on the inside of her mouth and trickling down her chin. She watched him smile at her with an evil look in his eyes.

He picked up the serviette, gently dabbed at her lip and said in a caring tone, "You have a bleeding lip, Amber," as he wiped the blood away.

Amber was frozen to the spot. She knew not to move or say anything.

The waiter came over and handed them both a menu. Geoffrey handed the menus back and said to the waiter, "Sorry, mate. We must leave. Just put it on my tab with the usual tip." Geoffrey then leaned over to Amber, dug his fingers into her arm to pull her up from the table and taunted, "Why are we leaving now honey? Because you just couldn't wait to fuck me. Isn't that right, darling?"

Amber stood up and walked next to Geoffrey while he kept a firm hold on her arm. Although she was scared, she could not help but feel excited when she was with him. His forcefulness and control turned her on even though she did not want to be turned on. She had never felt like this before and she knew she was becoming addicted to it. She could feel her body already reacting to his hold on her arm and she sensed he knew it too.

Geoffrey turned his head and saw the raw desire in Amber's eyes. It excited him even more. The fact that the way he treated her excited her, turned him on like nothing before. When he was hurting Amber, he saw the fear in Amber's eyes but at the same time, he felt her excitement, from being controlled and hurt, of being in pain and in fear. She loved it and he loved doing it to her. Right now, he knew she was aching for him. He felt his own excitement while he planned what he was going to do to her, starting in the car.

As they walked out onto the street Geoffrey's driver was waiting patiently beside the car. The driver opened the car door and Geoffrey pushed Amber roughly onto the back seat, resulting in her hitting her head on the side of the door. While Amber was lying on the seat holding her head, Geoffrey lifted her dress and ripped off her panties. Amber screamed with the shock of the movement and Geoffrey slapped her hard across the face. "Shut the fuck up. You want me, bitch," he said, whilst undoing his pants with his other hand. As he thrust himself inside her, Amber groaned and dug her nails into his back. "Scratch me, bitch. Hurt me," he said, and then he wrapped his hands around her throat until she blacked out.

Brett

Chapter 4

It was the best and worst time in Brett's life right now. He was about to reach the pinnacle of success in his career and he was passionately in love with the woman in the bed beside him. The problem with this perfect picture was that he was married to another woman, Jane, with whom he had two little girls, and they had just bought and moved into the dream home he had been working towards all his life. After sleeping in and then ordering room service, he casually flicked through his emails on his mobile. One of them was from his best friend, to whom he had confided his marital problems. This friend had recommended he go and see a family lawyer named Sarah Walters to get urgent advice. His friend urged him to do it ASAP, just in case Jane got to Sarah first, as he would be "begging for mercy" after that lawyer had finished with him.

Brett thought it was amusing that Dane would think Jane capable of anything like that. Firstly, poor Jane had no idea about Lisa, the girl in his bed, and he had already spoken to another friend, a lawyer, who had started putting things in place for him to have a smooth financial exit. As he was about to put his phone down, it pinged and an urgent email came through from his office. After reading it, Brett got up out of bed abruptly and paced the room, mumbling to himself.

"Why the fuck would they call a board meeting in two hours when they knew I was on leave?" Brett was annoyed and mumbling to himself, but knew he had no choice but to attend.

Two hours later, Brett strode into the boardroom looking like he owned it. He made obvious his anger at being summoned by his business partners to an urgent meeting at such short notice. Brett was the last one to arrive in the boardroom. He had dressed to kill in his couture suit, immaculately manicured hair and polished shoes. He was making it clear that someone was going to pay for him having to attend a meeting during his leave. Coffee and tea had already been served and the other board members were deep in conversation. At Brett's arrival, they all swung around and looked at him. By the looks on their faces Brett knew there was trouble. It did not worry him though; he was used to it. He decided to go on the attack before they did.

Once he reached the board table, Brett remained standing. He leaned forward, spread his hands on the table, then with one fist thumped a staccato on the French polished wood, demanding aggressively, "What is going on here guys? Why the fuck did you call me in when you knew I was on leave for three days? What is so fucking urgent that it couldn't wait?"

The company CEO, Ian Hammersmith and his right-hand man, Tim Breen, were sitting at the opposite end of the table. At Brett's outburst, Ian stood up. His reply was stern but patient, "We are aware you were on leave for three days, Brett. What you failed to disclose was that instead of being home to help your wife move into your new house, which was the reason you told us you needed to take some time off, you were in fact away on a trip with your PA."

Brett burst out laughing and then angrily responded, "And what the fuck does that have to do with you or the Board? It's none of your business what the fuck I do in my private life!"

Ian walked around the table and stood directly in front of Brett. Ian knew how to handle Brett and he spoke in a very controlled voice, "If you think that your reckless behaviour, which can only lead to a divorce, when we are amid one of the biggest deals of our careers is none of our business, that's bullshit! If your wife finds out about Lisa and decides to divorce you right now or in the next six months, it could blow up everything we have been working towards for the last ten years. You've not even tried to hide this fucking affair, you stupid prick. Why fuck your PA? She's telling everyone in this office that you're going to leave your wife." "I don't believe Lisa has told anyone about us," Brett replied, somewhat mollified.

"You idiot!" snapped Ian, hanging his head at Brett's stupidity. "She is telling the other secretaries so as to justify having an affair with a married man with two young children, because they are telling her she is an idiot!"

"How did you find out?" Brett asked, more calmly. He was starting to feel uncomfortable with what was being disclosed to him.

Ian laughed loudly and derisively, "You can't be serious Brett? You haven't even tried to be discreet. We all thought you would come to your senses, but to leave Jane with two little girls, to move to a new house alone, shows you are an arrogant prick and pussy whipped by Lisa."

Brett was stung as he responded back, "What fucking well gives you the right to comment on how I run my personal life and my marriage? You guys have no fucking right to do that."

"Oh yes we do Brett when it could affect our business! If Jane leaves you, her lawyers could issue subpoenas and injunctions and cause the same mess we went through with Daniel's divorce, five years ago. Don't you remember? That caused so many problems that it nearly forced us to pull out of the deal. Now here we are about to finalise the biggest project the firm has been involved in and you may be putting us in the same position again!"

Brett sat down. He had forgotten about Daniel's divorce and the problems it had caused. The endless subpoenas and injunctions from the wife's lawyers almost brought the business to a standstill. Whilst their business deals demanded confidentiality, any exposure was dangerous.

"I actually forgot about that, Ian. I'm sorry, but there's no problem. Really, Jane would never do that to me. She is not like that."

Ian returned to his chair, his anger abating now that Brett seemed to have finally understood the gravity of the situation. The other partners had all just been sitting back in their chairs, almost enjoying the sparring between Brett and Ian. Some of them understood that, should their private lives be investigated, they too would be on the receiving end of this lecture from Ian. None of them was an angel, but none of them was being as stupid as Brett. He had committed the ultimate management mistake of sleeping with a member of staff.

Ian placed his hands firmly on the table, emphasising his power and control. In a more modulated voice he laid out a number of demands. "Brett, the Board is asking you to end your relationship with Lisa. Having an affair is bad enough but having a relationship with an employee is outrageous. It is causing turmoil in the office. This affair has exposed us to possible legal action by Lisa, and may lead Jane to seek a divorce, which would have a devastating impact on our latest deal. This has to end Brett and if you don't agree to it, then you need to leave the partnership, so we are protected against your insanity."

Brett sank further into his chair. He covered his face with his hands and leaned forward, his elbows resting on the table.

Ian continued, "Brett, you have not thought this through. You have just bought the house you have coveted your whole life, you have two beautiful little girls and a wife who adores you. You are having an affair with your PA and you are deluding yourself that Jane will do nothing if she finds out. We need to face the position you are exposing us to."

Brett dropped his hands from his ashen face and replied with resignation, "Okay, I get it." Shaking his head, he said, "I will fix this. I get what you are saying and I will fix this."

"Go home then Brett. Go home and help Jane with the move. She is your wife and the mother of your little girls. We can all be shits to our wives at times Brett but think of your kids. There are limits to the conduct this Board will accept."

Brett rose from the table and said with determination, "I will fix this. I said I would and I will." He then proceeded to walk out of the boardroom and head towards the lift.

On entering the lift, Brett looked at his mobile and saw a message from Lisa, "Is the meeting over yet? Come back to bed honey!"

He smiled as he texted back immediately, "Leaving the office now, honey. Stay in bed. I'll be there soon."

Brett flung open the door to his car and slumped into the driver's seat. He turned on the engine and then called his lawyer. He was not as stupid as the guys thought he was. He had already sought legal advice on the best way to divorce Jane. He just thought he should wait, but as the partners were pushing him to protect their positions, he would have to bring it all forward and get Jane to sign the paperwork. His lawyer's advice was to get her to sign the financial agreement, so that his position and the company's position would be protected.

Brett spoke without any preamble as soon as his lawyer picked up, "Hey James, I need you to finalise and email me the financial agreement. We can't wait now. Can you send it ASAP, mate?"

James replied, a little impatiently, "Mate, as I told you, both of you need to get separate legal advice for it to be binding."

Brett dismissed James, "Leave that to me, I'll have it sorted. Just email it to me."

James was wary and tried to warn Brett of the legal fallout, "Brett, the whole thing could later be set aside by Jane if she said that she didn't get advice before she signed it or was unfairly pushed into this. Be very careful about how you arrange this."

Brett insisted, "Mate, I don't want any more advice I just want you to email the document. After that, it's no longer your problem." Realising that nothing he was going to say would change Brett's mind, James replied, "I'll send it to you with a cover letter, confirming everything I have just said to you about the implications this may have."

Brett smiled at what he saw as weakness. "I got it mate. Just send it!" and then he hung up. Feeling his phone vibrate, Brett looked at his mobile and read a text from Lisa, "I need to fuck you now." He pictured Lisa, waiting in bed for him and felt excited. He was now really annoyed that his partners had taken him away from her. He reached into his coat pocket, pulled out a blue pill and immediately after swallowing it he texted back to Lisa, "I'm driving back right now to fuck you baby X"

Brett looked at his reflection in the rear vision mirror and saw his leering smile spread ear to ear across his face. He turned on the ignition of his Maserati, revving the engine loudly whilst waiting for the roof to fold down and accelerated off.

Sarah

Chapter 5

Kate, Sarah's secretary, picked up the intercom and called Sarah's office. She said in her disapproving voice, "The first of your new clients today, Geoffrey Pemberton, has arrived for his appointment. He has a ghastly half naked girlfriend with him and they both look drunk to me."

Sarah laughed as she detected the disgust in Kate's voice and teasing her, replied tongue in cheek, "It could be his sister?"

"Yeah, right!" Kate said. "They have been practically having sex on the lounge since they arrived. We need to send them into you before they start taking their clothes off in front of our other clients in reception, who are feeling quite uncomfortable."

Sarah laughed but regretted it immediately when Kate slammed down the phone.

Geoffrey walked into Sarah's office with Amber, who was very amorous, draping herself around his shoulders, giggling and appearing to be in rather elevated in spirits, which Sarah thought could possibly be alcohol induced.

Sarah stood up and shook Geoffrey's hand. She introduced herself, "Good morning Mr Elliott, I'm Sarah Walters." Turning to Amber, Sarah held out her hand and said, "Pleased to meet you."

Amber looked bemused and asked, "Don't you remember me, Ms Walters?"

Sarah looked at Amber and was slightly embarrassed to reply, "I'm sorry, no I don't at the moment. Please understand, I meet a lot of people every day. Can you please remind me how we met?"

Amber was seething inside, *I can't believe I brought her a client and she doesn't even remember me. Then again, how tough must she be to not even remember me? Pull yourself together Amber, this is the lawyer you want, one that doesn't even remember who she destroys.*

"Look Ms Walters, I'll forgive you. If you just sort out my boyfriend's wife, all will be forgiven," Amber replied curtly.

Sarah took an instant dislike to the woman.

Geoffrey burst into a rush of words, "Ms Walters I'm separated from my wife whom I married seven years ago; I left her six months ago. I am the beneficiary of a substantial trust fund that my father set up for me. It distributes to me anywhere from two to five million dollars a year; my accountant will provide you with the details. All my assets, including my house, my artworks and cars are owned by the trust. My wife came into the marriage with her car and her clothes." Geoffrey paused, surprising himself with a fond recollection of his wife.

Sarah noticed and pressed him to continue, "And what would you like the outcome to be Mr Elliott?"

"I want to get on with my life. I have a new relationship with Amber. Katrina, my wife, is still living in the house with the kids and I'm still paying for everything. Katrina thinks we are getting back together but she should accept she has to move on. I want to be fair to her, to buy her an apartment for her to live in so I can get my house back. I'll pay her child support and I would like to have things sorted out legally between us as soon as possible."

Sarah needed more information and so she asked, "Mr Elliott, do you have a say as to what you receive from the trust fund per year or is it at the trustee's discretion?

"The trustee is happy to distribute anything between two to five million each year. I was the only child and the only beneficiary of my father's pet food business."

"Which pet food, as a matter of interest?"

"He was a smart dude my father. He invented the process to make dried and then wet pet food and then sold the patent to the major pet food companies. All he did was sit back and get royalties."

"I see," Sarah replied. "I won't go any further with your financial details until I have a discussion with your accountant. The Family

Law Act allows the Court to consider assets of the trust as part of the matrimonial assets."

Smirking, Geoffrey replied, "My accountant did bang on about something like that and said he would get everything together for you."

Sarah quickly changed direction and asked, "Please tell me more about your children. How many children do you and your wife have and what are their ages?"

"We have two children, Ben is three and Judy is five. I haven't seen them a lot since we split." Then he became agitated, "Amber and I went away for a few weeks to travel around Europe and when we came back I called her to see the kids. Katrina said they were so upset when I left that I needed to go and see them at home first, because I had never had them by myself before, so I gave up. I don't want her telling me what to do, and I don't want to see the kids in the house with her. I want to be able to see the kids when I want to, when it fits in with me. I'm the one who pays for everything and so why the fuck do I have to work around her?"

As charismatic as Geoffrey was, Sarah could see what a difficult man he could be, and she felt empathy for his wife and young children. "Mr Elliott, I can see where your wife is coming from. Your children are very young and need to develop a relationship with you, away from their mother, slowly and regularly. There are counsellors, who can help you both develop a plan for this. They can assist you in establishing a new relationship with the children and to eventually build up spending time with them away from their mother and at your home."

Geoffrey let out an impatient sigh, as if he were bored stupid by what Sarah was saying to him. He blurted out, "Katrina is just a sad sack of misery most of the time. She got postnatal depression after having Judy, then the depression got worse after having Ben, which then reached a pinnacle resulting in us breaking up. I just can't stand going over there to see the kids, when she is always so miserable. It's been four years now and she hasn't got better. I am not going to fucking counselling! I don't need counselling. It's her that needs the shrink. I am fine and have never been happier!"

Sarah felt sad for Geoffrey now. As offensive and annoying as he was, clearly something had gone very wrong in his childhood and he was an emotional disaster. He just could not understand his wife's depression after he had left her and their two young children so he could be with his girlfriend, with whom he had been having an affair.

Sarah addressed her client in a calm manner, "Mr Elliott, I really want to help you and your wife with the breakdown of your relationship. Where children are involved, their welfare will be our priority. In all my cases, I try to settle amicably, if possible. If we cannot settle, then you need to take this matter to court. You will have to go to counselling before we can start court proceedings. That is now the law in children's cases. The party seeking the orders is required to get a certificate that they have attempted to have the matter resolved by mediation with the other party before they can file in court for orders."

Amber asked abruptly, "How long will all that take?"

Sarah watched Geoffrey and was intrigued to see that he was totally in Amber's hands right now. The dynamic between them was unusual and Sarah could not help but wonder whether Geoffrey was playing games here. Sarah replied, purposely directing her answer to Geoffrey and not Amber, "The process can take days, or weeks and sometimes months. We will just have to take one step at a time and see how things go. As the children are young and you have not had them on your own prior to separating, you should start seeing them regularly for short periods, to build up a relationship with them. Eventually, when that goes well, then you can move onto overnight visits, and from there we can work out the future."

Amber jumped up from her chair. At the top of her voice, she screamed at Sarah, "You are just a self-righteous bitch! You don't even remember me, do you? You acted for my ex-husband last year and you took my kids off me and had me thrown out of the house! You ruin people's lives every day and you don't care, so why are you carrying on like we have done something wrong, because he left his wife and kids? We fell in love and no time is a good time to leave, is it? We don't want to go to counselling or settle. We are here for you to take this to court, get his kids and throw his wife out of the house. I want you to ruin her life, like you ruined mine. Don't get mad, get even, right Sarah?"

Amber's stinging words immediately restored Sarah's memory of her. With blonde hair now, not brown, and wearing far more tailored clothing than two years ago, Sarah recognised Amber White. Her husband had come to Sarah, a broken man. He had found out that

Amber had secretly started working as a prostitute in their house after he left for work. They lived out in the country and he was a farmer from a once wealthy farming family, that was now struggling in the unstable economy. Amber had married well but she could not cope with being a farmer's wife when times were hard. She became restless and despondent. More out of boredom than anything, he felt, she returned to her former occupation, from which he thought he had saved her, when he fell in love with her and took her home to his country property. When he discovered what she had been doing, he begged her to stop. She had just laughed at him, packed her bags and left him and their two little boys. A year later, when the man she had run off with dumped her, she sought legal advice to see what she could get from him. It was only then that she had tried to regain custody to improve her chances of getting part of the farm.

Sarah stood up, walked to the door of her office and opened it. Kate, sitting outside at her desk, looked towards the door, her eyebrows raised.

Sarah looked Amber straight in the eye and said, "Amber, I am sorry that you and Geoffrey have wasted your time coming in to see me. I'm sorry if you feel the way you do about how your family law case went, but I acted in the best interests of my client and your children. I do not act for people to get even or who otherwise seek to abuse the legal system."

Sarah then addressed Geoffrey, "I'm sorry, Mr Elliott, but I am not the lawyer you are looking for. If you think that I am prepared and willing to abuse the family law system to get what you want in a property settlement, you are wrong. You are not the first person and you unfortunately will not be the last who wants to mislead the court that you care about your children to obtain a better property settlement than you think you would achieve by being honest enough to admit you don't care less about your kids."

Geoffrey knew he should be offended by Sarah, but he found her arrogance extremely alluring. He liked how sassy the bitch was and how she was not going to take shit from Amber, let alone from him.

He attempted to calm her down, "Ms Walters, please don't give up on me so quickly. I am just looking for the right advice here. I will be an extremely good client for you. Surely we can come to some acceptable terms on what you will and will not do and I will pay you accordingly." Sarah was intrigued that Geoffrey had pushed Amber aside and taken control.

Geoffrey had come to the realisation that he was dealing with much more than he had bargained for and he could not help but feel an overwhelming attraction to Sarah. He would have loved to have been able throw her on her desk and fuck her right now. Unfortunately, he saw the feeling was not mutual.

Sarah was aware that Geoffrey was sizing her up and replied, "Mr Elliott, I am not the right lawyer for your case and you are not the type of client I will act for. Thank you for coming in but we should not waste any more of each other's time."

Amber stepped right in front of Sarah, put her hands on her hips and screamed, almost spitting into Sarah's face, "You can't refuse to take this case, bitch. There is the cab rank principle with lawyers and you have to act for us because we got here first before Katrina. You don't have to like us; we don't care if you don't. Just do what we pay you to do, like every other bastard you act for."

Sarah was not surprised by Amber's conduct. She now recalled her appalling behaviour during her family law hearing when she acted for the husband. Kate moved to Sarah's side as she corrected Amber in a calm tone, "Amber, the cab rank principle only applies to barristers not lawyers. We can pick and choose who we act for and if you have any doubt, you can call the Law Society and ask them."

Sarah exchanged a meaningful look with Kate, who said to Amber and Geoffrey, "I will see you both out."

Amber snarled in Sarah's direction, "You will regret this, bitch!"

Sarah simply nodded to Geoffrey, as Amber stormed out ahead of him. Sarah was not surprised when Geoffrey smiled at her, winked and left.

Kate walked into Sarah's office and sat down in one of the client chairs. "Wow! What was that about, Sarah? How do people think they can behave like that?"

"Some people think that money buys everything because it means everything to them. When it doesn't, they get angry and obnoxious."

"Well you handled it so well, Sarah. I would not have been so polite."

"Unfortunately, this business involves dealing with all sorts of people and it's usually at the worst time of their lives when they are highly emotional and feeling very vulnerable. I'm used to it, Kate. To tell you the truth, I found the dynamic between the two of them intriguing. The power shifted between them throughout the meeting, at Geoffrey's whim. I got the feeling he was playing with Amber like a cat with a mouse and he enjoyed it when she lost her temper. I wonder at the psychological dynamic behind couples like that."

Kate snarled, "I don't know how you find madness so interesting."

"It's like deep sea diving to me, looking into people's hubris or madness. You never know what you will find but you know there is lots of interesting stuff going on in there and you never know how it will manifest itself. My interest in the mind has helped me so much in both cross-examination and in settling matters. If you get past a person's facade and can work out what they really think and what really matters to them, then you can find their Achilles heel and that is where a good lawyer knows to aim."

"So where would you aim with Mr Pemberton then?" Kate said.

Sarah laughed as she replied, "He has some issues, I suspect from his childhood. He tries to appear as though he is in control and superior, but there is great insecurity there. If you threatened his trust fund he would lose it easily. Press on that button and the wife will get what she wants."

Amber

Chapter 6

Amber was still fuming with anger as she got into Geoffrey's car. She spluttered with indignation, "Who does she think she is? Bloody stuck up bitch. Like she does the right thing in every one of her cases? That's just bullshit. What right did my ex have to get the kids and the house and leave me with nothing? Best interests of the children, who is she kidding?"

Geoffrey leaned over and kissed Amber passionately. "I love you when you're angry, babe," he said as he slid his hand up her skirt. "Let's go home and fuck. You can take it all out on me, honey."

Amber pushed him away, which she had never done before. "Don't make fun of me! That woman was rude to me, to us, and you are letting her get away with it."

As though Amber had pressed a button, Geoffrey snapped from being passionate to aggressive, shouting in Amber's face, "That woman needs another client like a hole in the head. The two of you would constantly set each other off like firecrackers, so God help me and my case if you two were at it all the time! There are lawyers everywhere, honey. Who cares about the bitch? If you want me to, I'll get square with her for you, but I couldn't care less myself. I left my family to have fun, Amber. Remember what you said to me? We're here for a good time not a long time."

Amber was very aware that Geoffrey had left the perfect wife and family for her, within six months, when everyone else had told her she was an idiot and he would never leave Katrina. But what they did not understand were the tricks she had up her sleeve that every man loved.

She thought to herself, *God, men were stupid! Did Geoffrey really think women loved him?* She was basically homeless and penniless when she stumbled across him, drunk at a pub, on her way home after being dumped by her boyfriend.

His idea of flirting was to say to her, "Babe, I'm married with kids but I'm out for a good time not a long time. You up for it?"

"Well, I'm your good time girl," she had told him and he had fallen for it.

He had cut straight to the chase and replied excitedly, "OK, babe, my driver is outside. Let's go to my hotel."

They had gone straight to the hotel, where Geoffrey had the Presidential Suite. The doorman greeted him like royalty. She had been living in the hotel ever since. *Just like Julia Roberts in Pretty Woman,* she thought. And now he has left his wife. Who said that looks aren't everything?

Amber leaned over, gave Geoffrey a deep, lingering kiss and then, when he was starting to get excited, broke off the kiss and said, "I want you to get that bitch for me. How will you do it?"

Clearly annoyed at her withdrawal from him, he said, "I will honey. I'm not quite sure where or when yet, but I'll work it out."

"Promise me you will!" demanded Amber. "She got on top of me with my ex and she is now telling us she won't act for us! I hate her."

Geoffrey, who was getting more irritated pointed out, "You are the one who chose her, not the other way around, babe. I kind of like her. She's tough and doesn't take shit." Then he softened a little, "Darling, I told you I know how to handle these things."

Amber was determined to steer a tough course. She pressed Geoffrey, "Will we get the house back? I love that house and Katrina doesn't need it. You had it when you met her, so you should get it back, right?"

"I'll get Katrina out, eventually," Geoffrey said with a smirk on his face.

"It won't be easy if she gets a good lawyer," Amber warned.

"Trust me, they'll tell her to stay put but what they don't understand is how women think and how easily manipulated they are." Amber saw the glint in Geoffrey's eyes. She knew he was a bastard and a womanizer, but now she could see he had some real evil in him. She was seeing the side of him which excited and scared her.

Amber's questioning gaze had not gone unnoticed. Geoffrey's face flushed red and his eyes opened wide as he yelled, "Why the fuck are you staring at me like that, Amber?"

Startled by the change of tone in his voice, Amber replied, "I haven't seen you like this before."

"Like what?" he demanded.

"You have an evil look in your eyes today," Amber said quietly.

"That's because I am stupid! The bitch will get a lawyer and try and hide behind the lawyer and do whatever her lawyer says. When her lawyer asks for her to get the most she can of my assets, she will say to me that it's not really what she wants but what her lawyer says is a fair thing for her and the kids to have. I know the tricks and I also know how to break a woman's soul. I can make Katrina feel worthless, scared and vulnerable so that nothing anyone else says to her after that will make her feel safe again. After that, they'll agree to anything just to make it stop. I have many women who have tried to trap me and threaten me with lawyers before."

Amber shrank away from Geoffrey and he saw the fear in her eyes. He lunged at her and pulled her towards him by her hair. Amber groaned in pain and simultaneously in a reflex action put her hand over her mouth to smother the sound.

"Shut up!" Geoffrey barked at her. He slapped her across the face. He let go of her hair and Amber's head dropped to her chest. Her body slumped down in her seat and she sat staring blankly ahead as silent tears fell down her face.

Geoffrey was even more enraged. "Don't start crying, bitch! Why have you gone all goody two shoes now? You come and fuck up my marriage and now you say things like I enjoy hurting Katrina. You didn't mind fucking her husband, stealing him away from her and breaking up her happy family, did you? It's all your fault and you need to see that. You are the reason I left her and you are the reason she is upset. If it weren't for you, I'd still be playing fucking happy families. Now stop looking at me like I'm the monster and start doing some of the stuff you promised me if I left home for you, right fucking now!"

He glared at her and he leaned back in the car seat. He undid the belt on his jeans and then his zipper. Amber leaned over into his lap and took him into her mouth while continuing to run her hands over his groin. She felt him relax and lean back into the car seat, his eyes closed.

Moments later, Geoffrey grabbed her by the hair, pulled her head up and forced her to look at him. He spat out the words, "That's more like it, bitch, and you remember that."

He slapped her across the face with such force that her head reeled back, and she felt dizzy. He looked at her and saw the shock and fear in her face, which turned him on immediately. He leaned over and grabbed her by the hair again and pushed her head back down into his lap, warning her, "Don't you try and fuck with me again, bitch, or you will learn a new meaning for the word pain." He felt Amber's mouth around him again, enjoying her expertise at pleasing him.

Geoffrey knew he was becoming addicted to the adrenalin and desire that Amber stirred up in him. The roughness of the sex he enjoyed with her was a new angle in his life and he knew he was liking the bruises he gave her and the cut lips and scratch marks that appeared after they had sex. It was his form of branding her and every time he looked at the marks it immediately stirred up the desire in him again. At forty-two he thought that he had tried everything but Amber had released a side of him that had obviously been hidden. He had backhanded women before when they had annoyed him, but this was different and dark, and he loved it.

During the day he would fantasize about new things to do to Amber. The latest fetish he had thought of was getting one of her friends to fuck him while Amber watched. He wanted to watch her face as another woman turned him on to see if she felt threatened because he might enjoy fucking someone else more than her. The thought of it, together with Amber's lips around him aroused him to ecstasy and he felt himself explode inside her mouth, as he grabbed her hair in his hands oblivious of the fact that she was screaming in pain. He slowly opened his eyes, relaxed his hands and realized he had whole clumps of her hair in his hands. She sat back in her seat, whimpering as she ran her hands through her bloodied scalp.

Geoffrey glanced sideways at her then slapped her with an open right hand, forcing her to hit her head on the car window. He said, "Shut the fuck up you stupid bitch."

Looking out of the car window, Geoffrey saw they had arrived back at the hotel. As he got out of the car he said to Amber, "You are such a messy fuck, Amber." He then got out of the car and walked to the entrance of the hotel. As he was about to enter the revolving doors he turned around and saw Amber had still not moved and the car door remained open.

Annoyed, he walked back to the car and said to her, "Come on Amber, hurry up."

Amber looked up at him with pained eyes, "Why Geoffrey?" "I'm already feeling horny again, aren't you a lucky girl? Now come inside and clean yourself up, then I'll fuck you," he said as he walked into the hotel.

Amber continued staring at Geoffrey as he walked into the building. She slumped into the back seat of the car and felt completely exhausted and beaten when she heard the driver's voice coming from the car door. "Get out please Amber. Geoffrey has sent me a text saying he wants you upstairs."

Amber starred at him in disbelief. "You know what he just did to me. Can't you see I'm in pain?"

Without hesitation the driver replied, "You do it to each other. My job is to drive and that's what I do. Now get out of my car and go where you like, but don't think I will get involved in the dark web you've woven yourself into Amber."

Amber's phone rang which startled her. She saw it was Geoffrey and she answered it. "Darling, I'm in bed, waiting for you and you know I'm not at all patient when I want your body," and then he hung up. Amber, now knowing there was no alternative swiftly got out of the car and walked into the hotel.

Brett

Chapter 7

After the meeting with Brett, Ian Hammersmith and Tim Breen left the others in the boardroom to finish their coffee and croissants, while they went back to Ian's office. They were both looking very pleased with themselves. Ian took his seat behind his expansive, leather topped desk, while Tim closed the door and then sat across from Ian. Ian took out his mobile phone and checked his text messages.

There was a text from Lisa, "Brett's on his way back here now.

You obviously didn't scare the shit out of him like you said you were going to! LOL"

Ian laughed as he read the message aloud to Tim, then said, "So, Brett's going back to her now! He is more of an idiot than any of us expected. We all thought he would go for her, but no one thought he was going to leave his wife for her."

"Yep, he's a fucking idiot. The typical yuppie who drives a Maserati, buys a waterfront and starts to fuck around believing he has suddenly become attractive to women because of his good looks!" Tim scoffed.

"Never underestimate the power of the pussy, Tim. It has ruined many men and will continue to do so. There are always the secretaries wanting to jump executives, and desperate girls looking for a sugar daddy, so it's beyond me what he sees in it - but that's exactly why we had to do this. The guy is hungry and he's fucking smart, but sometimes he thinks with his dick and that's why we have to get rid of him."

Tim was concerned, "You know, when you first told me how worried you were about him, I really didn't think he was that big a problem. I mean, I know it was a pain because he couldn't help but leer at and occasionally even touch up the girls in the office, but I really didn't think he'd fuck up this badly. I cannot believe what damage he could have done to us if we hadn't hired Lisa. What happened to him? He wasn't always like this was he? I thought he was quite the devoted family man when he came to work for us and was absolutely in love with his wife."

Ian picked up his coffee, leaned back in his chair and put his feet up on his desk. "It seems to be the case of success going to his head, Tim. I have seen it before and we will see it again. Guys that start out being the straightest types you will ever meet turn into Narcissists as soon as they have money. I have thought about Brett a lot and I think it happens more to those who have come from nothing and covet being wealthy. They are the ones that become the biggest arseholes to deal with later."

Tim reflected on what Ian had said before he replied, "I really liked the man that Brett used to be, but I don't like the man he has become now. It's like someone else has invaded his body. I am really struggling to stay calm with him when he has become the most selfish prick I know and doesn't even care about his devoted wife, let alone his kids."

Ian elaborated, "Look we have taken Brett from basically rags to riches and that affects some people badly. It shows you the fibre of someone when they get some money and throw it around thinking it makes them look important. We need to face reality, get rid of him and get on with what we are doing. We will make sure his wife and kids are looked after and that's all we can do for this mess. It's a lot more than most business partners would do in the same situation. I have now moved on from feeling any- thing but annoyed with Brett and looking at him like a problem we need to exterminate. The process of hiring a hooker to be his secretary was the most fun I've had in years. Those interviews, I really did enjoy."

Tim laughed, "Do you remember when he first laid eyes on her? He couldn't believe we'd hired him such a good sort. I mean, surely, he should have thought something was up when he saw a 5' 9 supermodel sitting at the desk outside his office, in the same seat his last secretary sat who was sixty-five-years-old, dull as dishwater, stumpy and grumpy before she retired?"

"No, he is driven by his dick, Tim. She had legs up to her chin and boobs that spilled out of her very expensive blouse, so he was in heaven.

My wife always joked that she asks me for what she wants when we are having sex, because the blood is flowing to my dick and not my brain and I always say yes to everything." "Your wife is a very smart woman, Ian. I've always said that!

If I were getting sex from my wife she could have whatever she wanted too! But all jokes aside, and back to our problem boy Brett. We've got him now, on breaching the partner's code regarding behaviour that will put the partnership at risk during a deal and divulging confidential information. He is clearly a danger when he is willing to tell Lisa everything about all our deals and leave the due diligence paperwork where she could screen shot it, which she has of course.

"Ian swung his legs off the desk and leaned forward, resting his elbows on the smooth leather surface in front of him. "We need to mop this up Tim, and we need to do it quickly. Have you sorted out the payout?"

Tim nodded and placed a folder on Ian's desk. "It's sorted. He's fucked! Wherever he tries to turn, we have him cornered. He's breached all the essential terms of the partnership and we have it all from Lisa, and from others last year, who made the sexual harassment claim. He took out a loan for seventy-five percent of the cost of his new house from us. So, part of his severance package will be that we won't call on the mortgage but we will give him six months to sell the house and repay it. Then we'll pay him $5,000,000 for his share in the partnership."

Ian shook his head, "Come on Tim, why would he take that? He knows that if we pull off the next deal, we are going to make $500,000,000 and he has a ten percent share of that as well."

Tim was prepared for the criticism and replied, "He has breached every term of our partnership, save none. We have evidence of it all. He is usually a lot smarter than this, but he has been distracted by his ego. When he signed the partnership agreement he overlooked the clause that everything that is done on our server and from his work mobile which is supplied by the firm, in the case of a partnership dispute or criminal investigation, can be used by us without it being a breach of confidentiality. We therefore have evidence of everything he has done. So, if he leaves with no contest, he will have time to rearrange his affairs, or the alternative is we sell him up immediately to call in the loan.

As far as what his share in the partnership is worth, our partnership agreement provides that we can buy his shares at market value now because he has breached two of the essential clauses. Unfortunately, the shares can only be sold to each of us as and at the highest bid."

Ian frowned, "Tim, make sure if he is leaving Jane that he agrees that part of the money is paid to her. I am not going to leave his wife and kids penniless because he has fucked up; that is not what we are about and it's just not the way we are going to run this business."

Tim sighed as he stood up to leave. "I know you are right. I don't want to screw over his wife and the kids, but I would enjoy screwing Brett. Okay, well, we have room to move and we should be fair. Leave it with me, Ian."

Amber

Chapter 8

In the enormous hotel bed, Amber gazed lovingly into Geoffrey's eyes, luxuriating in the attention he was showering upon her, before she lay her head on his chest. She had never been with anyone who had been so totally consumed by her before and it had become intoxicating. Geoffrey stared intently back into Amber's eyes as he propped himself up on one arm next to her. Whether she had started out wallet fucking him was irrelevant, because he could clearly see from the way she looked at him that she was now in love with him. He ran his fingers through her hair gently as her hand stroked his inner thigh.

When Geoffrey made love to her, he devoured her. It had become increasingly rougher, but the nice surprise was that she surged even more with pleasure, which drove Geoffrey even crazier. Amber found herself becoming proud of the bruises and marks he left on her after he had beaten her and came to see it as a sign of his passion and lust for her. He had strangled her so hard this week while they were having sex that she had blacked out in the back of the car. After half an hour the driver had to get security to help put her in a wheelchair to get her up to the room. Geoffrey had apologised and explained it was because she had just turned him on so much and he was so in love with her that he had lost control of himself. He was the first man who had wanted her this way and desired her so much, that it made her feel special.

The last two months had been a dream run, as Geoffrey had treated her like no one had ever done before. Married guys had always been generous because they usually felt guilty, but he had treated her like a girlfriend.

Geoffrey stared deep into her eyes and asked, "Do you know how beautiful you are, Amber?" He gently brushed her hair away from her eyes with his fingers as she lay on his chest.

Amber smiled and leaned towards him to kiss him. She never thought she would be treated like this by a man. At times he made her feel like a princess; he took her shopping, bought her designer clothes and then took her to lunch at one of the most exclusive restaurants in town. They were now in the most beautiful hotel suite and Geoffrey had made love to her, whilst whispering to her that she was the most beautiful girl in the world.

Suddenly, Geoffrey gripped Amber's arm with his other hand while holding the back of her head by her hair. He asked in an aggressive tone this time, "Amber do you know how beautiful you are?"

Amber shook her head and raised her shoulders, as if to say, "I don't know."

Geoffrey pushed her off him and onto her back on the bed. With menace in his eyes and his voice, he persisted, "I said, do you know how beautiful you are, Amber?"

Amber shook her head again but this time whispered, "No." "Why the fuck can't you speak Amber? It's a simple fucking question, isn't it?"

Tears started to well up in Amber's eyes and she pulled herself up on the pillows to reply, "No one has ever told me I am beautiful before, Geoffrey."

Geoffrey leaned over her and he seemed to have calmed down. He stroked her hair gently again and then slid his hand over her face and down her neck. She felt his palm at the base of her throat. He caressed her throat and then moved his fingers lightly down her chest. "You have such beautiful skin, Amber. It's so soft."

Amber relaxed and smiled, sensing that he had now relaxed too. At times now, he was becoming very aggressive with no warning and this time had scared her.

Geoffrey continued to gently stroke her neck and shoulders, until he spread both his hands and laced his fingers around her neck. He squeezed tighter and tighter until she began to gasp and choke. He whispered hoarsely, "You have a beautiful neck, Amber. It's long and it feels really nice in my hands."

Amber was gasping for air and struggling to breathe. She tried to pull Geoffrey's hands away when, suddenly, he let go. She gasped for air and Geoffrey put his arm around her and patted her on the back as if he were comforting her.

"I'm so sorry, honey," he said. "I didn't mean to do that. It's just such a turn on watching you struggle to breathe and be so close to dying."

Amber tried to take deep breaths to regain her composure. She was trying very hard not to cry or scream in panic.

Geoffrey cupped Amber's chin in the palm of his hand. Then, his fingers gently traced the contours of her face until his hand rested on her neck and he began choking her again. He pinned her down across the shoulders with his other arm and looked intently into her face. His eyes were wide with a look she had seen only once before.

"Listen to me," he warned. "Listen carefully. You are mine. I have paid for exclusive rights to your body and if you ever think you can leave me you are wrong. If you ever try to fuck someone else, I will make sure your pretty face is not so pretty anymore and then no one will want you, not even me. If you try and leave me, just when you don't expect it you will wake up with me next to you again and I will have sliced your face with a razor blade so many times that no one will ever recognise you."

Amber was too scared to even breathe. She lay motionless and just stared back into the vacant black depths of his piercing eyes. "Don't ever forget that, Amber. No one will be able to protect you from me. No one will be able to help you. You will not be beautiful anymore, so no one will want you. If you ever try to leave me, just remember, you will never be the same." Amber knew what she had to do.

Men and women played this unwritten game and, if you played it right, a girl always got what she expected. She had watched her mother do it all her life and she had learned how to do even better than her. Although her mother was happy enough, she never really had a handle on what really made men tick and Amber did. Her mum always said that men wanted to feel needed and feel appreciated for them spoiling you. What her mum never under- stood was that what men wanted most was to be the best fuck you had ever had. It did not matter whether you were their wife, girlfriend, hooker or just a stray fuck.

If you could make them feel like they were the best fuck you had ever had, you had them.

Her mother had not wanted to use men, she had just been put in that position when her husband went missing at war. Fearing that every day, any day, she and Amber would be thrown out their home, she would try and stash away as much money as she could while trying to find another "Mr Right" just in case, like her father, he never came home. In her mum's case it was just a matter of survival and doing the best she could with what she had, and all she had at the time were her looks.

As hard as Amber tried, and no matter how many times Amber had looked at photographs of her father, she could not remember him. He had been drafted and gone to war when she was five years old and never came home. Her mother had waited for over five years after he had gone missing to accept what the military had been telling her - that he was missing and presumed dead. Amber knew that part of the reason her mother was in denial, at least publicly, was because if he was in fact found dead, then her mother had been told by one of the other military wives that she and Amber would be thrown out of their military house and his wage would stop being paid to her. The realisation that they could be homeless at any moment and without any money coming in drove her mother to what she had to do.

For the five years that her mother pretended her father was coming home, she had talked about him a lot. At least once a week she would sit with Amber and go through photos of him together, talking as though he had been here yesterday. Although Amber heard her friends and family telling her mum she needed to face the reality that her husband was gone, her mother's response was always, "He can't be." So, her mother just continued to publicly pretend that he was alive and coming home one day, and privately her mother started her own, very discreet business of escorting men.

Each day they lived with the fear that someone from the military housing would tell them that they had to move out of their home. The first day of every month when her mother received her missing father's pay into her account was a day of relief. The week before, her mother was always tense, touchy and angry. Amber prayed every night that her father would one day walk back through their front door, but as she found out very early in her life, prayers do not work.

Five years after her father's death, Amber's mother had finally found the next "Mr Right". Her mother had been friends with his wife, as they lived in the same street of military owned houses. When the wife had been diagnosed with breast cancer, Amber's mother helped to take care of her. After she passed away three years later, Amber's mother continued to comfort the grieving widower. After another six months, her mother finally realised that her husband was never coming home and she accepted "Mr Right's" offer of marriage. When Amber, who was by that stage ten years old, had expressed her surprise that her mother could marry her "best friend's" husband, her mother quite reasonably explained to her that he was a good man and that good men were hard to find.

Having accepted her mother's marriage, hoping it would bring peace and a new father to her life, Amber was left bewildered by what followed. After her mother remarried, no matter how many times Amber asked her, her mother would never again talk about her father, or go through the photo albums like she used to. To her mother, it was like Amber's father had never existed and that he needed to be punished for leaving her in such a terrible mess. Amber rarely went to school as her mother was unconcerned, as long as Amber did the chores at home. As soon as she turned sixteen and could legally work, Amber moved out. Her mother had not only disconnected from her father after she accepted his death, but also from Amber and it was like she was just a reminder of a life her mother wanted to forget. She had not seen or heard from her mother since she had left home.

Amber moved in with a girlfriend who worked at a supermarket. While her friend was at work, Amber started her own business at their apartment doing "massages" for the guys she met at the local pub. A few months later, she met and married her friend's brother. He was a nice guy and he took care of her. She had never been taken care of before and she thought, "this must be love". It took her years to realise that it was love, but on his part and not hers. As soon as she had been nurtured and cared for, so that she became a self-confident woman, she realised her marriage bored her stupid and the life of a housewife with kids was not meant for her. She left. She was attracted to what she had grown up with and "normal" had nothing to do with it.

Jane

Chapter 9

While standing on the verandah of her new home, Jane glanced across at the harbour and felt a wave of relief that the removalists had finally gone. She walked over and sat on one of the new chairs which she had had made to order. She was pleased with how wonderfully it had all come together. After three days of packing and unpacking, she was excited that she could finally relax and enjoy the serenity of their new home. She had already planned a surprise candlelit dinner on the balcony with Brett for tonight when he came back from his business trip. She knew how much moving into this house meant to him and she wanted it to be perfect.

Brett had told Jane many stories about when his family had moved back to Australia after living in New Zealand. His father had taken several years to re-establish his career and on weekends, because they had little money to do much else, his father would to take him fishing in the bay. This beautiful house Jane and Brett had just moved into was perched up on the hill above where Brett and his father fished. His father would say to him, as they stared up at the house from their tinny in the harbour, "When you live in a house like that, you'll know you've made it, son." Brett told Jane that he was determined to own the house from the first time his father had said those words to him.

Their new home was an old Federation house that was over a hundred years old and full of character but had been a much loved and renovated family home over the years. It faced north on Sydney Harbour, had a boatshed, jetty and pool, but the major source of amusement to their girls was the huge double glass door fridge in the kitchen, which put most shops and restaurants to shame. It was the biggest fridge Jane had ever seen in a home and it had its own gas engine outside on the verandah. Jane had spent nearly an hour trying to figure out how to turn it on. It had taken several phone calls to her handyman, who together with a plumber, had reconnected it.

The girls had exclaimed, "This is like having our own shop Mummy, isn't it?" They made Jane promise that they could organise the fridge just like a proper shop.

Jane felt relaxed and was enjoying her glass of wine and the view. She could not help but reflect, staring out at the magnificence of Sydney Harbour, how far they had come since moving into their first home. It was thirteen years ago when she had met Brett one morning on the peak hour train to work. Brett had stood up to let her sit down and she was, of course, very impressed but thought no more of it. The next day, the same thing had happened, but on that occasion, Brett had said, "I was hoping you would be in this carriage again." Jane had smiled at him and said she would make sure to take that carriage every day. When Brett had finally got up the courage to ask Jane to dinner that week, he had later told her that he had expected her to say "No." He had confessed to having watched her for weeks at the train station in the mornings before the coincidence of her standing next to him. Jane had been touched and overwhelmed by Brett's feelings for her.

The relationship had developed steadily and slowly in an old fashioned way. For the next two years, Jane got to know Brett and he told her about his troubled childhood. He said that his parents had moved to New Zealand when he was a toddler, after his father had inherited a vineyard from his uncle. Unfortunately, his parents had not realised that the local area only had one school and the pupils were all Maori children. Brett had been the only Caucasian boy and he had never been accepted by the other children. He had tried to make friends and fit in, but he had finally grown sick of being beaten up on a daily basis. He left home each day pretending to go to school, but instead he would spend the day in an old boatshed by the river. His sister, who had been a few years older, ran away from home after a few months with a teenage boy to escape the town. They were later married and were still together. He and his parents eventually moved back to Australia two years later, after his parents realised that they were unsuitable to running a vineyard and sold it.

Although Brett was tall, dark and handsome and Jane's white knight, his childhood had left him with a vulnerable side, which Jane felt she helped him cope with. By the following year they had become inseparable, travelling to and from work together, in the same carriage, every day.

One morning, an announcement was made over the intercom in the train, "This is your train driver and I have the pleasure of announcing that this is a very special day for a couple in carriage four. Not only is it the anniversary of when they first met two years go," as Jane and other passengers looked around trying to identify the couple having the anniversary as the voice had continued over the intercom. "But today Brett would like to ask Jane if she will marry him." Everyone in the carriage watched as Brett went down on one knee and presented Jane with a diamond ring, which was resting in a little blue Tiffany box. Jane of course had been surprised and overwhelmed as she looked at Brett and then at all the expectant faces in the carriage. She realised they were all waiting for her response so she said, "Yes!" which was greeted with clapping and cheering from the carriage full of people.

A woman standing near them said she had recorded the whole proposal for them on her phone and showed them. The camera had captured an extraordinarily romantic scene, full of the young lovers' happy faces and the smiles and congratulatory shouts of their fellow travellers.

They had moved into their first house after the honeymoon. It was a "renovator's delight" which was all they could afford. Having used every cent they had on the purchase of the house, they had nothing left to buy furniture. Being the thrifty girl she was, Jane had searched and found free unwanted furniture on Gumtree and eBay to furnish the house. She and Brett had recalled with a fond smile many times over the years how none of it matched. There had been a 1970s cane lounge with bamboo print, a wooden outdoor dining table and chairs, which they used indoors, and an old wrought iron double bed that collapsed when they were too affectionate in it.

Every weekend for months, they had renovated bits of the house with the help of family and friends. Jane had made curtains and Brett had put up a clothesline from Bunnings. Once they had finished the renovations, instead of feeling relieved and ready to enjoy the results of their hard work, they had found they were bored on the weekends. And so, they embarked on a course of buying and renovating one house after the next, working their way up the property ladder, growing more confident with more experience and more money to hire tradesmen. Now, finally they had arrived at the new house. It was their fifth home.

They had always had houses which were inland, with Jane hoping one day they may be able to buy a house with at least water views. Brett had driven Jane past their new home so many times over the years claiming they would one day own it, but as it was a harbour waterfront she had thought it was one of Brett's many ambitious dreams. Never had she really thought that she would be standing where she was right now, even though Brett had always said he would get whatever he wanted in life. For a moment, Jane felt a pang of guilt. Although the house was magnificent, nothing would ever replace the joy and happiness she had felt when they moved into their first little house. They were so happy, so in love and so ambitious about their future together. She wondered for a moment why she was not feeling that joy right now, even though she was mesmerized, watching the activity on the harbour. The constant activity was like viewing a peaceful movie which ran all day and night. A ferry tooted as it passed by, signaling the nearby jetty of its impending arrival. The yachts and boats were bobbing happily up and down. The full moon was reflecting on the water and cheekily teasing her with what looked like diamonds shining on top of the soft ripples of the aqua blue water of the harbour.

Jane had arranged for the babysitter to take the kids out to dinner. Jane wanted just the two of them to enjoy some time alone, to toast their new home. She wanted to surprise Brett with a candlelit champagne and lobster dinner, which was his favourite meal. Today was a special day, not only because they were spending their first night in the new home, but it was also the thirteen-year anniversary of when they had first met. She was unsure whether Brett would remember, but it had always been the most important anniversary to her. It was the day she had fallen in love with him - deeply, madly, truly.

They had been together thirteen years and married for ten of those years. Their marriage had not been boring, there had been more ups and downs than most roller coaster rides. They had ridden it through and Jane was proud that she had let go of a lot of things that would have ended most marriages, to keep them together. Brett had suffered from bouts of depression when highly stressed, and during those periods it was hard to know what to do. She had encouraged him to get help, but he always said that he knew how to get himself out of his black moods eventually, in his own way. *His own way* sometimes meant going on drinking binges for days and nights in a row, hardly speaking to her and sometimes not even coming home, but Jane put up with it over the years as he did eventually become normal again.

In Brett's defence, the other side of his personality was worth putting up with almost anything for. He had the gift of making her feel beautiful and loved when he devoted time to her. The way he could make her feel when he looked into her eyes, his soft lingering touch and his deep, long kisses that took her breath away, gave her the strength to endure the rest. With time, Jane had felt that she and Brett had developed an understanding that when she needed to let him go she could, trusting him to come back to her. Their daughters, Dianna and Jill, were eight and six- years - old, so she knew it was all worth it.

Jane had been pregnant three years earlier with twins. In a freak accident in their former home, she lost them. She still had no idea how she came to fall down the stairs that she walked up and down several times a day. She recalled nothing about the fall, just that she woke up in theatre with a doctor telling her she was losing the twins and if they did not operate immediately, she would bleed to death. It had seemed surreal at the time and it was a loss she thought she would never get over. The agony of the physical and emotional pain was exhausting for months after and it seemed at the time she would never recover.

Brett had been determined to move to a new house after the accident. Even though that particular house had been Jane's dream home, she agreed to it. She had loved that house and still did. Although she never talked about it, she continued to be struggling with the loss of the twins. The pregnancy had only been twelve weeks advanced, so Jane had not told anyone by that stage. Luckily, Brett had insisted they wait until twenty weeks before announcing it, otherwise Jane would have had to endure the pain of revealing her loss to her family.

Jane was willing to try almost anything to get over it. She had destroyed any trace of the twins, including the ultrasound photos, because although she wanted to keep them, they made her cry. The twins haunted her every day, especially when she saw a baby in a pram or worse, twins. She would see her twins on the ultrasound flash before her eyes, cutely snuggled together, the bigger one always moving much more than the little one, who always seemed to be looking at the screen. Brett suggested Jane go to a depression clinic, but she told him she did not want to leave the children for six weeks, so he booked her in to see a psychiatrist. From that time, Jane had been having regular therapy.

Jane came out of her reverie when her phone beeped, and she saw a text from Brett, "Just had to pick up some papers from Mark on the way home. Be there soon."

Brett had been away for the week of the move. When he was away, just the thought of Brett's arms around her was enough to stir her memories of him and suddenly fill her with delight. It was not great timing for Brett to be away, but as he said, the deal he was working on was going to make his career and set them up for the rest of their lives. The deal had taken longer than he expected but it was also going to be far bigger than he and his team had thought. The agency had not only taken off overseas but had disrupted several markets that they had not anticipated. The takeover offer, which they knew would eventually come by the international agency, was five years earlier than they had planned and many more times the price they had only dreamed of.

Jane had become worried that Brett was both enjoying and valuing his work more than his family in recent years. Since the girls had come along, he was spending more time at work and becoming more and more obsessed with his business. Although she always knew that Brett was driven, Jane had not anticipated the effect his ambition seemed to be having on his personality, in the last couple of years. The once grounded, unaffected and generous guy she had fallen in love with was developing into a show pony with grandiose ideas for their future. He had gone from driving a Ute to work, because he could throw his surfboard in the back, to driving a Maserati. Instead of a wardrobe of RM Williams shirts and pants, he now only wore Italian brand suits and silk ties. They used to travel economy, but now the whole family went business class and Brett travelled first class when he was on a business trip. He told Jane, recently, that when they floated his company, they were going to be able to fly in private planes, not "commercial" anymore. Jane wondered if she would ever get her old Brett back and realised, with a pang, how much she missed him and the simpler life they once had.

Jane's phone buzzed again and this time the text announced, "I'm home". She stood on the balcony and took a long, deep breath, feeling like an excited schoolgirl waiting for her first date to arrive. She loved Brett so much and she wanted him to love what she had done with furnishing the new house.

She heard the door open and saw him walk into the foyer. He had still not seen Jane, but he was looking down at his phone, which had buzzed, and then he smiled and walked towards the balcony.

Jane greeted Brett with a glass of champagne and said, "Here's to our new home, darling".

Brett took the glass and stared out over the water without speaking. He did not kiss Jane as he usually did. He turned and walked to the other side of the table, sat down and opened the folder he had carried in under his arm. He looked up at her and said, "Where are the girls?"

Jane was nonplussed by Brett's cool demeanour. "I arranged for the babysitter to take them out to dinner, so we could have some time alone. I have lobster and prawns ready for us to have here on the balcony with our champagne," she said.

Brett seemed wired and spoke very quickly, "We have some issues we need to deal with Jane and as the kids aren't home, we should deal with it now."

Jane realised that there was something different in his eyes and she did not quite know how to react. Brett took some papers out of the folder and flicked through the pages. He noticed Jane staring at him and said, "I'll talk you through this Jane, don't look so worried."

Tears started to well up in her eyes. "Brett, please can't we do this tomorrow morning? I would really love us to have some time to relax, have dinner and enjoy our new home first. I've been working for three days to get the house perfect for you and you haven't even noticed anything. You just can't keep putting work ahead of me. It's not fair Brett!"

Brett realised he needed to placate Jane. "Honey, if we can just get this document signed quickly, we can move on and enjoy the rest of our night. I want that just as much as you, but I can't relax until I get this business sorted out first. It won't take a minute and then the night is ours." He smiled at Jane, looking piercingly and lovingly into her eyes. He touched her face with his hand and then moved it slowly behind her head to bring her face towards him. He kissed her deeply. She melted into his body in his firm embrace. When she felt like this, in Brett's arms, she had often thought that if the world ended at that precise moment, she would have no regrets.

Sarah

Chapter 10

Sarah and her client were walking out of the Family Court at the end of the day. They were both extremely relieved that they had won the case. The judge had ordered that the children live with her client and spend alternate weekends with the father. Although they had been successful, the father was demonstrably angry to the point that he had been removed from the court by the court officers. His legal team had already indicated they were going to lodge an appeal. They were now heading to the pedestrian crossing to walk to Sarah's office.

Also leaving the court were the usual parade of lawyers, barristers and clients walking out in groups, and mostly in serious discussion. As the traffic lights turned red and the traffic slowed to a stop, a car screeched around the corner. Everyone looked up to see the car speeding directly towards them and suddenly mounting the footpath. They scattered like wind-blown leaves to get out of its way, amid screams, screeching tires and then scraping metal as the car finally crashed into the building.

Sarah had been pushed abruptly sideways by a security guard, just as the car hit the wall at the front of the building. She had fallen to the ground, hitting both her head and shoulder. Shocked, Sarah lay dazed trying to work out what had happened when she heard screaming and shouting. Concerned, Sarah looked around for her client, whom she had lost sight of.

A piercing pain shot through Sarah's head and she closed her eyes with the abrupt onset of pain. Sarah felt disorientated and faint. She saw flashes of darkness and bright lights before her eyes. As though submerged under water, Sarah heard a distorted voice asking her if she was alright. She managed to open her eyes and tried to lift her head to reply but felt nauseous and she gagged.

Sarah heard a woman's voice saying to her, "Please don't try to get up, the ambulance is on its way. I will stay with you until it comes." Sarah felt the woman's comforting hand on her shoulder. She closed her eyes and lay back on the ground. Sarah had a flashback and with explosive clarity, the bodies of her dead parents flashed before her eyes. It was not until ten years after her parent's death, when she researched newspaper archives that she found an article on their deaths in a car accident and a photo of them in the mangled car. The article stated that the accident had occurred late at night and they were not found until traffic passed the scene in the early hours of the next morning. They had crashed into a pole on their way home from work, with no evidence of the cause, other than the assumption that the male driver had fallen asleep at the wheel. It was confronting to read the article and to see the photo, but there had been an ache in her since she was a young child to know how they had died.

Sarah heard several voices near her and felt her body being lifted. Although she was conscious, she found she was unable to speak. The paramedics moved Sarah carefully onto a stretcher and headed towards the ambulance.

One of the paramedics spoke, "I'm giving you an injection to help you with the pain," as he put the needle in her arm.

Peter, Sarah's ex-husband rushed up to the doors of the ambulance. He had been walking back to his chambers after a court appearance in the District Court on the same street. As he walked towards the Family Court he had seen the commotion. The security guards informed him that Sarah was being taken to the ambulance and on to the hospital. Peter raced up to the ambulance and introduced himself to the ambulance officers as Sarah's ex-husband. He grasped Sarah's hand and she opened her eyes.

Recognising him, she said, "Peter, I don't really know what happened", before she drifted off into unconsciousness. As Peter looked concerned, the paramedic informed him that he had given her a sedative and that was what had caused her to fall asleep.

Geoffrey

Chapter 11

The following morning after reading the news online on his phone, Geoffrey picked up the newspaper from under the hotel door and flung it onto the bed. He was aiming at Amber and managed to hit her on the back of the head to wake her up.

"You may want to read the newspaper today," he said as he walked away from the bed laughing. He added, "Shit, I never asked if you read babe? Anyway, if you can't read, look at the pictures and you will get the drift."

"Of course, I can read," she replied indignantly.

Amber wriggled herself up into a sitting position and propped a couple of pillows behind her back before she picked up the paper. Pictured on the front page was a car crashed into a wall with an article about the incident.

Daily Newspaper

Lawyer struck by a car at the Family Court.

In a dramatic scene today at the Family Court in Sydney, lawyer and well-known media identity, Sarah Walters was hit by a car as she was leaving court with her client. It is alleged by witnesses that a man drove his four-wheel drive directly towards her and up onto the footpath. Crowds of people, who had been leaving the court at the end of the day, escaped injury. Having crashed the car into the wall of the Family

Court, the driver fled the scene. Police initially believed the driver to have been the husband of Ms Walter's client, who had just received a judgment in the family law court where he lost custody of his children to his former wife. However, he has been ruled out as a suspect, as he was detained by court officers at the time. Although the family law fraternity is in shock with the news, they are aware of the dangers of the jurisdiction, with its long history of judges and lawyers being attacked by unhappy litigants. Only last year, a judge had a bomb placed in his car, which luckily exploded after he had parked his car in the basement of his home, injuring no one. The threat, however, remains.

* * *

Geoffrey observed Amber's reaction as she read the paper. He was enjoying watching her expression which progressed from confusion, to surprise and finally satisfaction. Amber threw the paper towards him and got out of bed. She asked, "Did you arrange that?"

Geoffrey smiled at her, "I made a promise, didn't I?"

Amber hugged him and squealed. Then she asked, "Is the bitch OK?"

"It was just a warning. Now, come here and reward me for keeping my side of the deal."

Amber kissed Geoffrey deeply as he picked her up then threw her back on the bed. Amber looked up at him adoringly and asked, "Have you arranged something like this before? Having people attacked like that?"

Geoffrey had wanted to see Amber's reaction before he admitted to it, just in case she reacted differently. Now he was reassured she had enjoyed the attack on Sarah as much as he had.

"Of course, babe. I just wanted to see how you handled it before I went any further."

Amber pictured Sarah lying on the ground with the fuck scared out of her. She realised she had never felt so excited and asked Geoffrey, "Can we have her killed?"

"You be a good girl and we can do whatever we want, to anyone we want." Geoffrey stared intently at Amber before he said, "This turns you on, doesn't it babe?"

He could see the lust in Amber's eyes as she replied, "I love that you did that for me. I've never felt like this before," she gushed.

"Trust me honey, it will only get better." Geoffrey rolled her over and looked into her eyes. "Now, I think I deserve a reward for being a man of my word, don't I?"

Amber knew from looking into his eyes and feeling his hard- ness rubbing up against her exactly what Geoffrey wanted to her do and she was never more willing to give it to him. As always, the pleasure was mixed with pain and she bit into the pillows wanting to scream, but at the same time feeling the excitement well up inside her.

Sarah

Chapter 12

Sarah spent three days in the hospital after the accident, which seemed like an eternity to her. Her secretary, Kate, had brought her laptop at Sarah's insistence, but Sarah could not wait to get out. By agreement with the doctors, they allowed her to leave if she promised to stay home and rest. Of course, this was never going to happen.

Although the working week was nearly over, as it was early Friday afternoon, Sarah knew most of her staff would still be at work and she needed to go into the office to relieve her anxiety that everything was okay. As soon as she walked in and greeted her receptionist, she felt better than she had for days. She knew she was back in control and her concerns were alleviated.

Sarah flicked through her phone messages and felt extremely touched at how many people had taken the time to call her office to enquire about her and to leave a message. There were even messages from Chloe's school teacher, the security guard from the television station where she worked as a media commentator each week, and her yoga instructor Elizabeth. After flicking through all her phone messages, she turned on her computer and went through her emails.

Sarah smiled at the number of emails that continued to bounce up onto her screen, which brought home to her the large number she received each day. As she scrolled down she determined those that were urgent. One of them was from the Law Society with a heading "Important Updates". Once Sarah clicked on it she could only stare in shock at the screen. There was a photo of her at the scene at the Family Court; she was lying on the ground. She had not seen this before and was both startled by the look of fear on her face and embarrassed by the realisation that the photo had been published for all the legal fraternity to see.

Sarah sat frozen in front of the screen, staring at the picture. She realised how lucky she had been, let alone to have only suffered minor injuries. Like an emotional tsunami, a flashback hit her and she suddenly felt faint. She was sensing the agony of the memory of herself waiting in vain that night in 1984 when her parents did not come home. Her grandmother had found her staring out the window when she woke up at 6 a.m. Shortly after, she remembered the police arriving. Sarah had answered the door but they asked to speak to an adult. When her grandmother arrived at the door, the police had announced that Sarah's parents had been killed in a car accident, seemingly oblivious to the fact that Sarah's grandmother could not understand a word of English. It was not until Sarah had interpreted in Chinese to her grandmother that she had understood what had happened. Sarah recalled getting into the police car with her grandmother to go to the morgue and how the police had allowed her in, against all the rules, to interpret for her grandmother as no other interpreters could be located at the time.

Dealing with these flashbacks was something Sarah had had to learn to manage. Almost chanting to herself, she breathed slowly and deeply to regain her composure before reaching into her desk drawer for one of her pills. It only took a matter of minutes these days before she could refocus. In no time at all she returned her attention to the hundreds of emails she needed to address.

Time flew by and Sarah looked at her watch. She recalled her promise to Chloe that she would be home to make tacos with her for dinner. Motherhood was not an easy juggle for Sarah, but she could not imagine life now without Chloe. She had never imagined her life would be this way. Sometimes, Sarah felt guilty from a long run of having to work early mornings and late nights. Becoming a mother had made Sarah think about her parents more often. She now appreciated how hard it was to be a working parent and she wished she could tell them that. She wished that they could have had the joy of being grandparents and that Chloe could have felt the love they would have given her.

Sarah wondered if her father knew somehow that his decision to allow her to accept the scholarship, just before their fatal car crash, was a key factor in enabling her success. She knew that if she had not gone to boarding school, like her brother, Tom, she would have left school as soon as possible to get a job to help their grandmother support them. Sarah's brother continually reminded her, especially when he had hit her up for loans over the years, that the only reason she could finish school and go to university was because he had left school to get a job.

The anonymous benefactor of her scholarship had been unique in that she not only paid Sarah's school fees but she also covered all of Sarah's other costs. The scholarship paid for her education, uniforms, books and excursions, but also it meant that she did not miss out on anything the other children participated in, as well as music excursions to Europe, formal dresses and shoes, concerts and special events.

Feeling nostalgic and grateful, Sarah walked over to the fridge and picked up a bottle of mineral water which she drank while still holding the fridge door open and staring at the wine bottles. She thought about pouring herself a glass of wine to ease the discomfort she was feeling, but then she paused and closed the fridge.

For years she had drowned her emotional pain with alcohol, to the point she knew she was drinking excessively and becoming dependent on it. At the time, she thought it was better than the alternative. She had promised herself as soon as she had fallen pregnant, that she would never have a drink again to block out her pain.

She now only allowed herself to drink wine to relax and to enjoy herself. Realising that it was time to leave the office, she grabbed her handbag and headed to the door and home to Chloe.

Peter

Chapter 13

Peter did not know why he had chosen to turn along this street to reach his chambers. He had avoided walking this way since the attack on Sarah but because he was distracted, talking on his phone, here he was again. As he reached the street corner, near the dramatic scene where Sarah had been injured, he could still see Sarah's eyes, filled with shock and pain.

Unfortunately, death threats and verbal abuse were part of the life of those who practised in the highly emotional and volatile field of family law. Many from the profession, including Sarah, had personally experienced harassment and received death threats. The disturbing thing however was the police had still not identified the driver who attempted to run Sarah down. It had not been the person the police at first suspected and all other suspects had now been interviewed and excluded.

When Peter left their relationship, he felt that Sarah was relieved. When he went back to pick up Chloe from home for the first time after they separated, it was as though he had never been part of the family. Nothing seemed different for Sarah or Chloe, as they continued living in the same home and as a family unit, but his life had turned upside down. If it had not been for his secretary Kim, who had stepped in when she realised he was depressed over his marriage breakdown, he hated to think what he may have done to himself.

Peter knew Sarah would be in the building or "The Palace of Broken Dreams", the nickname given to it by the legal profession, most weekdays. He could not resist glancing up at the imposing marble and gold building, which looked more like a museum than a justice building. It was where couples came to have someone else make decisions about the most important things in their lives, their children and their assets, because they could not agree themselves. Pete never understood how Sarah coped with the bitterness and anger that rendered her client's emotional wrecks, raving lunatics or stubborn fools who preferred to spend their money on lawyers rather than give in to each other.

Peter stepped into the Love Bites Café, aptly named, as it was across the road from the Family Court. He usually went there to meet his clients when he had a case on in the District Court next door. As he looked around to see if his client had arrived, he was immediately drawn to a face staring straight at him. The man was sitting at a table towards the back of the café. It was a face Peter would never forget. The man looked almost the same as the last time Peter had seen him, even though now his grey hair gave him a more distinguished and elegant air. He was thirty years older now and dressed smartly in a suit instead of jeans and a T-shirt; but it was him. Anthony nodded acknowledgement of Peter's eye contact then abruptly turned away, continuing his conversation with the men sitting with him.

Clearly, Peter thought, Anthony did not want to take this any further. Maybe he needed to put their friendship behind him and Peter respected that. Just seeing Anthony, however, brought back the memories of their time together. Peter scanned the room and saw his client was not there yet; he found a table at the other end of the restaurant and sat down. He could not help but think about his friendship with Anthony and Anthony's sister Madeline, who had been his first girlfriend.

It had been a tough time in Peter's life. He did not fit in at school and he had been classified by his parents and school counsellor as "a troubled teenager." He had gravitated to the other "troubled" kids that smoked pot and drank whatever they could steal from their parents or their friends' homes. He had not been interested in girls until he met Madeline. They connected the first night they met and had talked for hours. She had a calming influence on him and he just liked talking to her. She eventually invited him home for dinner and her family was nice to him. He was there almost every weekend after a while and he got along well with her brother. Her family welcomed him and made him feel normal, unlike his own parents who seemed to have disowned him. After a couple of months, Anthony and Peter had become best mates. When he stayed at their house, he and Anthony would wait until the parents had gone to sleep then go into their wine cellar to get some wine, drink and play cards all night. Their friendship started as partners in crime, enjoying the spoils of deceit but it developed progressively into so much more.

One night, after drinking not only wine but moving onto vodka and smoking a joint, Peter and Anthony ended up in Peter's bedroom together, doings things to each other that seemed to come naturally. After that night, they realised how much they were attracted to each other, which almost came as a relief to Peter, as it explained his lack of interest in women. From then on, they spent most of their time planning their next interlude, to the ignorance of Anthony's parents and Madeline, who thought Peter was there to see her.

Their clandestine relationship went on for six months and Peter and Anthony developed a chemistry that neither of them seemed to understand. Peter knew, considering Anthony was so young, that it was wrong to do what he did with him, but he had never felt attracted to anyone like that before or since. Peter knew that the pain and intensity of this first love had never completely extinguished and Anthony had never left his memory.

In his early twenties, Peter had a couple of sexual encounters with males, but they were all one-night stands. He found himself attracted to men from time to time, but only if they reminded him of Anthony. Peter mainly dated women but found developing a relationship difficult.

Peter often wondered about Anthony and whether he was happy or not. It had concerned him deeply that Anthony had appeared in his life again today. He was already wanting to contact him after just seeing him again for a fleeting moment. He did feel concerned about whether he could stay away from temptation if he went ahead and contacted him, which could turn his life upside down. There was no doubt that Anthony had been the only special person in Peter's life, until he met Sarah.

Sarah was the first woman, since Anthony's sister, that Peter was able to develop a relationship with. He was forty-two-years-old at the time they met. The relationship with Sarah was totally different from anything he had ever experienced. While it lacked the excitement of the intense sexual intensity and satisfaction he had with Anthony, with Sarah he felt safe and that he belonged.

Sarah had said to him that, at times, she felt more like his sister than his wife. He felt attracted to Sarah, but she was right when she said their relationship was almost platonic. He did not realise it at the time, but Sarah read his lack of sexual appetite as unconditional love. She was relieved that, for once, a man was not constantly pressing her for time alone or for romantic weekends away, which disrupted her busy life. Instead, Peter was content to spend time with Sarah, whenever she was free, and never pushed her or invaded her space and that is how their relationship flourished.

After marrying Sarah and having Chloe, Peter loved being part of a family; he finally felt at home. When their marriage ended, he was devastated. He had known that Sarah was complicated, but as they say the brilliant always are. She had her demons, but Peter loved her anyway. Sometimes she would disappear before his eyes - she would just switch off and go somewhere else in her head. Her strength, loyalty and sense of what was right, far outweighed the problematic side of her. Peter knew that all her issues had something to do with her family, about whom she had refused to talk for a long time. It was only after Peter had pressed her for months that she finally confided in him. She told him her parents were killed in a car accident on their way home from work. After that, she had gone away to boarding school and drifted apart from her brother; it all seemed very sad to Peter.

Peter knew that he and Sarah had issues with intimacy and vulnerability but as their marriage went on, Sarah seemed to put up an even higher emotional wall. Eventually, the only person she allowed through it was their daughter, Chloe. It had caused their troubled marriage to become unbearable for him and he felt he had no choice but to leave when all intimacy had ceased for over a year between them.

Sarah's reaction to him leaving had not surprised Peter. To him she appeared relieved. She said she had always expected it, which made him even more convinced that she had never let him into her emotional world. Sarah had however, always made an earnest effort to encourage Peter's relationship with Chloe and did so even more after they separated. It was one of the most important things to Sarah that Chloe had both her parents in her life, having suffered painfully herself from the early loss of both her parents. As Peter drank the last of his coffee, he noticed Anthony leave the café from the other side of the room, evading Peter in the process. Peter shrugged nonchalantly, both comprehending but regretting the lack of contact. He pulled his briefcase up from the floor and stepped across to the courts to represent yet another battler fighting the system.

Anthony

Chapter 14

As if they had no alternative, Anthony's eyes were drawn again to Peter as he left the café. It was the first time he had been to a café at this end of town, and now regretted allowing his business manager to suggest it. He had known it was him as soon as he had seen Peter's eyes. No one had ever looked at him that way before or would again. As Peter walked closer to him at the counter, he could smell him. He had put on weight which suited him, his hair had become grey and he looked very conservative, but it was Peter. It had taken Anthony years to get over him. As close as he and Peter were, after Peter broke up with Anthony's older sister, he had disappeared from Anthony's life. As a fifteen-year-old boy, all Anthony could do after Peter left him was to block him out of his mind. Memories of Peter had haunted him in his dreams and sometimes he thought that he would never get over him, but he had - until now.

Seeing Peter again was bringing back all the anger, shame, humiliation and betrayal he had felt when Peter vanished from his life. He had gone through the confusion and the pendulum of emotions alternating between loving him and hating him, of missing him to giving anything to just see him again. Through it all, Anthony had believed Peter loved him and that something terrible had happened to him, to make him disappear as he did.

For many months Anthony had waited, believing Peter would come back but he never did. Anthony felt unsettled and confused as to why this surge of bitterness was suddenly racing through his mind. His life was perfect now and he did not need this. He had a beautiful wife who adored him, a stepdaughter, a beautiful home and a successful career. Why would he even care about Peter and what had happened so long ago, when it did not affect him now? He knew he needed to just get Peter out of his mind and let it go, but as he walked along the street, he could not help but reflect on how good Peter had looked. He looked like the successful barrister Anthony had heard about. Dressed in a classic suit, he was just like Anthony had imagined him at this age. He knew Peter had seen him and he wondered if Peter wanted to contact him. He wondered if Peter was in a relation- ship with anyone.

Anthony found himself reminiscing about all the nights he had spent with Peter. He wondered if he had he ever mattered to him or if he was just something he had used to entertain himself when he became bored with his sister. He was developing a dangerous and burning desire to look into Peter's eyes to see if they still had the same connection. He needed to feel Peter's touch on his skin. He realised the more he thought about him the more desperate he was to see him.

Geoffrey

Chapter 15

1968

Geoffrey stood at the school gates, the only boy wearing short pants. His mother stood next to him, stoic and emotionless. She was dressed like she was in her early twenties in a tight short skirt and low-cut blouse. She had never fitted in and now neither did her son. She must have known and felt her only child's total humiliation, his desire to melt into the ground, to disappear, to do anything except walk into that school ground as the only boy wearing short pants. If she did feel any empathy for her son she did not show it.

"Come on son," she said. She only ever called him "son" and her treatment of him had been mistaken, by many who knew them, for child abuse rather than love. But she loved him in the only way she knew how to love. It was the kind of love that knew no boundaries or limits but because of that it was blurred at the edges.

Geoffrey's feet would not move. They were stuck to the ground by some superhuman force. His toes were trying to grip into the ground like claws and he stood emotionless, staring at the boys who were staring back at him and pointing at his knees. He could not hear what they were saying but he knew what it would be. Every other boy was wearing long grey pants. The signature that marked the transition from primary to high school; the mark of becoming a man. He had already been taunted for being skinny and short in primary school and for his unfortunate lack of co-ordination, which caused his clumsiness, particularly on the football field where he would drop the ball, knock it on or just miss the pass altogether.

Last night he had gone to bed excited about starting the first day of the year. This morning, after he had been woken by his mother, he had seen her hanging up his freshly pressed uniform and to his horror he had seen his short pants from last year.

He had pleaded with his mother, "Mum, where are my long pants? You told me that you had bought them for me."

His mother had looked at him and laughed dismissively as she replied, "I did buy them at the end of last term last year. I thought you would grow and you didn't. They are way too long for you. You'll have to wear your short pants until you grow tall enough, son. Now hurry up and finish your breakfast or you will be late for school." She then turned and walked out of his room.

It was not until much later in his life that Geoffrey had wondered if his mother had known what she had done to him by making him wear short pants when all the other boys were wearing long pants. Why couldn't she have just had the hems taken up? Did she now know how humiliated he felt because he was not only one of the shortest boys in school, but he looked like he was still in junior school because he was wearing the junior uniform? Did she realise what she had done or was she just too busy with keeping up the pretence of her shitty life, when she felt she had deserved a whole lot better?

His mother often confided in Geoffrey, during his early childhood, that she found her life a misery and that she had been disappointed that his father had never been promoted in his job. She had insisted his father would never amount to anything because of his obsession with developing the stupid idea he and his mate had for a dry pet food that could be stored and kept for months. She felt that she deserved far better than the miserable life they ended up with.

All she cared about was finding a way for Geoffrey to become a success. She latched onto that hope when the teachers told her that he had something special about him. The teachers were convinced that Geoffrey's poems and stories were creative masterpieces and that he demonstrated an imagination far beyond his years. They had recommended he apply to a selective school for gifted and talented boys. Soon this became all his mother cared about - that maybe he would get her out of the suburban shitty life that she had married into instead of what she deserved.

It was only when he went to the school interview that his mother finally made sure he had long pants to wear. It was only when the school board told his mother, after reading his work, they believed he had extraordinary creative talents, that his mother suddenly cared openly about him. She did not bother telling them that she never once helped him with his homework, read anything he had ever written until the very night before, or cared about anything else except herself. For the first time in his life, as Geoffrey got up from the interview table, she went to hold his hand to leave the boardroom. Never in his life had Geoffrey had a memory of his mother touching him.

Two years later, when Geoffrey was fourteen years old, his mother finally gave up waiting for him and his father to come good. One Saturday afternoon, as she walked out the front door of their home with her bags already packed, she announced to them both that she had decided to leave. They watched her leave in a limousine, his father later finding out she had emptied their bank joint accounts.

Upon her leaving, his father's reaction was to say to Geoffrey, "I hope she is happy now," as he walked back out to the garage to continue working on his dog food formula. Geoffrey never saw his mother again.

Eighteen months later, his father went on to realise his dream, and his dried dog food invention made him millions. His father lived on happily, remarrying, and eventually dying twenty years later. On his death bed, his father had apologised to Geoffrey for his mother's abandonment of him. He left Geoffrey with a large managed trust fund that his father hoped would ensure his future happiness and security.

Anne

Chapter 16

Anne and Anthony drove into the circular driveway of their home, still looking as happy as newlyweds even though they had been together for several years. He had called her after his morning coffee meeting with his lawyers in the city and said he wanted to have lunch with her at home. He was still grappling with his emotions from seeing Peter, after so many years. He knew that going home to Anne would help to settle him down again. On the way home, he had repeated to himself again and again that his life with her was his future and that Peter was his past.

They were the perfect looking couple. Anne was tall, thin and beautiful with shiny, long brown hair and striking emerald green eyes. Anthony was the archetypal tall, successful businessman in his grey suit and with his hair slightly greying at the temples. Anthony leaned towards Anne as they stopped the car in front of their beautiful homestead. He put his arm around her shoulder and kissed her lightly on the cheek.

After Anne's husband died unexpectedly of a heart attack at the age of forty-two, her life was difficult as a single mum. The fact that Gary's wealthy parents had hired a lawyer for them to apply for custody of Jessica was the straw that nearly broke the camel's back for her. That was when she thought she was going to completely break down. If had not been for the help of one of her sister's client's, the lawyer Sarah Walters, she knew she would not have had the strength or money to battle the parents for Jessica. Sarah managed to reach an agreement with Gary's parents' lawyers for Anne to have custody of Jessica if she transferred the funds she received from his life insurance policy, which she and Gary had taken out and paid for.

Anne commenced looking for work and applied for several jobs thereafter, eventually obtaining a position with Anthony's firm as a receptionist. For the first six months, her relationship with Anthony was purely professional, although the fact they got along very well was obvious to all. It was at their first office Christmas function that they kissed. It was a kiss that shocked them both, but the chemistry had been established.

Almost from that very first night, they had never been apart. Her daughter, Jessica, had bonded with Anthony almost from the first moment they met, when Anthony gave her a pink bike for her birthday. Life with Anthony took Anne from struggling to pay the rent and juggling credit card bills and school fees to a life of luxury as the much loved and cherished woman of a very wealthy man. Anne could not believe how lucky she was that Anthony had taken Jessica on as though she were his own child. She was amazed at how understanding Anthony was of Jessica's teenage moods, which were becoming more and more unpleasant, lately. Anne knew that Anthony's love for Jessica was unconditional and deep and it was obvious for all to see. Well it was obvious to Anne.

Jane

Chapter 17

As quickly as Brett had taken Jane's breath away by kissing her, he had jolted her back into reality by ending the kiss and sitting her down abruptly. The look in his eye changed as he grabbed the papers in front of him. Jane did not know what to say. He saw the confusion in her eyes and that seemed to make him more uncomfortable.

In a sudden burst, he stood up, picked up his champagne glass and drank it in one gulp, before saying forcefully, "Jane we need to sort out our financial situation. As you know, when we bought this house I had to borrow most of the money because I needed my cash for the deal my company was working on."

Jane noted that he had just referred to the money they received from the sale of their last home, her dream home as "his" cash. She had become aware that over the last few years, Brett had started to refer to their house as "his" and that "he" was going to buy a new car. She now realised it was more than just a slip of the tongue. He viewed his income and their assets as his entirely. This was all in contrast to the talks they had had when they decided they were ready to have children. They had a long and serious discussion, because at the time Jane's career in marketing had taken off much faster than Brett's and she was earning the much higher income. It was a major decision they had made together for her to stop working after she had their first child but one which they felt was important for them as a family. Until recently, Brett had always referred to their home, cars and his business as theirs and the change was now evident and concerning to Jane. She realised that as he was becoming more successful he did not regard her contribution to their family as being as valuable as his.

Jane are you listening to me?" he demanded. "That deal now looks like becoming the biggest deal of my lifetime and my partners want me to make sure that there will be no unforeseen problems in the future with you and me."

Jane was confused. "I don't know what you mean Brett? Why would we have problems?"

Brett looked straight at Jane. The look in his eyes was a combination of anger and frustration when he said, "Jane for the last couple of years it has been a nightmare living with you. We have struggled to keep our marriage together. How can you say we have not had problems?"

Jane felt angry at Brett's retort and defended herself, "Brett, I was so excited about us moving into our new home, about you having the home you had wanted since you were a boy. I have worked endlessly for three days to get everything moved in and perfect for you so that we could have a beautiful night tonight. What's happened since you went away last week to Melbourne?" "Jane, you have been lost in space for so long, you have no idea where we are as a couple. I am trying to complete a deal that could set me up for the rest of my life. I don't know if we will last, so it's hard for me to convince my business partners of that." Jane was furious but knew that she could not show it or Brett would respond badly. She held back her anger, even though she was pushed close to tears.

"Brett, what are you saying? I don't know what you're saying!"

"Jane, what I am saying is that I want you to sign a financial agreement. I have it here and what it says is, if we break up you will not get any part of my business partnership and the deal I have been working on with my partners. They need to know that the deal will not be interrupted by us breaking up and lawyers getting involved in a divorce case."

"Brett, you're scaring me!" Jane exclaimed. "Why would we get divorced, we have just bought a new home, we have children. Why would we get lawyers involved and how would that affect your business and your partners? We've been together for thirteen years. Why is this now an issue?"

"Jane, there have been changes to the Family Law Act since we married. Now you can make agreements while you are married, not only before and after."

"Why would anyone want to do that?," Jane asked.

Trying to look and sound calm Brett replied reassuringly, "So that if a couple break up, certain assets can't be taken by the other person. My partners are insisting on this, so that if any of us gets divorced the business isn't fucked over by our exes or drawn into a Family Court dispute."

Jane was confused. This was the last thing she had expected from Brett tonight.

"Look Jane, this is just to keep my partners happy. Anyway, when you read it you will see that it protects you and the kids too. You and the kids will get to stay in the house until the kids turn eighteen and I will pay you child support if we break up. You will be safe and secure and I will be able to satisfy my business partners that our marriage will not interfere with our business plans, should we break up. If we stay together, nothing changes, so it's a win-win for you."

Jane got up from the table, walked inside and sat on the lounge. She was feeling unsettled and needed to be somewhere comfortable. She closed her eyes, sank back into the sofa and put her legs up on the ottoman.

Brett followed her back inside and argued, "Jane, please don't carry on with your usual floppy emotional bullshit. I know you're okay. This is no big deal. You need to just sign this. If you love me like you say you do, I don't see the big deal."

Brett walked back out onto the verandah, poured himself another glass of champagne and skulled it. He picked up the bottle and brought both the bottle and the glasses inside with him. He filled up one glass and handed it to Jane.

"Please Jane," he pleaded, "this should be a celebration. Don't make it anything else. Sign the document and we can then have dinner before the kids get home and everything will be normal. You know I love you."

Brett leaned towards Jane and touched her face before kissing her lightly on the lips. No matter how many times he kissed her, for her it was always the most beautiful feeling; his soft lips ever so gently touching hers and pulling away to kiss her again. Unfortunately, no matter how he behaved Brett never failed to take her breath away when he kissed her.

Jane looked into Brett's eyes and saw what she needed to see. He loved her and she needed to do this for him. She would do anything for him and he knew it.

Brett walked over to the table, picked up the document, handed it to Jane and said, "Sign where the stickers are. There and there." Jane signed. Brett walked away and swiftly placed it back into his folder.

To Jane's relief, Brett then walked back to her, reached out to help her up from the lounge and took her hand as he led her into the kitchen, turning to say sweetly, "Honey I'll get us another bottle of champagne and let's have the lobster on the verandah to celebrate our first night in our new home."

Jane heard the bottle pop and realised she needed to get through the evening as though she were okay with what had just happened and deal with her feelings later. This was how she had kept their relationship together for most of her marriage. She had developed the ability to push away any rising feelings of anxiety, like when Brett did not call her for days when he was away on business, when she found a woman's jacket in his suitcase that did not belong to her, and receipts for jewellery he had never given her. She had made the decision some time ago and she had kept her family together, so far. How long she could keep it up for she did not know, but for now she was going to fight for her marriage and her family to stay together. Hopefully, Brett would eventually see how much she loved him and how much she had gone through to help him in his career and to keep their family together. He had said to her when he married her that she would make the best wife in the world and she was determined to be just that.

Anne

Chapter 18

The school nurse had called Anne to say Jessica was not feeling well and that Anne needed to come in as soon as possible. As she was picking up her handbag and keys to leave the office, Anne realised she had just been thinking yesterday how easily Jessica had gone through her school life. She could not remember the last time she had to pick Jessica up from school because she was sick. She had noticed that Jessica was not her usual happy self that morning, but Jessica told her she was fine when she had asked her if she was okay.

Anne parked the car and headed to the medical clinic at the school. The receptionist was waiting for her and greeted her, "Hello Mrs Shaw, Jessica is with Dr Quade and they are waiting to see you. I'll take you there now."

"Isn't Dr Quade the school psychologist? I'm sure I met him at the start of school year cocktail party."

"Yes, Mrs Shaw he is," the receptionist confirmed.

Just as the receptionist walked from behind the reception counter to take Anne to Dr Shaw, two policewomen arrived. One of them announced formally to the receptionist, "Hi, we are here to see Dr Quade. We spoke to him this morning and he's expecting us."

"I'll let him know you are here. I will be back in just a moment, officers. Please just take a seat."

Anne whispered to the receptionist, "Why are the police here?" "I am sure Dr Quade will explain everything," she replied. "He just asked me to take you into his office."

When she returned from taking Anne in to Dr Quade, the detective that had addressed her earlier asked, "Is that the mother of the girl Dr Quade called us about?"

"Yes," the receptionist answered.

"Sorry, we had hoped to get here before her," the detective said. "This is never easy for anyone."

Jane

Chapter 19

Jane was feeling guilty that she had doubted Brett. Since she signed the financial agreement a few weeks ago, he had been more attentive than ever. Maybe it was just as he said, that his partners were making life difficult for him and the stress had been affecting him. Jane did not read the document she signed, but Brett said she and the girls would be okay.

Days later, whilst she reflected on signing the agreement without reading it, she had a flashback to a segment on her favourite radio programme by the lawyer, Sarah Walters. Sarah had said that you should never sign a legal document without reading it first. At the time, Jane recalled thinking, *who would do that?* Now she had done it herself.

Brett had been so attentive to the girls recently, reading to them and helping them with their homework the past couple of weeks. He was usually too exhausted from work to be bothered with "playing babysitter", as he put it, but lately he had been different. In the last two years he had been away for work more than any other time in their marriage and it had been hard for Jane and the girls. Having him home after work each day lately, acting like a normal dad coming home for dinner and helping with homework, was just like old times and Jane hoped it would last.

At times, when Brett was away for weeks and had been too busy to even call her, Jane had felt neglected and unloved, but she would never bother Brett about those feelings. Although she wished Brett would be more aware of how much she missed him when he was away, and how keeping in contact with her during these times would make her feel supported, she knew she had to accept him for the way he was and not how she wanted him to be. Brett had explained to Jane that when he was on a deal it consumed him, and when he was with Jane that consumed him. He could not balance both. Sometimes, at the end of his business trips, he would go on a trip to a health resort in Los Angeles. That also sometimes upset Jane because he had never asked her to join him. She knew he had a group of friends that he met up with, but he told her it was a boys' thing, even though women also went to the resort.

There was an incident, a year before, that had caused her to feel insecure and she had discussed it with her psychiatrist. He wanted Brett to come in and discuss it with him, but Jane knew Brett would never agree to see him with her. It was an incident that occurred when they went to a wedding of one of Brett's friends in Ireland. As they were walking into the hotel to check in, two women walked up to Brett and proceeded to hug him and ask why he had not returned their emails.

One of them said very loudly, in her South African accent, "But why did you miss Anne's birthday, Brett, in LA? We all agreed to meet up after in July and you just didn't show? Anne said you definitely confirmed you were coming."

She then realised that Jane was standing there, and she looked at her and said to Brett, "Who is your friend, Brett?"

Jane had stepped forward and said to her, "I'm not his friend, I'm his wife."

"Oh, you must be newlyweds then! Is that where you've been Brett, getting married?"

Instead of replying to her, Brett said, "We have to leave now. Nice to see you but we have to get going."

He grabbed Jane's hand and started to walk towards the lifts. As they were walking, Jane turned around and called back, "We're not newlyweds, we've been married for nine years and have two children." She had seen the shock on their faces. When they got back to the room, Jane had been very upset and confused. She asked Brett to explain why the women thought he was going to a birthday party in July and that he was not married. He replied that he had met them at a health resort, hardly knew them and that they had clearly mixed him up with someone else. When Jane asked about the emails he had simply replied, "I'm not entertaining any more madness." He said he was going to do some work and reply to some emails, slamming behind him the bedroom door of their suite. Jane found the hardest part about Brett's work was that she had no idea what he did when he was away. She was home with the kids, so he knew exactly where she was, but on some of his long trips, Jane would be lucky to know what country he was in.

Sarah

Chapter 20

Sarah was leaving the Family Court for the day and was now heading back to her office for her pro bono meetings with clients. Once a month, Sarah set aside an afternoon to see people for a free legal consultation if they had called in to her radio or television appearances. Before she started with the appointments, she noticed she had missed a call from Peter. She checked to see if he had left a message in case she needed to return his call. She was proud that they had worked hard together, with a counsellor, to overcome their issues and jointly parent Chloe. Of course, because of Chloe, he would always be a part of her life. She often wondered whether Peter would settle down again with another partner.

Sarah had seen her friends having to cope with handing over their children to their exes and the new partners and it was extremely difficult to get used to. She often wondered if all those people who wrote articles about "conscious uncoupling" and "moving on" after separation had been through the experience themselves. She still recalled her friend Carolyn calling her in tears one Christmas day. She had arrived at Sarah's home after dropping her young sons to her ex's home on Christmas morning, following the court orders. Carolyn had recounted to Sarah how it took all her strength to smile as she walked her boys to her ex-husband's door and handed them over to him and his new young wife.

Sarah always tried to find the good in a bad situation and she would often say that the one good thing that came out of her divorce was having first-hand experience. She knew she had developed a deep understanding of the emotional pain that her clients went through and how that affected them. It had given her the ability to see things from a totally different perspective. The pain of having to leave the family home, the solitude of being alone at night, the agony of watching your child miss the other parent and the tiredness of doing it all on your own, were experiences that Sarah could now relate to with her clients.

Sarah thought moving on with her life after her separation would be easier than it had proved to be. In the first year, although she had sorted out the financial settlement with Peter, generously and swiftly, when it came to handing Chloe over to Peter on the first Christmas morning, she was a mess. Sarah and Chloe had spent a wonderful morning together but instead of the joy of the day continuing, making lunch together and pulling apart bon bons, she had had to drop Chloe to Peter's house. She felt empty handing her over to Peter that day. Instead of the perfect family Christmas Day as they had spent the previous year, Sarah went to the office to take her mind off her sense of loss. It was bittersweet when she called Chloe later in the day and heard how happy Chloe was with Peter, while Sarah was feeling lost and lonely.

Sarah buzzed Kate to let her know she was ready to start the first of the conferences booked in for the afternoon, which was tight with back to back appointments. After the final conference Kate came in to give Sarah her phone messages but said, "You'll have to return them in the car. You need to jump in the car and head to Justice Myer's house ASAP".

Sarah looked at her watch and realised she was due at the judge's home in little more than an hour. The week before, Sarah had received a formal invitation from Justice Hilary Myer from the Supreme Court to ask if she would join her for dinner at home. It was an invitation with the grace and formality of a bygone era. Sarah was both surprised and flattered by the invitation. Hilary Myer was one of the very few women to be appointed Chief Justice of the Supreme Court and she had come from a long line of Supreme Court judges. The first time Sarah met her was when Justice Myer was one of the guest judges at Sarah's university graduation ceremony, so many years ago. She remembered that when she walked onto the stage to receive her law degree with first class honours, the judge had handed it to her with tears in her eyes. She also told Sarah how proud she was of her finishing at the top of her year. Since that time, Sarah had rarely appeared in the Supreme Court, so she did not know Hilary Myer well.

Sarah picked up her bag, car keys and headed towards the lift. As she pulled out of the car park, she called Peter. He picked up immediately and was clearly happy to hear from her. "How are you Sarah?" he asked cheerfully. Just hearing Peter sounding so happy made Sarah feel happy herself. Peter was never down, but he rarely sounded as happy as he was right now on the phone.

"I'm busy as usual, Peter, and rushing to a meeting but all is good. You sound happy."

"I had a great day in court today. You know how it is when you get justice in an unfair situation and how happy that can make you feel?"

Sarah could picture him with a huge smile on his face as he said it. "I don't know what you did, but I am just so happy to hear the joy in your voice, Peter. I haven't heard that for a while. It must have meant something to you."

That was the thing with Sarah, she analysed everything. Peter thought he had just had a good win, but now he was thinking about her question and he realised she was right.

"I just helped a dad to keep seeing his son when his ex-wife tried to get an AVO to stop him and portray him as something he wasn't. I know that if I hadn't been at court today and just happened to finish my case early, so I was able to help him pro bono, she would have got the AVO and he would now not be seeing his son."

Sarah sighed deeply as Peter spoke excitedly to her about his day. It was this part of Peter that she had fallen in love with - his desire to help those that the legal system was failing. He was one of the few barristers that always did pro bono cases on the hop while they were at court, in between their paying clients. He had said that some of them were his most rewarding cases. "Well then, he was a very lucky man today, Peter."

"Thanks Sarah. I was calling you not just to share my victory but also to let you know the wife was really upset when she lost the AVO and as she left the court she said to my client, "I'm hiring Sarah Walters, the best lawyer in town and she will make sure I get what I want. I'm sorry to interfere Sarah but I just have to tell you his side of the story in case she tries to hire you."

"Well that's a problem easily fixed, Peter, isn't it? Now that you have talked to me about the case I have information I would not otherwise have had.

That makes me ethically conflicted and I now could not act for her. Do me a favour and email Kate with your client's name, so Kate can deal with this if she tries to make an appointment."

Smiling to himself Peter replied, "Thanks Sarah. I needed to just give this guy a break because he married such a wicked witch." He laughed, then added, "Sarah one other thing. Elizabeth, the yoga teacher who used to come to our house to give us yoga lesson years ago, called me to ask how you were after she saw the news about the attack on you. She was relieved to hear you were okay and asked me to send you her regards. She said to also let you know that her sister, Anne, who you helped with her custody case years ago, has remarried a great guy and she and Jessica are really happy."

"She left a message at my office too. I'm sorry I just haven't had a chance to get back to her."

"I don't think she expects a call back. She was happy I could give her an update, but while I was talking to her she asked how Chloe was and said she has now started yoga classes for kids. She asked if Chloe might like to go and try it. Can I book her for this weekend when I have her?"

"Of course, Peter, I think that yoga would be great for Chloe to try. Please send my best to Elizabeth when you see her and tell her I'm so happy for her sister and niece. It's nice to hear that people do find happiness again after going through a difficult divorce."

As she hung up, Sarah reflected on how much she had enjoyed her home yoga classes, but like everything else, she had no time to continue doing it. She thought to herself that if Chloe enjoyed it, then perhaps she would make time to book private lessons at home for them both. As usual, the thought entered her mind just as she reached her destination and flew out as quickly as it had arrived.

Sarah

Chapter 21

.

Driving down the street looking for Justice Myer's home, Sarah finally spotted number 42 and pulled over to park her car. She leaned over to the passenger seat to pick up the bottle of her favourite French champagne and the bouquet of flowers. After getting out of the car, she headed towards the imposing security gates of the Hilary's beautiful home. Sarah announced her arrival through the intercom and the towering iron gates opened. As Sarah walked through to the manicured gardens, she was taken aback at the immense colour and beauty of the gardens. Her eyes flickered as they followed the endless lines of rose bushes which continued until they reached various flowering shrubs and magnificent trees. The gentle fragrances reminded her of being in the garden with her father as a little girl. A wave of nostalgia and abiding loss swept over her. She thought wistfully of the small garden her father had tended so lovingly as a distraction from his financial pressures. She could not help but think how much she would have loved holding her father's hand right now and what she would have given to be walking in these gardens with him.

As she glanced up towards the front door, she saw Justice Myer standing there smiling. It was not until this moment that Sarah realised just how attractive she was. Sarah had only ever seen her when she was wearing her court gown and wig. Standing there with her hair out to her shoulders and wearing a cream tailored dress, Sarah thought the judge looked not only elegant, but quite beautiful.

"You didn't need to bring anything, Sarah!" the judge admonished her, as Sarah handed her the flowers and champagne.

With a broad smile, Sarah said, "I'm sorry but it's something that was drilled into me as a child, judge."

Hilary smiled as she agreed, "That's exactly how I was brought up. Now come inside and you must call me Hilary. It's just the two of us for dinner. I know you must be wondering why I have asked you to come to my home to see me, so I shall get us a drink and we can sit down and I'll explain."

Sarah followed Hilary into the most elegant room she had ever seen. It was a room of grand proportions, beautiful artwork and exquisite furnishings. From a domed ceiling, a magnificent crystal chandelier was suspended over a long antique dining table which had been disproportionately set for two. A butler discreetly appeared and took the flowers and champagne from Hilary.

"Thank you, Steve," Hilary said, "and could you please bring us a glass of champagne."

They sat down at the dining table, and Sarah noticed a gift wrapped box in front of her on the table.

"After I have explained why I invited you here, Sarah, I would like to give you this gift. But first, let me give you some background." "Sarah, I'm sorry that I didn't meet you one on one like this before. I'm doing so now because I have an inoperable and terminal illness. This isn't how I had planned to meet you for the first time, but that's the card life has dealt me. I hope we have as much time as possible together before my illness advances to the final stage."

Before Sarah could respond, Hilary continued, "Don't be sad for me. That's not why you are here. There is something far more important."

Hilary leaned over and touched Sarah's hand as she began to speak, "Sarah, the last time I saw you was at your university graduation and I was so proud of you."

Sarah interrupted, "Hilary, I remember that. I will never forget it. My parents had died, and my grandmother and brother were unable to attend and I remember feeling alone and sad that all my friends had their family there and I had no one. Then, when you handed me my degree, you had tears in your eyes and you told me you were proud of me. Even though I didn't know you, when you looked at me and held my hand, I felt that you were genuinely proud of me and that made me feel like someone cared."

Hilary had tears in her eyes, which she dabbed at with her white embroidered handkerchief. Sarah could not help but think that Hilary even cried elegantly. The butler had arrived with the two glasses of champagne and he looked concerned. "Ma'am is everything alright?" he asked.

"Thank you, Steve. Yes, it is more than alright," she assured him. He smiled and left.

"I'm sorry if I upset you, Hilary," Sarah apologised, feeling awful. Hilary waved away the apology with a smile and continued to speak in her gentle but assured tone, "I'm sorry I have left this for so long, Sarah. I would have given anything to hug you that day and tell you how very proud I was of you. In the box in front of you is a family heirloom. I took it with me to give to you that day but when you were announced as the honour student of the year and received the University Medal, I didn't want anything to distract you from that moment. After that, no time seemed the right time to give it to you, until now."

Sarah wondered if she had just heard correctly. "Hilary, you brought the broach to the graduation ceremony to give to me? Why would you have done that, when you didn't even know me?"

"Sarah, I gave you the scholarship to go to boarding school. I have been watching your progress since you were eleven years old."

Sarah was completely taken aback and did not know what to say except a very meek, "Thank you".

"It has been my pleasure," said Hilary "I have followed the progress of you and all the girls to whom I have provided scholarship over the last thirty years, and it has given me more joy than anything else in my life. You were my youngest scholarship recipient and the application was sent in for you by a teacher at your public school, Ms Kris. My scholarships are given to students recommended to me by teachers, who they feel are special and deserving."

"I remember Ms Kris. She taught me in Year 6 and she was also the sports mistress," Sarah said with a degree of fondness. "Ms Kris called me and told me she thought you were a special child and that my scholarship could change your life. She told me about your parents and how concerned she was for you because of the bullying at your school. I was the one who tele- phoned your father and talked him into agreeing to you going to boarding school. I'm so sorry he and your mother passed away in a car accident."

Sarah looked down at the floor, pained by the mention of her parents' accident and, at the same time, overwhelmed by the tremendous acts of kindness to her from both her teacher and Hilary. She raised her head and said, knowing her words were inadequate.

"I don't know what to say, Hilary. I am so grateful to you and Ms Kris. I felt truly alone after I lost my parents, but I needn't have been. I had both of you caring for me, I just didn't know it. I'm so pleased I know that now."

"After your parents passed away, Ms Kris contacted me and we arranged for you to go to school as soon as possible. I have monitored you since then. As you were my only scholarship recipient with no parents, I promised your grandmother that I would watch over you and make sure you had everything you needed and whatever the other girls had. The school sent me your reports and photos each year. I attended all your school events and speech days. I was bursting with pride at each one of them!"

"Why didn't I get to meet you then Hilary? Why now?" "When I started the scholarship," Hilary replied, "I wanted to be a silent benefactor. I started it after I lost my daughter. Mary was stillborn. I was given an emergency caesarean, which resulted in some problems, preventing me from having any more children. I thought that providing a scholarship would, in a way, allow me to remember Mary and to be a kind of surrogate parent to other girls. It helped enormously with my grief. I stayed anonymous because I didn't want the parents or girls to feel indebted to me in any way. It was a gift and as rewarding to me as it was to them." While Sarah listened to Hilary's heartbreaking story, she realised what a beautiful person she was and what terrible hardship she had experienced. Instead of becoming bitter about her loss, Hilary had dealt with it by creating a scholarship to watch other people's daughters benefit from the education that her daughter had missed out on.

Sarah snapped out of her reverie to hear Hilary say, "It was only when your parents died, and your grandmother asked me to watch over you that I felt it was okay to play more of a role in your education."

Sarah recalled her first work experience, which was at a legal office. She asked, "Did you arrange my work experience with the law firm when I was in Year 10? That changed my life and was the reason I went into law."

"Yes, I arranged that." Hilary laughed, pleased at her handiwork. Continuing on she said, "As you were a fantastic debater and public speaker and academically advanced, your careers advisor at school thought law was a natural choice."

"They were so kind to me there, Hilary. That was the first time I had been in a legal office. I was completely overawed and they knew it. My work experience with the family law partner, Michael Jacobs, was what made me decide to become a lawyer and to specialise in family law."

"I was very excited when I was told you wanted to do a degree in law when you finished school, as it seemed a natural fit for you. I was surprised when you chose to take the job in a specialist family law firm for your first position, when I knew you had received several job offers after winning the University Medal. I was informed you were adamant that was the field you wanted to specialise in."

Sarah nodded before she went on to explain to Hilary. "My best friend at boarding school was there because her mother had died of breast cancer after her parents' divorced. After she passed away, and while my friend was grieving and living with her maternal grandparents, her father, who had been overseas for most of her life had started a family court case for her to live with him. Their mutual lawyers had agreed the best result was for her to go to boarding school and be with neither of them. My friend had confided in me that her father had been physically violent to both herself and her mother for as long as she could remember. Her mother had been unable to prove it in court, so her grandparents had agreed she should go to boarding school, even though it upset them greatly, as they did not want to risk her being sent to live with her father.

I had discussed this situation with Michael and, with great patience, he explained the difficulties of the family law system to me. After I realised how difficult it was for people like my friend's grandparents to win such cases to protect their children, I decided that I wanted to work in the area of family law to help as many people as I could, and to at least try to eventually change the system that was obviously flawed."

Hilary looked out the window at the heavily laden branches of the flame tree, whose leaves were turning to amber. She turned back to Sarah. "I am so glad you told me the reason for your choice of jurisdiction Sarah. It explains much about you and why you are such a special person."

"I'm not special, Hilary. I think we all try to find our place in life where we can help others if we can."

"Not everyone thinks that way Sarah and that is why I have asked you here today. I have three scholarship girls, aged fourteen, sixteen and seventeen now and I am asking you to take over the control of these and future scholarships. I need someone who will continue my work and I know you would be perfect, but I do understand if you are too busy to do so. I know you are a mother, so please feel no pressure to say 'yes'."

Sarah stood up and walked over to Hilary and asked, "Can I hug you, please?" Hilary reached out for Sarah's embrace.

Sarah said, "I have never been so honoured. I promise to do my best to continue your legacy. I can never repay what you have done for me but if I do this for you, I can at least feel I'm trying."

Hilary smiled and picked up the gift box, which she handed to Sarah. Sarah opened it to see, resting on a bed of dark blue velvet, a beautiful brooch with a gold cross.

"That has been passed down in my family for hundreds of years to the next family member who became a lawyer. I have no children to pass it down to, so I am passing it to you. To continue the tradition, I would like you to pass it down to your daughter or one of the children who are our benefactors, who becomes a lawyer."

Sarah had tears in her eyes as she said with heartfelt emotion, "I am so touched, Hilary."

Hilary looked delighted and said in a much brighter tone, "Well, now that we have the formalities out of the way, Sarah, let's have a lovely dinner. For the rest of the night, let's talk about your daughter and all that has happened in your life. I want to hear everything."

Anne

Chapter 22

The moment Anne saw the police, she felt uneasy and confused. *Why were the police waiting to see Dr Quade too?* She was suddenly feeling nervous.

"Mrs Shaw," called the receptionist, "Please come with me to see Dr Quade." Anne followed her down the hallway to the doctor's room.

Dr Quade was an impressive man. Tall, with an athletic build, silver fox hair and dressed smartly in a navy-blue suit, he had a presence. At the same time, he came across with a gentle and caring demeanour. He greeted Anne warmly and ushered her into a chair across from his desk.

He sat down and searched her eyes, before saying in a kindly voice, "Anne, as you know, I am the school psychologist. About six months ago, Jessica told a friend of hers about things that were happening at home. That friend told the school headmistress, out of concern for Jessica. Jessica initially denied that anything was wrong but was encouraged by the headmistress to come and see me. Jessica agreed to that and, as a result, I have spent time with Jessica a couple of times a week over the last few months. Today, she made great progress and finally told me what she had been keeping from everyone, all this time."

Anne felt a surge of anger as she cried out, "Why was I not notified by the school of this? I am her mother and I should have been told there were concerns and that she was seeing you for treatment." Without shying away from her gaze, Dr Quade replied, "I completely understand how you are feeling towards me. I am sorry that we did not notify you until now, but Jessica maintained there was nothing wrong and threatened that if we told you she was talking to me, she would stop immediately. As she is over fifteen years old, she is entitled to confidentiality. We had no choice. We are only able to breach the confidentiality of a student if we fear she is in danger of taking her life and that was not the case."

Dr Quade took a deep breath and said, "I know this will come as a great shock to you Anne, but your husband has been sexually abusing Jessica."

Anne slumped back in her chair and found herself staring vacantly at the wall behind Dr Quade's desk. She felt like she was dreaming. Overwhelmed by the rush of emotions, she felt numb. Her head pounded. *This can't be happening. This is what happens in movies, on TV, not to me, not to us.*

She rose to her feet, exclaiming, "No! You must have the wrong child. This can't have happened between Jessica and Anthony." Anne picked up her bag and started to stride to the door. Something in the calm insistence of Dr Quade's voice stopped Anne in her tracks.

"Anne, Jessica is in the waiting room outside that door. I do not want you to walk out there and tell her you think this must be a mistake. That would be terrible for her. I need you to come and sit down again and listen to me. I know you have had a huge shock, but I am going to help you and Jessica through this. Please come back."

Dr Quade walked over to Anne and put his arm around her shoulders, gently guiding her back to her chair. The smell of his aftershave was strangely comforting for a moment, until Anne realised it was the same as Anthony's.

The doctor continued, "Anne, I want to let Jessica come in now and tell you herself what has been happening over the last eighteen months, since she was thirteen years old. She didn't tell you or anyone else because Anthony convinced her that if she did, you would blame her and hate her. Jessica needs you now."

The two police detectives knocked briefly before entering the room. The shorter one addressed Anne, "Hi Anne, this is Milly Smith and my name is Jan Brown. We are detectives with the Child Protection Unit. We are here because we were called by Dr Quade. We believe Jessica would like to speak to us and we would like to speak to Jessica. You can stay with her during our interview."

Anne did not know what to say but then pulled herself together, "If that is what Jessica wants then I will support her. I have just found out about all of this and it seems surreal right now."

Detective Brown replied, "We understand. Like I said, we are from the Child Protection Unit, so unfortunately, we see shocked mothers like you all the time. We are here to help, and we will do all we can to protect your daughter."

Dr Quade stood up and walked to the door, where he suggested, "Look, how about I give you detectives a little time with Anne while I go outside and see Jessica. Just let my secretary know when you are finished."

The other policewoman, Detective Smith, thanked him then turned to Anne. She began, "I know this is hard, Anne, and what will happen from now on will require all the strength you can find. Please let us help you. Please keep this to your very close friends and family, you will find that people's reactions may surprise you and you don't need any more surprises right now. And most importantly, you will need a very good lawyer."

"Why do I need a lawyer? What do you mean? Am I being charged with something?"

Detective Smith shook her head. "Of course you are not being charged. This is about you and Jessica financially. Do you have a lawyer you can talk to?"

"I can call the lawyer I used when I got custody of Jessica.

She's a friend of my sister."

For the first time, the detectives looked concerned. Detective Brown asked, "Anne, do you understand what is happening? Your daughter told Dr Quade that she has been sexually abused by your husband for the last eighteen months. We will be interviewing your daughter and we expect to be charging your husband very soon. You can't and should not go home if he could be anywhere near you or Jessica. You will need to find some- where else to live until this is dealt with. I know that Anthony is Jessica's stepfather, but does Jessica have any contact with her biological father? As she is a minor we should contact him. Do you have any details for him?"

Anne shook her head. "Jessica's father passed away a few years ago."

Anne started to feel the reality of what had been her perfect world caving in around her. Jessica abused by Anthony, her daughter abused by her husband. How could this have happened? Anne started to shake and cry until she began sobbing uncontrollably.

Detective Smith put her arm around Anne. She could not imagine how much pain Anne was in, but she knew from her training that to keep a mother strong, you needed to keep reiterating the need to protect her child.

"It's not your fault Anne. Please don't blame yourself. We will do our best to make sure he is stopped from doing this again and punished for what he has done to Jessica. Please stay strong to help us do that."

Anne lifted her head and stopped crying. She realised that although she needed to release her tears, she had to put her own emotions aside and focus on helping Jessica. "Thank you," she managed to say to the two women detectives.

Anne

Chapter 23

Jessica hesitated at the door to the office but then walked towards her mother with her arms open and then put them around her.

"Sorry, Mum, I'm so sorry. I didn't want to ruin your life. I didn't want to upset you but I couldn't do it anymore. I couldn't live with him anymore. I thought I should run away and leave you and Anthony to be happy, but when I told Dr Quade he said that wouldn't make you happy. If I ran away it would hurt you more than anything I could say to you about Anthony. Is that true, Mum? Do you still love me?"

Anne suddenly realised how selfish she had been. Jessica had only been thinking of her and Anne was thinking of herself. She should be thinking about Jessica and what had happened to her. *How could I have let this happen to my little girl?*

Anne hugged Jessica with all her strength and vowed, "Jessica, I love you more than ever and always will. I will be there for you and we will get through this. I'm so sorry this has happened. Please forgive me for not seeing it."

Jessica and Anne embraced each other and cried. Dr Quade ushered the detectives out of the room, and said, "Let's give them some privacy and time together, detectives."

Detective Smith stopped Dr Quade and said, "I think Anne needs some help, Dr Quade. They need somewhere to live now."

Do you think she is up to sorting that out while we arrange to arrest and question Anthony? Hopefully there is family they can stay with as they will need support through this."

Dr Quade replied, "I know from Jessica that her mother is very close to her sister who has a house where they stay often. It's about half an hour's drive away. I am sure that, once she gets over the initial shock she will call her and arrange to stay with her. Detectives, can I ask you to take a break from interviewing Jessica and her Mum for today? I know Jessica wants to speak to you as soon as possible but I think she and Anne need some time to deal with this. Could this continue tomorrow, back here? I will make sure that I have Anne and Jessica here for you, at the same time tomorrow."

The detectives looked at each other and nodded their agreement. Detective Smith spoke for the two of them, "Sure, Dr Quade. Whatever you think is best. I know this sounds like I'm being cold, but please try and get her to think about calling her lawyer. I have worked many of these cases and her husband is going to get very angry about all of this. I'm scared he'll cut her off financially and I think she and Jessica have enough to deal with, without also having nowhere to live and no money to support themselves."

"I will do my best, detectives," promised Dr Quade. "See you tomorrow."

Jessica

Chapter 24

Dr Quade walked over to Anne and Jessica, who were sitting close together on the lounge.

"Ladies," he said, "I am going to leave you alone for a while. I'll be in the building, so when you want me back, please let reception know and they will call me." He turned and closed the door behind him.

"Jessica, I am so grateful that Dr Quade helped you." Anne tried to hide the hurt she felt over Jessica confiding in Dr Quade and not her.

Jessica had a pained expression on her face. "I was sent to see Dr Quade a few of months ago, Mum. My girlfriend and I had started speaking about guys and contraception. She asked me if I had discussed it with you and I said I couldn't. She said she and her mum had discussed it a few times, because she was now seeing a boy regularly and her mum was getting concerned. She asked me if I was seeing someone and I don't know why, but I just started to talk about what was happening at home. She wanted to take me to the police, then and there, but I talked her out of it. I didn't know that she went to the school Principal, who called me in. I denied it to the Principal and she really acted quite cool about it. She told me that she thought it would be good for me to have someone to talk to, confidentially, about my life. It would be just between me and Dr Quade, she said, so I agreed.

"Dr Quade has been unreal to me, Mum. First, I told him that the guy I liked was someone my age. He picked up on things and eventually, he asked me if I would like to talk about who it was and whether the relationship was appropriate. When I finally told him it was

Anthony, I felt such a surge of relief and emotion. I knew then that I had to tell you, and Dr Quade and I discussed how I should do that."

Anne felt sick and sad as she listened and admonished herself for letting these terrible things happen to her daughter. She hugged Jessica and said gently, "Jessica, you don't need to tell me anything more now if you don't want to. I am here and will always be here for you. We can't go back home right now. Are you okay with that? I will call Elizabeth. We can go and stay with her until we sort something out."

"I'm sorry Mum." Jessica whispered into the warmth of Anne's shoulder. "I know you love our home. I didn't want to ruin this for you."

"Darling Jessica, you have not ruined this, Anthony has. You are my life; houses are just bricks and mortar. You are the most important thing and wherever you are is my home. All that matters is that you are safe."

Jessica raised her head, looked Anne directly in the eye and said, "Mum I never want to go back there. I have dreaded every moment there for as long as I can remember."

"Okay, Jessica. We will stay with Elizabeth until we have somewhere else to go."

"Mum," urged Jessica, "you know you need to get a lawyer, like the detective said. Anthony threatened that if I told you about any of this and if you left him, he would make sure we had nothing. He told me no one would believe me and that we would be out on the street with nowhere to live and no money."

Anne tried to calm her down. "You know we are going to stay with Aunty Elizabeth. Her home will always be our home. She will help us through this."

With Jessica next to her, Anne called her sister, Elizabeth, who picked up almost immediately, as she always did when Anne called her.

"Hello, Anne," Elizabeth said, in her almost fairy godmother like voice, "I was just thinking about you!"

Trying to remain calm because she knew Elizabeth would sense the distress in her voice, Anne said, "Elizabeth, something has happened. Jessica and I need to come and stay with you, is that okay? Can we come now, please?"

Elizabeth sensed the gravity of the situation. "Anne, where are you and Jessica? Can I come and pick you up? Of course, you will come and stay with me. You know my home is your home, always and forever."

"We are at Jessica's school, Elizabeth. We will drive to you right now."

After the call ended, Elizabeth walked outside onto her verandah and sat down. She hoped that nothing serious had happened and that whatever the problem, they could hold their family together.

Anne had struggled so much as a single mother and every- one had been so happy for her when she seemed to have finally found happiness with Anthony. Anne walked out to reception and asked them to let Dr Quade know that she and Jessica were ready to see him. When Dr Quade returned, she told him she had arranged for her and Jessica to stay at her sister's house.

She explained to him, "I need time to absorb what is happening and Jessica and I need to talk. Can we come back tomorrow, when we have had some time together, please?"

"Of course, Anne. I'm so glad to hear you have somewhere safe to go. If you need to talk to me anytime, here is my mobile number." Dr Quade handed Anne a business card. He surprised Anne with the question, "Anne, are you going to tell Anthony today that you know what has been going on? If you are not up to that yet, how will you explain to him that you are not coming home tonight?"

Anne looked shocked. "I hadn't even thought that far ahead. I don't think I can talk to him, Dr Quade. I will have Elizabeth call him and make an excuse, I think, because Jessica said he would be angry if she told me."

Dr Quade advised, "I think if you can hold off confronting Anthony until you are ready, that would be a good thing. How Anthony will react is an unknown, but we can assume he will not like this and will react defensively, at the very least."

"I'll get Elizabeth to sort it out for now. I just couldn't deal with him tonight."

Sarah

Chapter 25

Sarah woke up at 6 a.m. every day but on Tuesdays she worked for an hour at home before she woke Chloe up to get her ready. She had made a commitment to Chloe that at least every Tuesday she would take her to school rather than the nanny. Sarah knew that it was important to Chloe that Sarah was a part of her school life as much as she could be.

At 7 a.m., she went in to wake up Chloe and to her surprise Chloe was already awake and sitting on the floor of her bedroom in the Lotus position. Sarah could not help but giggle as she saw her, and Chloe swung around to see her at the door.

"Good morning, Mummy, I am doing my yoga which I learnt with Elizabeth on the weekend. It's called the Lotus position and it's good to start the day off with centering your thoughts."

Sarah smiled. "I think it's wonderful darling. If you are happy to get up this early, maybe we could do this together in the mornings?"

Whilst Chloe was getting dressed, Sarah made her breakfast as well as her morning tea and lunch for school. Chloe loved Sarah to surprise her with her lunch, which could range from a ham sandwich to sushi. Such simple things make Chloe so happy, Sarah thought. She always left a note in Chloe's lunchbox when she made her lunch, which Chloe adored.

Sarah picked up her car keys and Chloe's bag and made her way to the front door of her apartment. She called out, "Come on Chloe, we'll be late, honey."

Waiting patiently but still no Chloe, Sarah urged, "Please hurry for Mummy or we'll be late."

Chloe yelled back, "OK, Mummy, I'm coming. I'm just getting my stuff for news, today."

"Darling, have you brushed your teeth?"

"I only have one pair of hands, you know. I can only do one thing at a time! I'm going as fast as I can."

Here we go again, Sarah giggled to herself after Chloe quoted her favourite line and thought, *how do I argue with my daughter, who is a mini me?*

True to her word, Chloe bounded down the stairs, carrying a rolled-up piece of cardboard for news and beaming from ear to ear. "Let's go! I'm in a hurry. I have news today and I'm first. Don't make me late!"

That's my girl! Sarah thought to herself.

Once in the car, Chloe started to talk about what she was showing for news. She and her nanny had been working on it for the last week and she seemed very excited about showing it to her class. In her seat next to Sarah, she unrolled the cardboard and Sarah saw the heading and the family tree complete with photographs. She recognised the photos that Chloe had used, and they brought back so many memories.

Sarah touched Chloe's hand and said, "Oh darling, that is an amazing job you have done. It's just beautiful. After you have finished with it at school can we get that framed so that we can hang it up at home?"

Chloe beamed. "I would love that. I want to have it at home, so I can show it to everyone who doesn't believe me when I say that my grandmother was born in Hong Kong and my great grandmother and great grandfather were born in China. Everyone thinks I'm joking and I wish they wouldn't laugh at me."

Sarah was delighted to hear that Chloe was so proud of her Chinese heritage.

Chloe said, "Mummy, we are studying family trees and our teacher went through her family tree and her mother is from Hong Kong. Her husband is Australian like my Dad. She said she can't wait to have a little girl and she hopes she looks just like me."

"That is lovely of her, Chloe. She must like you very much to wish she had a little girl just like you."

Chloe dismissed the compliment, as Sarah knew she would, and this reminded Sarah how much alike they were. Rather, Chloe told Sarah more about her teacher, "Mum, my teacher has a jade bangle just like you do. She wears hers every day. I told her you have one. Why don't you wear yours every day, Mummy?"

"Darling, my bangle is very old and special. It was your great grandmother's and she gave it to my mother and I want to give it to you one day. I don't wear it every day because I don't want to break it before I give it to you. I want you to wear it when you grow up."

Chloe screamed with excitement. "Oh, Mummy that is exactly what my teacher said you would say. I am so excited, I can't wait to grow up and put it on." Chloe beamed and reached out to rub Sarah's arm.

Sarah laughed and patted Chloe's head. Then she asked with some interest, "Have all the children in the class finished doing their family trees? Are there any that are really interesting?" "Oh yes, Mummy. Nicole's great-grandfather invented the weighing scales that they use in the grocery shop and Tina's grandfather started a building company that builds tall buildings everywhere. They have photos of them, like I have a photo of my great-grandfather on his potato farm in Scotland."

Sarah laughed at Chloe's innocence in her comparison and thought it was so sweet. They had just approached the school and Sarah could see so many of the little girls carrying a roll of cardboard too. Chloe was diligently rolling it back up and securing the elastic around it just as they pulled up to the front of the school.

Sarah hugged Chloe and said in a soft and emotional voice, "I'm so proud of you. I am so lucky you are my daughter."

"Got to go, Mum!" was Chloe's detached reply, as she wriggled from Sarah's arms, jumped out of the car and ran through the school gates, full of a child's expectations for the new school day. Sarah waved goodbye from the car even though she knew Chloe would not be turning back to see it. She then set her navigation to Hilary's home as she had asked Sarah back to her house to formally meet with her accountant regarding the scholarship fund. Sarah was excited and honoured to fill the position. Although she was sad that Hilary was ill, she was hoping that she could make their time left together as productive and meaningful as possible. She was honoured to be given the opportunity to assist the person who had given her an education and changed her life, just as she had done for many other girls. For the last twenty-four hours, Sarah had reflected on Hilary's generosity to girls she did not even know and on Hilary's humility as a benefactor. Hilary, unlike most people, sought no acknowledgement from her charity work.

Phillip

Chapter 26

Phillip Thompson, a successful entrepreneur and business media identity, sat on the deck of his hundred and fifty-foot Riviera power boat, while his young, tall, sexy, bikini clad girlfriend, Stacey, went to get him another beer. Known to his friends as Phil, he could afford anything but his drink of choice would always be Australian beer. Stacey had been his girlfriend for the last eighteen months and he knew he had to end the relationship soon. Firstly, she was starting to act as though she was the lady of the house and secondly, he was getting bored with her.

Phil was first attracted to Stacey because she was fun and easy going, pretty and she got along with everyone. He liked the fact that she was old school and believed that waiting on him hand and foot was a woman's role. She never complained about getting him a beer or about him not coming home at night. Once, when he confessed to having a one-night stand during an interstate trip after Stacey found some incriminating Polaroid photos in his suitcase, she forgave him. He realized that he was really going to miss her but Phil would infamously say, "Every girl has her use by date, some stay fresher longer than others, but when your time is up, it's up."

Having been born into humble beginnings, his mother had always held high hopes for Phil to become a success. His father had been a very handsome, muscular and fit Aussie bloke. His father had the good looks but had not been given the opportunity for an education and accordingly, he worked in a factory.

If asked whether he was close to his mother, Phil would respond with, "No, but she is my mother". Those who knew Phil, knew that his mother was the force behind him as well as the devil within him. She had been obsessed with him his whole life. She would not have cared if Phil had become a school teacher or entrepreneur - she would have followed his career with equal enthusiasm. However, as luck had it, she loved the idea of her only son being not only rich but also a well-known business identity. She loved the attention she gained from being his mother.

The newspaper articles about Phil were as much about his business success as his notoriety as a serial womaniser. The fact he was not in a stable marriage annoyed his mother, but many believed Phil enjoyed her disapproval. After his failed marriage and dozens of beautiful live-in girlfriends, Phil was just a bad boy. Phil did not inherit the chiselled features, muscular toned body or height of his father, but what he lacked in looks he made up for in charm. Phil had the gift of the gab, the power to sell anything, or in other words, he was a successful conman. He boasted that he could sell women anything from house alarms to convincing them that he was "the one", even when he was the opposite of what they had been looking for in a man. His PA, Carol, had worked for him and watched Phil's development of his business empire, along with his successful pursuit of women, for over twelve years. When she first started working with him, he showed her the house alarm he was selling. It seemed quite ordinary to her and similar to what you could buy at the local hardware shop. When she watched him train the sales team, she started to see the secret to his success. His salespeople were all very attractive young men and women who wore beautiful suits so that they looked extremely successful. They were trained to be charming and even flirtatious. He instructed them that when entering a home, they should insist on taking off their shoes so that housewives and househusbands thought that their houses were "special". Then the sales pitch would proceed where they sold a gadget that cost him five dollars in China to make, for one hundred and fifty dollars installed.

The special bonus to their customers was that for a monthly service fee of only fifty dollars a month, they should monitor the alarm back to base so that they would get a call if the alarm was activated. This business was such a success it made him his first thirty million dollars in three years, after which he sold it to start his money lending business.

Phil had the same ability to charm the women he wanted to have in his life. Carol had often said that any woman that Phil set his sights on had no hope of evading his grasp. Phil would be unrelenting in the pursuit but the women he pursued were special.

Carol recalled when Phil had found his first wife, Cara. Carol and the rest of his staff had received telephone calls to assist him when Phil had met her for the first time. Phil had seen her at another table having lunch with a group of people, who he had found out were her family, at one of his favourite harbourside Sydney restaurants. He asked the Maître d', whom he knew well, who she was. The Maître d' replied that he did not know her but believed she was a model, as her table had been booked by one of their other regular customers, a well-known modelling agent. The agent had asked for a waterfront table as the model was bringing her parents and sister, who were visiting from London, to dine with her.

Phil had the Maître d' introduce him to her. She responded politely to him, but she was elusive and returned to her discussion with her mother and sister. Cara had decided to reject his advances as he looked like a player, even though she had to admit she was attracted to his rugged good looks, larrikin charm and soulful blue eyes.

Realising that he needed some help, Phil went back to his table and enlisted the aid of Carol and all his staff. He made several phone calls. Once Cara left her table to go to the bathroom, Phil went and sat at her table and began chatting with her parents until he could see her returning, at which time he got up and left the restaurant.

Later, when they were leaving the restaurant, Cara was surprised to be told by their waiter that Phil had paid their bill and had left a note for her. The note invited her and her family onto his boat, which had conveniently been brought to the Marina in front of the restaurant, for a cruise around the harbour.

Cara's mother and sister were giggling like schoolgirls when they watched Cara read the note. "Tell us what it says Cara," they both teased her.

She replied, "He has asked if we want to go for a trip around the harbour in his boat, which is parked at the front of the restaurant." They all got up and walked over to the balcony of the restaurant and saw Phil sitting on the back of his 150- foot boat. Phil looked up just at that moment and caught them looking at him and the boat. Phil grinned broadly and started waving to them. "Well, we have to go now", Cara said.

Sensing their complicity, Cara asked her sister and mother, "Did you know about this?"

Her mother replied, "Darling, this may never happen to you again. Enjoy it, because we most certainly will. We are going to have a very nice afternoon and I am dying to see what he does next!"

As Phil saw Cara waving and then walking towards the boat, he knew that he now stood a chance of winning her over. He had already assessed Cara's mother and he liked her. She would have been a stunning beauty in her youth, and she now had all the elegance and style that only came later in a woman's life. She still had a sparkle in her eye and would want her daughter to have interesting adventures in her life.

Cara's sister and mother led Cara onto the wharf and up to the boat. Phil helped them onto the boat and they were greeted by the Captain and his staff with glasses of champagne. After welcoming them on board, Phil set out to try and get some time with Cara to himself. He suggested to Cara, in front of her family, "Cara, the Captain was wondering if your mother and sister would like to drive the boat?"

The Captain caught the ball and ran with it, accustomed as he was to being Phil's wingman. "It's an amazing view from up there. You will really enjoy it."

Cara's mother smiled and replied for herself and her daughter, "We would love it Captain!" as she linked her arm through the Captain's and walked with him to the stairs, her daughter following. Over her shoulder, Cara's mother shot an encouraging smile at Cara and an approving wink to Phil.

Cara watched as they walked away. Standing on the deck and staring out to the ocean, she was feeling completely overwhelmed by the situation she had found herself in. As much as she was annoyed at Phil's behaviour, she could not help but be flattered by his attention. Cara felt uncomfortable. As a beautiful model, she constantly attracted the attention of men who thought they could win her over with their wealth and influence.

Phil knew that he needed to get into Cara's heart and soul, and to do that, he would need to know what made her tick. She was not a girl he would win over by just standing on his wallet. She was deeper than that; she was intelligent and wary. Phil sensed it would take some time. Luckily, for the things he really wanted, Phil could be a very patient man. Phil moved closer to Cara, who continued to stare distractedly at the open water, either not noticing him or pretending not to. He removed his jacket and placed it on her shoulders and as he did so, Cara turned towards him. Phil looked directly into her wide, deep, almond shaped brown eyes and for the first time he could see the vulnerability in them. Phil placed a hand on both her shoulders and, as he looked deep into her suspicious eyes, he said in the most caressing way, "Cara, I fell in love with you the instant I saw you. I have never felt so connected and attracted to another human being as I am to you right now."

Cara looked at him as though she wanted to believe him but doubted every word, "Why me? You don't even know me!"

Phil replied by simply taking her into his arms and kissing her deeply, but gently. He felt her gasp as her body surrendered and she melted against his chest. He was surprised at how powerful the attraction between them was and how desperately he now wanted her. He had no doubt that Cara would soon be his wife. He drew back and looked into her eyes, which now expressed her confusion.

Phil put his arms around her as he reassured her, "Cara, there is no explaining chemistry, but I knew we would have it. I am going to marry you. You are the reason I have worked so hard to be successful, so I could shower the woman I knew I would one day fall in love with, with everything she could ever want. Will you give me that chance, please?"

As happy as Cara felt, she had tears in her eyes and her body felt like jelly. She had never been kissed like that before and all she wanted to do was kiss him again. Everything he was saying was too good to be true, but he seemed so genuine that she wanted to believe him. She replied nervously, "If you kiss me again, I will think about it", but she knew she had already fallen for him.

Phil smiled and felt genuinely happy. He really believed, in that moment, that he had fallen in love with Cara.

While it lasted, it was a fairy tale love story for Phil and Cara but not for Phil's mother. None of the women in his life was ever good enough and she made sure they all went, in time. She was horribly racist and some thought that when Phil married Cara, it was just to spite his mother, as, although extraordinarily beautiful and well educated, Cara was part Indian. This was much to Phil's mother's horror, which reached a pinnacle when Phil told her that they were having a baby. She had exclaimed at the time, "For God's sake Phil, you can't be seriously breeding with her?" When Cara was in labour, giving birth to their first child together, his mother was in attendance and announced very loudly for all to hear, "I hope the baby isn't caramel, like everyone keeps telling me it will be."

The room went quiet, as the obstetrician announced to Cara, "I can see the blonde hair! Not long now."

The baby was born not long after and she had porcelain skin, blue eyes and blonde hair, which shocked everyone and provided Phil's mother with a great sense of relief.

Sadly, for both of them the fairy tale only lasted for another four years after the birth of their daughter, due to Phil's untameable bad boy nature.

Phillip

Chapter 27

Sitting on the deck of his boat, Phil had a beer in one hand while he was dictating orders to his PA, Carol. She was efficient and as hard as stone, and she liked to think of herself as his protector. Phil let her believe it. It was the privilege of the wealthy to have staff to do their dirty work, like sack other staff and give the bad news to his girlfriends that they were over. It was a trade-off where Carol could feel important and Phil did not have to face most of the realities of life. He paid her well for it.

Carol, like his mother, liked to take the credit for Phil's success. She liked to let everyone know how close she was to him. She enjoyed his success as much as he did, relishing in her title as PA. She would often talk about her lunches with PAs to the other powerful men in Sydney and how exclusive and powerful their little group was. She had once boasted to a Maître d', and it got back to Phil, that no one got to these men without going through one of them and so these PAs held the real power in Sydney.

Whenever the stakes were high and Phil knew she had to not just lie to his wives, girlfriends and business associates, but actively mislead them, he would, without even addressing it with her, give her a substantial bonus that month. Right now, she earned double what her university qualified husband did. She had to hide it from him because she knew if he really knew what her job entailed, he would make her resign, or worse, leave her.

The fact her husband had such high morals and was such a nice guy made her job with Phil more attractive to her. She would often tell her friends she had the best of both worlds, spending her days with a charismatic bad boy and her nights with the nicest man in the world.

Carol enjoyed sorting out the problems in Phil's life and negotiating property settlements with his exes was what she enjoyed the most. Phil would always give her a best and worst-case scenario to negotiate and she got a bonus the closer she got to the best- case scenario. If Phil felt guilty, which was not often, the deal he offered would be reasonable. If for some reason he felt no guilt, even though he was always the one ending the relationship, then he could become mean and vengeful. With one ex, who got a new boyfriend way too soon after she should have, in his view, he went out of his way to get her back, just so he could dump her again. The poor girl had to spend a few weeks recovering in hospital after a total breakdown.

Amazingly, the women Phil had serious relationships with, or married, were beautiful and successful in their areas of life. They ranged from a model, a high-profile CEO and to most recently a PR executive who became his manager, (now former manager of course). He never once owned up to his part in a failed relationship or to the embarrassment and emotional damage he caused after each relationship ended, which was in deep contradiction to the emotional side he showed to the women in his life when he was courting them.

Stories of how he had hired out entire restaurants for a private dinner date; organised private designers to arrive at the women's offices or homes with racks of clothes and accessories to dress them when he had asked them out to an event; had new cars delivered gift-wrapped in an over-sized bow; and for one of the women, a single mother, he had sent a pony to her daughter's school as a birthday present.

Stacey walked up to Phil while he was still speaking to Carol and handed him another beer. She interrupted them, "Phil can I talk to you?"

Phil looked at Carol and asked, "Are we finished?"

"I think so for now," but she was clearly annoyed at the interruption.

Stacey, excited, said, "Good," and she sat down at the table waiting for Carol to leave, which she did, promptly.

Phil took a swig of his beer and then looked at Stacey. He could see she was looking nervous. "What's up babe?"

Stacey held up her hand. She was holding a white stick as she said in almost a whisper, "Darling, I'm pregnant".

All his friends had told Phil that at thirty-five, Stacey would be a worry about wanting to have children. Phil had been unconcerned because he was certain he had made it clear to her that he did not want any more children or to get married again. He had been constantly encouraged to get a vasectomy by his minders but of course he would not have it, seeing it as a threat to his manhood.

Phil's jaw dropped and Stacey was unnerved by the look of dismay written all over his face. "You're not happy?" she asked, her bottom lip starting to tremble.

Phil was decidedly unhappy. "You told me you were on the pill, Stacey! Go get yourself fixed up!" He stormed off.

Stacey's face crumpled and she burst into tears. She pleaded with him, "I was on the pill, Phil. I told you when I was really sick with strep throat that the doctor said we needed to use contraception if I was on the pill, because this could happen and you said it was just bullshit."

As he walked to the bar to get another drink, Phil recalled the conversation and realised that this had been a mistake by both of them. "You know what I said to you when we first started seeing each other, Stacey. I don't want any more children. I like being with you because you're easy to be with, but I'm not in love with you. I told you that. I didn't lead you on or lie to you."

Stacey composed herself, hoping she could talk Phil into agreeing to let her keep the baby. She said, in a calm voice but pressing her point, "You said you liked being with me. We might have something that's different from what you are used to, but better. This baby wasn't planned but not all kids are."

"I'll arrange to get you fixed up and we are now over."

Stacey tried to stand her ground and declared, "No Phil, I love you. You can't do this! I want this baby." She looked at Phil and could see the coldness in his eyes.

Phil moved his face within inches of Stacey's and spat out, "Do you think you are the first fucking girl to try and fall pregnant and trap me? Carol will arrange things for you, as she has done for many of my other girlfriends who thought they were too fucking smart. That's the end of our discussion and our relationship." He turned brusquely from her and walked outside to the back of the boat.

Stacey burst out crying and ran downstairs towards the main cabin. She threw herself on the bed and sobbed.

Outside, Carol shot Phil a weighted look. He glared straight back at her and said, "Don't say a thing, Carol! I know you told me and warned me. I don't need to hear you are right again. Just fix this up. That's your fucking job, so just do it."

"Sure Phil, because it's always that easy," she retorted. She looked down at the list in her lap, repressing her laughter as she asked herself, *When will he learn? Here we go with another girl-friend exit deal, if we're lucky another BMW and a $30,000.00 kiss off after the visit to the clinic. Am I a secretary, or am I just as bad as he is by helping him continue his serial reeling in and disposal of women and babies?*

Phil interrupted Carol's thoughts to ask her, "Carol, go and talk to Stacey. I did make the ground rules clear at the start and she has broken them, not me."

Startled by his transparent take on the situation Carol lifted herself out of her emotional ruminating and responded, "I agree." Stacey knew the score. Carol had spoken to her about it, more than once. She, however, had pointed out to Phil not so long ago to be careful with Stacey, as she could predict that a situation was about to arise. She said, "The problem is women grow addicted to the lifestyle you give them and they want it to go on forever."

Phil had had enough. *His secretary was employed to take care of shit not lecture him* he thought to himself. "Look after this, Carol."

"Sure." Carol smiled sardonically to herself.

Sarah

Chapter 28

Sarah had been looking forward to seeing Hilary again at her home. On the drive there this time, she noticed how beautiful the suburb was that Hilary's home was in. It was the first time it dawned on Sarah, since moving to the city, that she rarely took a drive out to the suburbs or even the country and this was some- thing she should do with Chloe. As she walked up to the gates, she felt saddened by Hilary's illness but honoured that Hilary was entrusting her with the administration of the scholarship. The meeting today was for Sarah to meet Hilary's accountant, Sam, and for him to explain the scholarship trust to Sarah.

On her arrival at Hilary's house, Sarah found Hilary as gracious and elegant as usual. Sam was charming but at the same time, as sharp as a tack. He was someone, thought Sarah, she could trust. Sam assured Sarah that the financial side of the trust was secure. He said that with the funds Hilary's estate would be leaving, the scholarship could continue indefinitely for at least one additional girl every year.

Hilary was relieved that Sarah and Sam were getting along so well, which she had hoped would happen. Over dinner, Hilary explained to Sam, in Sarah's presence, why she had chosen Sarah to take over the administration of her scholarship trust.

"I chose Sarah because I know Sarah will instinctively be able to choose the girls who are in trouble but who hide their problems. She will be able to determine which girls we need to help the most to change their lives. I was from a home where things were perfect, so I really relied on others, like Sarah's teacher, Ms Kris for this."

Sarah felt embarrassed and touched at the same time, that Hilary could see how and what she could contribute from her own journey. Hilary made Sarah want to be a better person and, for this, she was grateful. After meeting Sam, Sarah knew she would be able to not only honour Hilary's work but to continue to grow her legacy, helping young girls in need. Sarah felt this was something she had been missing in her life.

Hilary got up from the dinner table, went to the end of the room and opened a drawer in an antique chest. She took out two photo albums, returned to the table, and positioning them in front of Sarah and Sam, proceeded to open the first album. Sarah saw photos of herself as a schoolchild. Hilary went through each page of photos, all of which recorded highlights of the various stages of Sarah's school career. Tears welled in Sarah's eyes, because she could recall exactly the moments Hilary's camera had captured, but she had been unaware, in those moments, of Hilary's identity and presence. The last photo, this time taken by a professional photographer, showed Hilary handing Sarah her law degree. It was a full history of Sarah's academic success, compiled with love and pride and Sarah was moved beyond words.

After closing the albums, Hilary handed them to Sarah and said, "Please give these to your daughter, Sarah. I'm sure she'll enjoy looking at them as much as I have."

Sarah was overwhelmed and a tear tumbled down her cheek as she thanked Hilary for the photos. Sarah paused as an idea popped into her mind. She asked, "Can I bring Chloe here to meet you, so I can take one with the three of us?"

"Of course!" Hilary replied. "I would love to meet your daughter, Sarah."

"Let's make it soon then," Sarah said, "because as soon as I show her these photos and explain who you are, she will want to meet you and she will bug me until she does. I only realised on the drive here how I have been a negligent mother in not bringing her to see some of the most beautiful parts of our country."

Hilary nodded and suggested, "What about Sunday for brunch? Would that suit?"

"That's perfect. Chloe will be so excited," replied Sarah. "Great. I just wish I had done this sooner," Hilary said, a warm smile spreading across her face.

Sarah embraced Hilary, assuring her, "We are going to get to know each other and enjoy the time we have. You have my promise that I will do everything I can to make sure that the legacy you started is carried on indefinitely."

"I know you will Sarah."

Feeling embarrassed that she had to rush off, Sarah said, "I'm sorry that I have to leave now Hilary, I wish I could stay longer with you and Sam, but I need to prepare for a live television interview. I'm doing a 6 a.m. spot on the Morning Radio Show on the changes to financial agreements. No matter how many times I do this, it still takes me hours to translate the legal jargon into something the public can easily understand."

Hilary smiled fondly at Sarah. She was so proud of her pro bono work on her radio and television appearances, which she knew was undoubtedly helping a lot of women and men in need of legal advice, that they otherwise had no hope of accessing. She had no doubt Sarah would one day be a judge. What Sarah did not know was that she had not only invited her to her house for Sam to explain the scholarship trust to her, but for Sam to meet the person to whom she was going to leave her entire estate to when she passed away. The final thing she wanted to do for Sarah, was to leave her with a home that she and Chloe could feel safe and secure in, like many generations of her family had done before her.

Jane

Chapter 29

Jane was driving home after dropping her girls to school. This was one of her favourite parts of the day as she could turn on her favourite radio station on the drive home. She was hoping Sarah Walters' regular segment would be on. She was pleased when they announced it in the ad break and found it a coincidence that Sarah's topic this week would be financial agreements. Jane always felt that coincidences were meant to be noticed, and so she turned up the radio.

As she listened, Jane felt a connection with Sarah. Jane had always liked Sarah's segment but now that Jane had a legal concern, Sarah not only sounded like an intelligent and very practical lawyer, but genuinely concerned about the people who called in for her advice. What concerned Jane though, was what Sarah was saying about getting independent advice, and that it was essential for a financial agreement. Jane wondered why she had not had to do that with Brett. She thought perhaps she should email Sarah and ask her or maybe make an appointment to see her, as it was something that was really bothering her.

One of the things Sarah said had stuck in Jane's head, "When discussing as terms of a financial agreement, both parties get to see what the other party sees as a "fair thing," if or when things did not work out, and that would say a lot about the other person."

Jane agreed with that and realised she really had no idea what was in the financial agreement she had just signed, as far as what it provided for her and the girls. Brett had claimed the financial agreement provided that she got to keep the house and he would pay her maintenance, but now she realised that she had not read it before she signed it. She did not have a copy of it and she certainly did not get independent legal advice - all the things that Sarah said should have happened.

Jane wondered if she should bring it up with Brett. Maybe she could ask him for a copy of what she had signed. Surely, he would not mind if it said what he said it did, she thought. Jane had a feeling, and she knew that when she had that feeling, she was always right and that when she ignored it, she always regretted it. She had brushed the feelings aside because of the kids but the nagging in her head would not let up and she knew that she had to do something to ease her concerns. As soon as I get home, she told herself.

Sarah

Chapter 30

Sarah finished her pre-recorded radio segment at 6.30 am and by 8 a.m. that morning she had headed back home to pick up Chloe for school. She was now pulling over to the car drop-off line at Chloe's school. The car door was opened by one of the school mums, who leaned in and pulled out Chloe's bags. Chloe jumped out and after being handed her bag, started to run to the gate singing out, "Bye, Mum!"

As Sarah drove off, a call came in from Phil Pemberton, one of her regular clients. Although Phil was as bad a boy as they come, like most bad boys he was charming, seductive and demanding. Sarah said, "Good morning Phil, to what do I owe this pleasure?"

A seductive voice replied, "I'd love to say I'm calling just to say hello, but unfortunately I have been unlucky in love yet again. I have another personal issue for you to legally finalise for me."

Before Sarah could get a word in, he added, "Don't say it, Sarah! I know I'm an idiot, but just fix it please. Quickly. I've just broken off with a girl that I've lived with for eighteen months."

Sarah said, a sardonic smile spreading across her face, "Thanks for taking my advice this time and ending it before the two-year period."

"Yes, I thought I was doing okay, but she's just told me she's pregnant. I told her I don't want it, so she knows how I feel, but I don't know if she'll still have it now. She's a simple, nice girl and I should not have let it go on this long. I'll get my PA to call you with the details, so you can work out a deal. I can see you any day next week to sign the paperwork."

"Phil," Sarah stopped him short, "I won't be able to work out a fair deal until there has been a decision made about the baby. It will be a completely different scenario if she decides to keep the baby. As you had been living together when she fell pregnant, then she has rights under the Family Law Act. We'll need to go through the same procedure that we went through with your ex-wife when we work out a settlement with her."

Phil, furious at the situation he found himself in, complained, "I told her I didn't want to have any more kids or to get married again! It's just bull shit that because she decides to break our deal, I'll have to pay for it. This will send my ex-wife off her head, not to mention my kids. It will be a disaster if she wants to keep the baby, but there's nothing I can fucking do about that, is there?"

Sarah responded to his angry outburst with her usual calm, professional advice. "I can see your point of view and I'm really sorry this has happened, but we will just have to deal with the situation as it presents itself. Talk to her and let her know how you feel, with as much empathy as you can. Let me know how it works out. Whatever happens, we will deal with sorting something out."

Phil appreciated Sarah's calm take on it all. "Sorry, Sarah, I will. I was kind of shocked when she told me, and I probably sounded angry at the time. I do care about her and want her to go on and have a family, but with someone who loves her. This isn't what she's looking for. I feel like she was trying to trap me, not because of any malice or greed on her part, but she wrongly thought, as a lot of girls do, that a baby would make things better and create a bond between us that we didn't have."

"Well tell her that, in just that way. Then the decision is hers."

"I'll do what I can, Sarah. I'm not good with emotional stuff, as you know. I'm a better ex, I know that much."

"That's what I'm here for." Sarah hung up and continued driving towards her office.

Phil was one of Sarah's "repeat" clients. Although Sarah had advised him that the divorce rate for second and subsequent marriages was even higher than for first marriages, Phil did not seem to learn a thing from his failed relationships. Even though many of Phil's girlfriends did not have rights to a property claim in the courts, as such, Phil always liked to have an exit agreement in place to clear the path anyway. This was to let both of them move on with no unexpected media to upset his ex-wife, children or agent.

Although Phil was a complete relationship failure, he refused, no matter how many of his advisors suggested it to him, to try therapy to deal with his issues with relationships. He was, however, prepared to make up for what he lacked in emotional skills with monetary compensation. This was, of course, the easiest way out of everything in his life.

Many of her staff had asked Sarah how she could act for Phil and men like him. She would tell them that it was part of her job, but, if she was honest with herself, she actually enjoyed acting for him. It took all her self-control not to accept his incessant offers to take her on a date. After his divorce, and just for a Nano second, once, she'd had that unrealistic urge to see if she could be the one to tame him and sort out his demons. She quickly realised she was just dreaming and his form over the last few years had proved she was right. *If only Phil wasn't such a dysfunctional guy,* she thought, *but then he wouldn't be Phil, would he?*

Sarah recalled the first day she met Phil and the memory brought a smile to her face. She had been asked to act as a mediator in his dispute with his second ex-wife, a very beautiful and successful model. Both their lawyers suggested Sarah be appointed as a mediator to avoid the matter going to court. They all met in Sarah's boardroom and when Sarah walked into the room to meet them, Phil stood up and just stared at her in front of everyone, including his ex-wife.

Sarah, feeling uncomfortable, had asked, "Do I know you?"

Phil almost whispered to her, his gaze fixated on her, "You are exquisite." Sarah ignored the remark and moved into her mediator introduction.

The ex-wife whispered to her lawyer, but Sarah overheard her say, "He says something like that to every attractive woman he meets." Her lawyer also thought the fact that Phil, being slightly distracted and smitten with the mediator, may work in their favour. Phil's lawyer wanted to get the deal sorted so he could move on to sorting out Phil's business empire and knew, with Sarah's help, it would get done.

The mediation had been progressing well and after two hours Sarah announced that there would be a break for morning tea. She directed the two parties to their separate conference rooms while she stayed seated in the boardroom. As both legal teams and their client's left the room Kate entered with Sarah's coffee and croissant. As she placed them on the table before her Sarah stood up to take off her jacket placing it on the back of the chair behind her as she sat back down.

Just at that moment Phil walked back into the boardroom unannounced which took Sarah by surprise. She stood up as she said to him sternly, "You should be with your legal team. You cannot be in this room without them."

Phil stood transfixed starring directly at Sarah. She watched his eyes slowly navigate up and down her body before she recalled that she had taken her jacket off. He replied slowly as if speaking to himself, "Under that sheer, silk blouse you are wearing a white silk lace teddy. Under that killer suit you're dressed like an angel". Surprised by his astute description of her clothing Sarah inadvertently replied, "How did you know that?" before regretting asking the question as soon as the words left her lips.

Smiling and evidently very pleased with himself Phil replied enthusiastically after clearly having regained his composure, "I have bought more women's clothing and lingerie for the ladies in my life than anything else Sarah. I know my stuff and I would love to see everything you are wearing right now on my bedroom floor." Knowing he was in deep trouble, like a naughty school boy Phil threw a cheeky smile as he dashed quickly out of the room.

Kate could not help but burst into a giggle as Sarah looked at her and said, "Not a word."

At the end of the four-hour mediation and just before lunch, the lawyers came back into the room and announced to Sarah that a settlement had been reached.

The parties stood and walked from the room but Phil dropped back and approached Sarah. "Now that the settlement is over", he said, "will you go to Paris with me tomorrow? I'll fly you there first class, then take you shopping to buy more beautiful things for you to wear as we clearly share the same taste in ladies' fashion." Sarah laughed, "Mr Pemberton, that is a kind offer, however, I am married", she said as she pointed to her engagement and wedding rings.

Phil replied, "Well, you could excuse me from not noticing them as I didn't bring a magnifying glass! But I do know you could fix that minor technical problem quickly. It takes about two hours, from your form today. We could still make the flight tomorrow, if you get started this afternoon."

Phil was now even more attracted to Sarah. The ring on her finger was modest by any stretch of the imagination and this woman could have any man she wanted. A beautiful, intelligent woman not attracted by the lure of money, was going to be harder to get than most, but he always found the way.

Sarah, with a broad smile on her face, shook her head from side. This elicited a subdued, "I gather that's a no", from a chastened Phil.

Phil, however, regrouped and suggested, "What if I start using you as my lawyer from now on? At least I'll have an excuse to call you and you'll have to take my calls until you do get divorced."

Sarah replied, "I have to tell you, Mr Pemberton, from my observations today, you have a very competent lawyer acting for you already."

"Yes, he's good but he hates my ex and she hates him, so it never stops with my ex wanting more money and constantly changing arrangements with the kids. I'll suggest I'm sending that stuff to you from now on and he'll be bloody relieved. By the way, Sarah", he added, with determination rather than humour, "I hope you know you will marry me one day." He turned and left the office.

Overhearing the conversation, the barrister acting for Phil's ex-wife asked Sarah, "How do women who go out with him, not see his form? If he was a horse, you wouldn't back him but these beautiful and successful women fall for him!"

Sarah's reply was equally insightful, "Everyone loves a hundred to one shot, Tim. I mean that's the one that you always remember, isn't it? The horse everyone else thought was a dud that turned out to be a champion."

Tim nodded and sighed in agreement, "Yes, that is the dream indeed."

The next day, a very large and extraordinarily beautiful bunch of flowers arrived at Sarah's office with a card saying, "Thanks for getting me out of jail with my ex. I look forward to working with you. Phil X"

While Sarah was advising Phil over the phone on his latest break up, she had no idea he was thinking that during all these years, he had never gotten over his obsession with her. She was one of the very few women he admired and was in awe of. After hearing her voice again, he felt the same pang of desire surge through him and this time he was determined to win her over. The fact that she had knocked him back years ago, when she had first started acting for him and continued to do so, had baffled him. Whenever he had to use her services, he thought about how he would lure her into his life, and he knew one day she would relent.

Sarah

Chapter 31

It had been a long day for Sarah, starting with her pre-recorded radio interview, taking Chloe to school and an urgent application at the family court for an estranged husband to pay the kids' private school fees and enormous mortgage repayments, which he had stopped after leaving the family home. Then Sarah had a conference with a new client to apply to the family court for an urgent application for a sterilization procedure to be performed on a sixteen-year-old child, the daughter of her clients. The principal of the girl's school had notified the girl's parents that she had become sexually active with a boy in the same private special school she was attending.

After getting back to the office from court and finalizing the urgent application, Sarah had just sat down at her desk with a well-deserved glass of Pinot Gris, when her phone rang.

An articulate and authoritative female voice announced, "Hello, Sarah, it's Carol, Phil Pemberton's PA."

"Hello Carol, it's been a while since we have spoken." "Probably a good thing", Carol replied. "However, we have another situation and Phil has asked me to call you to give you the story about his now ex-girlfriend, Stacey."

Sarah's mind clicked into action and she could not help trying to picture what Carol the PA looked like. She had been Phil's henchwoman for over ten years now and they had spoken from time to time on the phone but had never met. Sarah found it extraordinary that wealthy people could find employees who would deal with all things unpleasant such as this.

"Yes Carol, Phil called me and said you would be in touch. How is Stacey?"

Carol spoke at some length, never for a moment dropping her authoritative voice, which came with some attitude. "Look, I think she will be okay after she gets over the shock. She's not a bad person, she's just, let's say, a little simple and naive. Funnily enough, they got on like two mates - drinking beer, watching the footy and the races. I think Phil thought it was perfect, as he didn't have to change his act to be with her. She was like a mate with fringe benefits."

"I see," Sarah said, somewhat taken aback by Carol's idea of perfection in a girlfriend for Phil.

Carol continued, "Anyway, it's over and he doesn't want the baby. She has now accepted that, and I think she will terminate." "Carol, you can never underestimate a woman in love or scorned. She may turn and become unfriendly and that's where I come in to help. It is far better to settle with someone who is heartbroken but still in love and hurting, than someone who is angry. Once they get angry, they can try and get even and that is never pretty. If she doesn't that's great but just in case can you give me this girls' history, as far as you know it, from both a personal and professional level. Also, any details about her date of birth, finances etc. Everything you can think of. Email it to me as soon as you can."

Carol said she would do so, then added, "I don't think she'll be like that, but you could be right. She seems too, you know, too dumb to be that smart."

"In my experience, in over twenty-five years of doing family law, it's those people that can be manipulated more easily in this type of situation. It may surprise you, but many people can be carried away by the advice of their well-intentioned friends or family or are just plain greedy or think they know it all. These people can be driven to seek huge settlements because they have read, in the papers or magazines, about people getting half or more of their partner's assets no matter what the facts of their particular situation."

"The media can create the illusion that you just have to live with a wealthy person for a couple of years to get half of their assets," Carol replied.

"And then the problem is, once you are in litigation, it quickly starts to cost enormous amounts of money in legal fees and you need to weigh up the cost of the legal case and what the other side is seeking to get. I have had cases where one party may have demanded what they want, and think they deserve, being up to ninety per cent or most of the assets, even I have advised them that was not what they were entitled to or likely to get in court. In most cases you will find they have been misled by greedy friends, family and in some cases, lawyers, into believing they will get this kind of revenge. Once they have started the exorbitant demands, it's hard to back down without looking silly. By contrast, the sensible people will assess the situation, deal with it realistically and take proper advice. She will also want to keep her dignity and pride. She will not sell it down the river by going for more than she is entitled to or let it be a *New Idea* story or television interview." Carol seemed to understand what Sarah was getting at, "I hope Stacey does this sensibly, for her sake. She'll get much more, if she can manage to be reasonable with Phil, than if she tries to play hardball like his ex-wife did. That just made him really dig his heels in."

"That's because with his ex-wife, Phil was punching far above his weight and he knew it very shortly after he married her. He left her because he thought she would leave him. When she handled it with grace and dignity, even when it was revealed he had been having an affair for the final six months of their marriage, it drove him crazy. The sad thing is, she told her lawyer and me that she never would have left him and that she would never get over him. We both believed her. He was just an insecure idiot."

Carol was impressed with Sarah's insight and she agreed with her, "You're a psychiatrist too, aren't you?"

Sarah laughed. "It's just the observations you pick up doing what I'm doing. I 'll start on drafting some papers but will need those details from you to finish it. I'll email you a draft when I'm done. Until then, tell Stacey that Phil wants to sort something out for her that's fair and that he is working it out and will have something to her soon."

"Okay, will do, Sarah. I'll wait for your email and I'll tell Phil we've spoken."

Stacey

Chapter 32

Stacey was lying in her bed at home hiding under the doona and crying. Phil had spoken in such a calm and detached way, she knew that there was no going back, even if she did not go through with having the baby. She had been stupid and lost the best thing that had ever happened to her.

Stacey loved Phil, but if she was honest with herself, she knew he did not love her. He did tell her he did not want any more children, but she had thought that he might change his mind, if it happened.

She had made the mistake of telling her little brother. He said to tell Phil that if he did not give her a million dollars, she would have the kid anyway then take him to the cleaners. She thought that was the most terrible thing she had ever heard.

"It's what girls do all the time," her brother said, like it was no big deal at all.

Stacey wondered whether she really wanted to be a single mother. She knew a lot of people would think she had tried to trap Phil. She knew that was what his PA thought. She had said as much to her today: "You're not the first to try this, Stacey."

Stacey wanted to call her Mum, but she knew her Mum would just say, "I told you so." She told Stacey right from the start, "Milk it for all it's worth, honey. His form tells you that he isn't a stayer, he's a sprinter and he'll be sprinting from you in no time. Have a good time get what you can and learn. Guys like that can teach you a lot."

She thought about calling her friend Kerrie. She was smart and had been through a divorce. She had told Stacey she knew all about the woman's rights, but Stacey knew that once she made that call Kerrie would insist on her getting as much as she could out of Phil. *Maybe she should see a counsellor, talk it through with someone who would understand and not judge her.* Her thoughts were interrupted by her phone ringing. It was Kerrie. Stacey paused before answering, then realised she had to talk to someone.

"Hi Kerrie, how are you?"

"Stacey, what's wrong?" Kerrie had detected things were not right. Stacey was taken aback.

"Nothing, why do you ask that?"

"I know you and something's wrong. Has he dumped you? Should I come around?"

Stacey could not hold her emotions in check any longer and burst into tears. "Yes, we broke up today. I'm shattered. I've really stuffed this up and now I don't know what to do."

"You'll be okay, honey. We all knew this wouldn't last. I know you love him, but you'll be far better off than when you met him. Remember, when you met him, you had just broken up with Reese. He left you a month behind in the rent and the car payments. You were broke. Phil came along and took you away from all that worry. It's like you've had a holiday from reality but now you have to face it again."

"I'm pregnant," Stacey whispered.

"Oh shit, Stacey. That would do it! That would make him run. Okay, I won't ask you why, but I will say that you need to get it sorted."

"Kerrie, do you really think I can't have the baby on my own? Lots of women do."

"You don't want to be a single mother like I had to be Stacey. It sucks like no tomorrow. Even if he paid you maintenance and gave you a house, you'll have to bring up a child alone. You shouldn't do this to yourself. You're a beautiful girl and you'll find someone to have a real relationship with, and kids. Phil was never the one for you honey, never ever. You don't want step-children, ex-wives and all that stuff when you aren't even married."

Stacey asked in a scared whisper, "Kerrie, will you help me? I can't do this by myself!"

"Yes, of course I'll help you. I'll come and get you now. I'm happy to talk to Phil, to sort things out for you. Phil's a player, but he's not a monster."

Stacey started crying. "I should have called you straight away, but I thought you would tell me to have the baby and get everything I could out of Phil, to hurt him. I'm sorry, I just thought that's what you used to say about your ex."

"That was different. My ex was a bastard and deserved all I gave him, for what he did to me. He cleaned out our joint accounts, stopped paying the mortgage and car payments and took off overseas with the cash while I was on unpaid maternity leave. I was fighting off the bank, who were trying to throw me and the kids out of the house, and the lease company that was trying to repossess the car. Only with the help of the Ombudsman was I able to hold off the banks for enough time to sell the house to pay off the mortgage and car, so that I could pay the bond on an apartment for me and the kids to live in, until I could go back to work full time. Your situation is different. This won't be a war. Phil will be feeling guilty and that's the time to get a deal done with him. Trust me, he'll get over the guilt quickly, so we need to work out what you need, and he'll look after you."

I know how these men think, Kerrie said to herself. She knew Phil would be wanting out of this as quickly as possible. She did not blame him, really. Never for a minute did Kerrie think Stacey would pull this old trick out of the bag, but she knew it was all fixable and that everyone would be fine in the end. She knew that she should go and pick up Stacey before her brother got in Stacey's ear again. If he tried to get her to milk Phil, Kerrie knew that he would get Phil's back up and he would do what most men do - cut off the money, bleed her dry, drag out the settlement while she starved and then try to pay her nothing.

Brett

Chapter 33

Brett knew he had successfully calmed the waters with Jane last night. He had arranged an early morning flight to get him out of the house before Jane and the girls usually woke up. He thought he had managed to get away without waking them, but as he was leaving he heard Jane and the girls calling out goodbye from the door. He waved to them as he got into the hire car to head to the airport.

As soon as he got into the car he pulled out his mobile and called Lisa. "I've just left home and will be at the airport in about twenty-five minutes." He sat back and picked up the newspaper, smiling to himself that everything was working out beautifully.

Brett walked into the business class lounge, straight up to Lisa and embraced her like a long lost lover. They both sat down staring into each other's eyes and he took her hand and held it tightly.

"How did it all go with Jane? How did she take it, Brett?" "She wasn't happy, but she signed it. I told her I would look after her and the kids, and I will."

"Did you tell her about us or just that you're leaving her?"

"Darling, you know I can't tell her about you yet, we discussed that."

"This can't come as a surprise to her if you haven't had sex in years, can it?"

Brett had forgotten that he had said this to her and Lisa could see the look of surprise on his face. "That wasn't true, was it?" she asked.

"Of course it's true! Look Lisa, Jane has signed the papers and we will be together soon. Just be patient. Not much longer now."

Brett leaned over and kissed Lisa. She responded passionately, which he was relieved about and he relaxed. For the next couple of days he was going to be in heaven with her catering to his every whim. Lisa had a body that was every man's dream. She made him feel like he was a sex addict. He just could not get enough of her body and she loved it.

Jane was now signed up, so if she found out about Lisa somehow, there was no way she could get nasty about it and fuck up his plans. He was relieved he had managed to convince the company's in-house lawyer, Mike, to witness Jane's signature and sign the statement that Jane understood the financial agreement, in exchange for a promise of a promotion. He knew the poor bastard was now panic stricken that he could lose his practising certificate if Jane contested it one day, but Brett assured him she would not do so. He had shown Mike, on his laptop, that he had access to Jane's emails and mobile phone records, so that if she sought legal advice, they would be the first to know and intervene accordingly. Life was good, and these were happy days.

Stacey

Chapter 34

Stacey answered the door looking a mess. She hugged Kerrie and started to cry. Kerrie held Stacey until she felt she had calmed down.

"I've made an appointment with a doctor for you in an hour. She wants to talk to you, to check how far pregnant you are, so she can give you the options. You will feel better after that."

"Thanks Kerrie for always being calm and practical, no matter what."

"This isn't the first time I've been through this with a friend. I just don't want you to make a mistake that will ruin your life forever. Now you need to get ready and I'll take you."

"You're right, Kerrie. I'll have a shower now. Whatever I decide to do, I need to see a doctor."

"Good girl," Kerrie said before she realised it. *Well she is just a kid*, Kerrie said to herself and she went to the kitchen to make herself a coffee.

Stacey got dressed and she and Kerrie got into the car. At the surgery, the doctor took Stacey and Kerrie into her consulting room. She asked Stacey why she had come to see her.

The doctor appeared concerned as she asked, "When was the first day of your last period Stacey?"

"I don't know."

The doctor pressed Stacey to remember. "I need that date to work out how pregnant you are. When was your period due?" "I really don't know." The doctor looked puzzled. "What do you mean, you don't know?"

"Phil hates me having my periods, so I just keep taking the pill and don't take the sugar tablets, for months at a time. I noticed last week that my boobs had become bigger and sore, so I googled it on the internet and it suggested that I could be pregnant and to buy a pregnancy kit. I did, and it was positive."

Kerrie interrupted, "How could you be pregnant if you were taking the pill?"

Stacey looked embarrassed. "I had a really bad case of the flu and was on strong antibiotics and I learnt from googling that it affects the pill. I had to take two prescriptions because I just wasn't improving."

"Such a common mistake," the doctor said. "You should have been warned by your GP. Your doctor didn't tell you to use other precautions?"

"I had forgotten about that, but he did. I remember telling Phil and he said he had never heard of anything so stupid in his life and that he wasn't going to start wearing rain coats at his age."

Kerrie was shocked but also relieved that at least Stacey did not try to trick Phil into this.

"OK, Stacey, let's get you into the other room and we'll do an ultrasound, so we can determine the term of gestation."

The doctor was careful not to call the foetus a baby at this stage. Kerrie turned to the doctor while Stacey was getting into a gown. She asked, "Do you think it's a good idea for her to see the baby? Once she sees it, she may get attached."

"This is really the only way to get an accurate reading and that's very important for her options. By looking at her, she looks about four months to me. She has that glow and her breasts are swollen and much bigger. How on earth could Phil have not noticed?"

"Too pissed probably," said Kerrie "and just enjoying it."

Stacey came back into the room and lay on the bed. She was secretly excited at the thought of seeing the baby.

The doctor informed Stacey, "Stacey, if the embryo is young you will not see much. I'll be the only one looking at the screen at this stage. Then we can discuss the options and we'll go from there."

Stacey was disappointed, but said, "I understand".

The doctor started the ultrasound machine and peered at the screen. Her face was like stone and neither Kerrie nor Stacey could read anything from it. Finally, the doctor told them, "I'm going to ask for one of the other doctors to come in and have a look. I would like a second opinion." The doctor went out and after a couple of minutes, returned with a male doctor. She operated the monitor and they both stared at the screen with steely faces. They nodded to each other and headed for the door. Before she went through it, the doctor turned and said, "You can get dressed now Stacey. I will meet you and Kerrie back in my room, where we will have a chat."

Stacey got up and dressed, then both she and Kerrie went back to the doctor's room. The doctor walked in a few minutes later, carrying the ultrasound images in her hand.

The doctor sat at her desk, her face set with a serious expression. She said, "I'm so sorry, Stacey, we could see the foetus, but we couldn't find a heartbeat. I don't know how long it has been since the heartbeat stopped, but we should get you into hospital as soon as possible, as the foetus could cause an infection in your uterus. You would be in and out the same day, if all goes well. I made a call and I can get you in tomorrow."

Stacey's voice quavered, and she began to cry, as she tried to clarify, "So what you're saying is that the baby is dead and I have to go to hospital tomorrow?"

The doctor nodded. "I'm so sorry Stacey, but we need to get you into hospital ASAP. You said you weren't feeling well and we hope it's not due to this, but we need to make sure it isn't." Stacey stopped crying and asked, "How old is the baby?"

"You were about sixteen weeks pregnant."

Once Kerrie dropped her back at the apartment, Stacey took one of the sedatives the doctor gave her and she got into bed and closed the door.

After Kerrie dropped Stacey home she felt relieved. Although it was bad news, she could milk this for all it was worth with Phil to get Stacey back on her feet. She knew Phil would feel relieved but also guilty, and that would encourage him to give Stacey a better farewell package than otherwise.

Stacey had given Kerrie permission to let Phil know about the baby. She did not have health insurance, so Phil would have to pay the hospital bills. Kerrie called Phil's mobile and Carol answered. Kerrie launched into attack mode, "I'll just get to the point and say that we have been to the doctor and Stacey will need to go to hospital tomorrow because the baby doesn't have a heartbeat and therefore needs to be removed as soon as possible." Kerrie was happy to use the baby word now with Carol and continued, "I will pay whatever it costs for her stay in hospital but I would like to be reassured I will be reimbursed."

"Of course," Carol said. "Phil will do that."

"I know Stacey is staying in Phil's apartment right now and that he would like her out. What thought has been given to alternate housing for her?" Kerrie replied.

Carol realised Kerrie was a tough opponent, "Kerrie, I get it. Let me know what you want me to arrange. If it's fair, it will be done, I'm sure. She can keep the car, which I will transfer into her name and I can organise a deposit into her bank account immediately, or I can arrange to lease another apartment for her for twelve months. Whatever she prefers."

Kerrie realised that Carol had probably done this so many times before that she had the real estate agent on speed dial, so she took the plunge. "Look, Stacey is too upset to ask for anything now, but as her friend, I'm trying to help both her and Phil. How about you arrange a nice apartment within fifteen minutes of the city, with the rent prepaid for twelve months and put a hundred thousand dollars cash into her bank account."

Carol attempted to sound shocked. "A hundred thousand dollars! Are you serious? And the car and an apartment for a year!" Kerrie could see right through Carol's response and put the cards on the table. "Okay, I'll spell it out for you. Make sure it isn't a shoe box you rent her. The hundred grand is for the pain and suffering of losing a baby with Phil. I'm sure if you want to cut it down to fifty grand, I'll get fifty for Stacey from a women's magazine for the story. If Phil would prefer that."

"Okay," Carol replied after quickly realising Kerrie knew what she was doing. "It won't be a problem. The lawyer will want something signed. Can you find her a lawyer to sign off on it for her?"

"Yes, I can," replied Kerrie, pleased with her success. "I have a friend who is a lawyer and I'm sure he'll do it."

Carol could not help asking, "So what is your cut for negotiating this deal, Kerrie?"

Kerrie was not surprised by Carol's question. Although she did not like Carol or secretaries like her, who disguised their sadistic and vile tendencies by saying "they were just doing their job", she did not believe it was easy for anyone who had essentially sold their soul to the devil to earn more than they ever would for being an ethical and moral PA. Kerrie decided to say what she had been waiting to say, now the deal had been done.

"Carol, I know that it's probably something you haven't had as part of your life for a long time, but I am just being a supportive friend to Stacey. I won't let the likes of you and Phil walk all over her and spit her out after Phil's decided he doesn't want to play with her anymore. Unlike you Carol, I'm just being a decent person." Kerrie then hung up, very pleased that she got that dig in, hoping it would wake something up in Carol whilst knowing it wouldn't.

Carol hung up from Kerrie and smiled. She knew Kerrie had enjoyed having a go at her about what she did for Phil. Kerrie was not the first and would not be the last to do that. What Kerrie had done though, was to reduce the end of the relationship to financial terms, and this in essence let Phil off the hook. Once money was handed over, that relieved Phil of any guilt or responsibility for the end of the relationship as far as he was concerned, and this was Carol's job.

Phillip

Chapter 35

After a long and frustrating but productive day, Carol phoned Phil to let him know about Stacey and the arrangements she had sorted out with Kerrie. Carol was proud of her ability to sort out every problem in Phil's life. She now regarded herself as totally indispensable to him unlike his wives and girlfriends.

While listening to Carol, Phil was secretly relieved the baby had died but asked, "Should I call Stacey, Carol? Ask her friend if she thinks I should call or see Stacey. I like Stacey, you know. She wasn't a bad kid and I don't want to look like a monster here." "I know that Phil, but I think seeing Stacey would just give her hope. Better to just be cruel to be kind. Any kindness by you now would let the poor girl think she had another chance with you, and she has been through enough."

Phil was furious but did not want to show it to Carol. He could tell that Carol was starting to judge him and she had no right to do that. She was his PA and her job was to support him. *If it weren't for him she would be unemployed, the stupid bitch.* The only thing she had going for her was that she had been loyal without question. She had lied to his ex-wife, his girlfriends and his friends, whenever he told her to. She had flowers delivered and booked flights and hotels for his dalliances with women. He knew she enjoyed the power of booking the abortions and sorting out the appropriate kiss off presents when needed. She had no right to now act like she could judge him.

"Let me know when it's done, Carol. Then we need to talk."

Carol hung up. She knew Phil was angry with her and she was beyond frustrated with him. He had no idea how much he needed her and how devoted she was to him. Even though she loved her job, she was finding it harder and harder to clean up his personal life without feeling like a monster these days. She had done it for twelve years and she was getting tired of it. She had even started to see a therapist about it.

Her therapist had told her that in his view, Phil was a sociopath and narcissist and as such, he would never feel guilt; that he used people without remorse and he would never change unless he went into therapy, which was unlikely. Carol had at times thought about quitting, but she knew she would not get paid anywhere near even half of what Phil paid her and she needed the money. Apart from that she knew that she also in love with Phil and leaving him would devastate her. Annoyed with her situation, she picked up the phone and called Sarah's office.

"Kate, can you please let Sarah know that Stacey has had a problem and that the pregnancy is no longer. Also, we have sorted out something with Stacey and I will email the details through. I have asked Stacey's friend to send the details of the lawyer Stacey will be using and I will forward them onto you, so Sarah can sort this out with Phil."

"OK, Carol, I will wait for the email and let Sarah know."

Katrina

Chapter 36

Katrina was surprised when Geoffrey called her on the way home from dropping the kids to pre-school. He had not called in a couple of weeks and his call had unsettled her, particularly as he said he wanted to come and talk to her. Just hearing his voice still upset her to the point she felt like crying. The thoughts that had tormented her for the last six months invaded her head: *How could he leave me? How could he leave us? What did we do wrong?*

The words of her counsellor came back to her. "Katrina, you did nothing wrong. The kids did nothing wrong. You will never understand why Geoffrey left you because there is no way to explain madness."

The counsellor's words were comforting but how could she ever get Geoffrey's parting words out of her head? "Katrina, I don't want to live in a child care centre anymore. I just want to go and have some fun. I'm leaving, and my lawyers will be in touch to sort out a payout for you."

She had since discovered that he had been having an affair, which was the real reason he had left. He had fallen in love with the woman, she was told by his friends. They encouraged Katrina to move on and protect herself and the kids financially. But she was finding it emotionally difficult to accept her marriage was over. The questions in her head showed no sign of relenting. *How could he have been having an affair for months and I didn't know?*

As her counsellor had said, she had made so much progress in the past six months. When they first separated, all she could think and talk about was Geoffrey and her hopes of him coming home. She told the counsellor there was not an hour that went by, either when she was asleep or awake, that she he did not pop into her head. After three months, she noticed a couple of hours could go by, if she was busy, where she did not think of him and now she could get through a day without a thought or a tear. She knew she just had to keep working to get through this for the kids' sake.

Phil

Chapter 37

Phil was the happiest he had been in a long time. He could not believe how lucky he was that Stacey lost the baby. He thought he had even sounded sincere to Carol about feeling sorry for Stacey. He was now determined to concentrate on Sarah and he could not wait to let her know how nicely things had worked out.

Sarah was heading to court when her mobile rang. It was Phil Pemberton; she had been waiting for his call.

"Hi Phil, how are you?" she inquired.

Sarah heard a loud sigh before Phil boomed into the phone, "I'm a relieved man, Sarah. We have sorted out a deal with Stacey. It was probably a little more than I thought was reasonable, but as you can understand, I don't feel I'm in such a great place to negotiate."

"I understand Phil. If you can be generous in these difficult circumstances, I'm sure it helps."

Phil told Sarah the details of the deal. "I believe my PA, Carol, is emailing the terms to you. I need to give Stacey the money ASAP, so can you please try and get this done quickly. I hope that's OK."

Sarah understood. "That's fine. I'll get it done ASAP. I'm just off to court now but it will be finished by this week. Stacey will need a lawyer to sign off on the settlement though."

"Yes, she knows that. Her friend that is helping her says she has organised that. She is going to email me the guy's details and she will forward them to you. I have been very lucky, this time."

You have been lucky this time, by the sound of it, although I haven't seen what you have agreed to give her, Sarah thought.

"You know, Sarah, maybe I will see that psychiatrist you were talking about. I don't want to hurt anyone like this again. I don't know why I do it." Phil sounded truly repentant, and Sarah was pleased.

"Let's talk about this, Phil, when you come in to sign up. It's really good to hear." Sarah smiled to herself, thinking that perhaps he may be on the way to reforming.

As he hung up the phone, Phil wondered why women always fell for that line after he had a breakup. It seemed to him that all you had to do to get a woman was to tell her you were thinking of going to therapy and they forgave all your sins and believed you would turn into a perfect gentleman for them. It had worked for fifty-three years now so Phil was not going to change something that wasn't broke. What he was going to do though, was to make Sarah fall in love with him. He had done his research and, apparently, the only true love of her life had been her ex-husband who was regrettably still involved in her life. No one else had made any headway into Sarah's heart but he was going to ensure it would open up for him very soon.

Katrina

Chapter 38

As usual, after she picked the kids up from pre-school, Katrina took them to the park. As they arrived, she was surprised by a call from her gardener, Mick. "Hi Katrina, I don't want to scare you but when I was mowing the lawns, I saw a man inside the house in the lounge room that I didn't recognise. I went inside and asked him who he was, and he said to me, 'I'm the owner of the house, you idiot. Just mow the lawns like you are supposed to and leave me alone.' Katrina, do you know who this is? Were you expecting anyone?"

"No, I don't," Katrina replied, very concerned with what Mick had told her. "I have no idea how he would have got inside the house!"

"That's all I needed to know," Mick said "I'll call the police and wait for them. Where are you?"

"I'm at the park, with the kids. Should I come home now?" asked Katrina.

"No, you stay there and keep the kids away, in case there's a scene. I'll speak with the police and let you know what happens."

Mick went to his car, which was parked in the driveway of the house picked up his phone and called the police, who said they would come to the house, straight away.

Just as Mick finished his call, the man walked out the front door of the house. He proceeded to walk down the street, but when he saw Mick he started to run. Mick chased after him for three blocks until the man jumped a fence and ran into a neighbour's backyard. Not wanting to be accused of trespassing himself, Mick buzzed the doorbell on the house but there was no answer. He then went around the side of the house and looked over the side gate. He could see that the back of the house led to a reserve and he realised the guy had got away. Mick headed straight back to Katrina's house hoping the police had arrived.

He arrived at the front yard just as the police were pulling up. Still catching his breath, he went through everything with the police, concluding with the chase, "He just walked out the front door like nothing was wrong but when he saw me on the phone, he ran. He went three doors up and jumped the fence, which leads to the public reserve."

The police and Mick went inside the house but as far as they could see, nothing had been stolen or damaged. They could see no sign of forced entry or disturbance. The police began asking the usual questions about what he was doing at the house and who resided there. Then they asked him to go to the station to make a formal report and to provide a description of the intruder.

After leaving the police station, Mick called Katrina and asked her to meet him at the house, to explain what had happened. He was concerned for her. He knew the separation had been devastating for her and he was very worried that this was more stress for her to handle. The thought of a strange man in her house would scare any woman but for Katrina, in her fragile state right now and having two little kids, it could just be too much.

Mick had felt protective of Katrina since Geoffrey left. He did not understand what was wrong with the man, leaving his beautiful family like that. Since Mick's wife passed away three years earlier, he had not been able to even think about another woman. Lately, though, when he saw Katrina he not only felt like putting his arms around her to protect her, but he had also started to feel attracted to her. He could see she was heartbroken over her marriage ending, so he knew that now was not the time.

After speaking to Mick, Katrina called Geoffrey to let him know there had been an intruder at the house. To her surprise, Geoffrey insisted on coming over to see that she and the kids were okay.

When Katrina arrived home, Mick was sitting in the drive- way waiting for her. She was so relieved that he was there, and this surprised her. She did not want to be alone right now. Mick helped her get the kids out of the car. Just as they walked into the house and closed the door behind them, the doorbell rang. Mick went to open it and saw Geoffrey standing on the doorstep.

"What the fuck are you doing in the house, Mick? Your job is outside so get the fuck out!" Geoffrey said.

Mick was shocked to see Geoffrey and to be spoken to so aggressively. He turned and walked back into the house without responding. Geoffrey called out to him again, "We need to talk mate. Come outside away from Katrina and the kids so we can sort this out."

Mick turned around and walked out onto the verandah to confront Geoffrey. As he did so, Geoffrey slipped past him inside the house and slammed the front door and deadlocked it. Geoffrey yelled out from behind the door, "Fuck off, mate. This is my wife and children. I'm here now so go home."

Katrina came running up the hallway shouting, "What are you doing Geoffrey?"

"I have just thrown Mick out of my house, Katrina. If he thinks he's going to go from gardener and handyman to man of the house, he has got another think coming. Geoffrey turned to look at Katrina, smelt her Chanel No 5 perfume. and noticed how hot she looked. The excitement of the moment had brought a nice red flush to her cheeks and she was wearing what she looked best in – tight blue jeans and a sheer white blouse. With a huge grin and his blue eyes lighting up with mischief, Geoffrey recalled how much he enjoyed pulling off her jeans and how her nipples were always so responsive.

He had a sudden urge to grab her, pull her apart like a warm chicken and devour her, but instead, he said to her, "You look beautiful today, Katrina. How about you get me a beer and I'll stay for dinner. When you've put the kids to bed, I could even give you one tonight, honey."

Katrina could not believe that the man she had married, and had two children with, was speaking to her like this. He had never spoken to her this way before but since their separation, he had almost become feral. The odd thing was, although she felt furious that he was using those words with her, at the same time, part of her wanted him to stay and have dinner with them and for him to make love to her.

Katrina shook her head. She knew there was no point trying to put their relationship back together, but she thought maybe she should give it one last try for the kids. She did not want to argue with Geoffrey, but she needed to resolve this now.

"Geoffrey are you saying you want to come home to us?," asked Katrina, looking straight into his annoying, hypnotic, blue eyes.

Geoffrey had to hold himself back from bursting out laughing and he wanted to say, *Fuck no, but I thought I'd give you one, right here, right now on the fucking table because looking at your legs right now I remember how I used to like them wrapped around my neck and I can see you could do with a fuck.* Instead he replied, "Katrina, I think it's something we could work on." This was part of his plan to lure her in so he could to get her out of the house. She was close to breaking emotionally, he could tell, and it would not be long before he broke her - but he just could not get over how good she still looked.

Katrina tried to take his comment as something positive. She touched his arm. "Geoffrey we would need to go to counselling to work through what happened. If we don't, I won't know why you needed to have an affair and what part I played in that. If you will do that, then we have a chance of fixing this. Will you go to counselling?"

Just as luck would have it for Geoffrey, Mick started banging on the door again and shouting out to Katrina, "Are you okay Katrina? Please, just let me know you are okay."

As she went to the door, Geoffrey placed his hand over the deadlock and said, "Don't unlock it Katrina or I'll kill him. Tell him to go away."

"Mick please go, I'm okay. I'm talking to Geoffrey and I'll call you later."

"Katrina are you sure I shouldn't call the police?"

"No Mick, I'm fine. It's best if you go now."

Mick could tell from the tone of Katrina's voice that she was upset but not fearful and with that he walked back to his car. He was going to drive down the street and wait until the bastard left. He could not believe the man. Geoffrey had abandoned his family and because he was there helping Katrina Geoffrey decided to throw him out. The guy was unbelievable.

Katrina looked at Geoffrey. He was very pleased with himself and looking like the cat that had swallowed the canary. Katrina said to him, "I don't have any beer Geoffrey and it wasn't very nice of you to do that to Mick when he has been so kind to me and the children. Why did you make him leave?"

Geoffrey had been consumed with jealousy when Mick answered the door to his former home. It had surprised him. He knew he had to pull himself together and realised it was probably best if he left.

"I'm sorry, Katrina. Now I can see that you and the kids are okay, I'll go."

Katrina felt confused and wondered why Geoffrey had come to the house. She needed to clarify with him why he was there.

"Geoffrey, do you want to try to reconcile with me and work through this?"

Geoffrey looked bored and got his keys out of his pocket as he replied, "No, I don't want to do that Katrina."

"Do you want to speak to the police about the break in?"

"No need to. As long as it's been reported to the police, that's all that can be done," he said as he was walking out the door.

Katrina followed him out and she said to him, "Mick reported it to the police."

"That's his job Katrina. That's what he gets paid for," Geoffrey said, before he got into his car and drove away.

But you don't pay him anymore, Katrina thought as she walked back inside the house, unsure whether she should be laughing or crying about what had just happened. Mick had been kindly working for free after Geoffrey left.

Mick saw Geoffrey drive away from the house. He walked back to the house and knocked on the door. As Katrina opened it he could see the surprise on her face. She smiled and gave him a hug.

"I thought it was Geoffrey coming back again and I'm so relieved it was you. Would you like a cup of tea?"

Mick smiled at Katrina. "I'd love that." Why on earth Katrina had been married to such a revolting man was beyond him, but he realised at that moment that not only did he care about her, but she really needed him in her life.

Geoffrey

Chapter 39

Geoffrey sat in his lounge room, pondering over how his plans had progressed and if changes needed to be made. Things had not gone as he thought they would, but it would do for now.

He thought about the conversation he had with Sarah Walters and muttered under his breath to himself, *Fucking lawyers, they think they are so smart. The old fashioned way is best, just scare the fuck out of women and they run scared. Then tell them they need something smaller and more secure, which always ends up costing jack shit compared to the mansion you just got them out of.*

Amber had even suggested to him that he encourage Katrina to see a counsellor or shrink and offer to pay for all the therapy, like a really nice, caring husband would. Then after Katrina had spilled her guts to the therapists, he could subpoena all the records and make her out to be depressed and a danger to the kids.

"It will scare the fuck out of her and she'll settle for the kids and some lose change," Amber said. That was the thing with Amber, she was ruthless when it came to fucking people over. It showed a loyalty to him that he liked. She would do anything for him and he knew it.

As he had planned, Katrina was now heartbroken and feeling vulnerable and unsafe. She was very close to becoming completely broken. With the intruder that he had organised, she would start feeling nervous and unsafe in the house. Now would be the time to talk her into moving into a security apartment for her and the children's safety, while the divorce was being sorted out.

If Katrina played this the way he wanted, he would pay her maintenance, and occasionally even give her one if he was horny.

He smiled as he recalled how hot she looked the other day. It had actually surprised him when he felt a bit of tingle following down the hallway. *If she would just stop crying and being miserable, she was not a bad sort,* he thought to himself.

He knew that Katrina was not strong enough to put up a fight, even if she were to hire a lawyer to stand behind her. It was only a matter of time and his problems would be solved with her.

Geoffrey had also worked out last night what was next for Amber. He was going to fuck her best friend and do it in front of her by arranging a threesome. He knew Amber loved him, so he knew she would hate it. But he also knew that she would do anything to keep him, so she would not only not show upset she was to him but even pretend to enjoy it. As he thought about how it would tear her apart, he started to smile. He would arrange for Amber to video him fucking Sally so that he could replay it repeatedly and watch her while she was with him. It would fuck with her head, over and over again.

Geoffrey reflected on what his doctor mate said to him recently when he once again tried to talk him into a vasectomy. He told Geoffrey that he needed to realise he followed a pattern with a woman, "You pursue women who aren't initially interested in you. Then you make them love you just so that you can destroy them."

When Geoffrey replied, "I like it. I just like fucking women over", his mate was stunned. Geoffrey went further and said, "It's not a crime, so why the fuck should I stop?"

Geoffrey enjoyed watching Amber writhe in pain, wanting to cry out but being scared to. He enjoyed playing the game with her and taking her from being no one to feeling like she was a princess. He loved lifting women to heights then watching them fall. Amber had been the easiest woman to make feel special. All he had to do with her was buy her dinner and drinks. When he first took her shopping for a new dress and shoes, she looked as happy as a little girl with her first doll.

Geoffrey really believed that Amber would eventually kill herself when he left her. He had already enabled her into a Valium and Xanax addiction when she was clearly unstable emotionally. The nutty ones are always the best fucks, he thought. They were also the hardest to get rid of. Luckily, he had developed the perfect exit strategies and they seemed to be working so far.

Jessica

Chapter 40

Jessica and Anne were relieved to be leaving the school and heading to Elizabeth's house. When they got into the car neither of them spoke. They needed the comfort of silence to regroup. They knew that when they arrived at her home, they would have to explain to Elizabeth what had happened, but they knew she would cope better than they were.

Elizabeth's home was a beautiful wooden homestead on five acres, only twenty minutes away, and this gave Anne and Jessica enough time to compose themselves. Anne parked the car in the driveway and switched off the engine. She turned to Jessica and smiled as she pointed to the house and said, "I can see Elizabeth on the veranda." Jessica smiled and got out of the car. She walked towards the verandah, waving to her aunty.

Elizabeth saw her, stood up and greeted them, "Hello ladies, I made some iced tea and thought it would be nice to sit out here on the balcony."

Elizabeth's verandah had the homely and calming atmosphere they needed. The large timber verandah wrapped around the house, and it looked out to the impressive vegetable garden which Elizabeth prided herself on. While sipping their iced tea, Anne thought of the many times through the years that they had enjoyed sitting here, drinking tea and laughing or crying, as the occasion demanded. *At least some things never change,* she thought to herself.

The three of them sat on the comfortable armchairs, Anne beside Elizabeth and Jessica in her favourite armchair, on her own. Anne opened the conversation, "Elizabeth, Jessica and I can't go home because Anthony has been…" At that point, Anne's voice began to quaver, and she could not continue. Elizabeth leaned over and put her arm around her.

"It's okay, Anne," she soothed. "If you can't tell me now, we'll try this again later." Elizabeth had always had the patience of a saint. In fact, she was the kindest, most generous and under- standing of human beings and Anne thought the epithet of "saintly" was never more fitting.

Anne recovered a little and said, "Elizabeth, Anthony has been sexually abusing Jessica; he has been hurting her and I didn't know. We can't go back, and we're very scared about what he'll do when the police go to see him."

Elizabeth had not expected this. Shocked, she said to Jessica, "I'm so sorry that this has happened, Jessica. I'm so sorry." As she spoke, Elizabeth stood up and walked across to Jessica to comfort her. She wrapped her in her arms and held her close.

Whilst Anne and Elizabeth had been completely devastated by the revelations, Jessica seemed to have developed a new strength. She pulled back from Elizabeth and said to both of them, "It was not your fault that neither of you knew about this. No one knew. I understand now that Anthony was very clever about it all. He's a smart, evil man. He tricked us all. I don't blame anyone but him. Sometimes, I used to blame myself, because I felt bad about keeping secrets from Mum, even though Anthony told me what we were doing wasn't wrong. He said that if I told Mum, it would hurt her so much that she would never talk to me again. He said he could convince her that I was lying because I was jealous. It wasn't until Dr Quade started to help me that I could see how Anthony had begun grooming and controlling me to protect himself, not me or Mum."

When Jessica finished telling Elizabeth what had happened, she stood up and insisted in a low, firm voice, "I am going to make sure he goes to jail. He won't win. He told me no one would believe me, that they would think I was lying, but Dr Quade believed me and you and Mum believe me. I know I can make a judge believe me."

Jessica slumped back into her chair, as the effects of the revelations and the enormity of the process ahead were beginning to weigh on her. "I don't want to talk anymore today. I know I must talk to the detectives tomorrow and that scares me. Dr Quade says that I've spent eighteen months blocking it out every day, as it happened. He said our mind copes with what it can handle at the time and blocks out the rest. It's been painful for me to unlock all my emotions and relive it all when I told Dr Quade, and then Mum and now you."

Fatigue overcame her, and Jessica excused herself. "Can I please just go and lie down for a while?"

"Of course, Jessica," Elizabeth replied. "We are here to support you and love you. You know where your room is, honey." "I love you Elizabeth and I love you Mum. I've always felt so safe here."

Elizabeth and Anne watched Jessica walk inside. Jessica had always had her own room at Elizabeth's home. Elizabeth's husband had died two years after they married, and she had never remarried or had children. Jessica was the closest thing she had to a daughter of her own. At times, Anne had felt jealous of their connection, which seemed to have grown closer as Jessica grew older. Right now, she was so grateful for her sister's support and could not imagine coping without her.

After Jessica left the verandah, Anne was the first to speak, "I can't believe I didn't see it, Elizabeth? How could I have been blind to what was going on? I don't know if I'll ever be able to forgive myself. I thought Anthony was my dream man, he seemed so kind to us both. How could this happen?"

"Please don't beat yourself up. Jessica needs your support right now and if you beat yourself up, you'll be no good to her. Neither of us saw this and we're both going to feel terrible guilt, but right now we cannot indulge in self-pity. We must stay strong and focus on Jessica. She's a strong girl and we're going to help her get through this in the best possible way."

Elizabeth reached out and pressed Anne's hands between hers as she knew she had to pull her back to the practicalities of Jessica's situation. "After the police have interviewed Jessica, they'll go and charge Anthony. You and Jessica should stay here with me until the police arrest him at least, don't you think?"

"The police told me I need to get a lawyer. The detective said once the criminal proceedings start, it may affect my family law rights somehow. I told the detective that I had a family lawyer who acted for me before and that I would arrange to see her."

Elizabeth agreed, "I think you should get Sarah here as soon as you're up to it. She will know exactly what you should do. Do you want me to call her for you and make an appointment?"

"Yes please."

"OK, I'll do that tomorrow." Elizabeth assured her, "We'll get through this one thing at a time. I know Sarah will guide you legally, and while she does that, you're both safe here."

"What if Anthony talks the police into believing that Jessica is lying? Or, what if this goes to court and they find Anthony not guilty? How will Jessica cope with that?" Anne asked.

"If Jessica wants Anthony charged and the police are willing to do that, then they must believe that they can convict him. That's their job, and we'll have to leave that up to them. We'll do our job, which will be to take care of Jessica while she goes through this by giving her our love and support."

"I hope that's enough, Elizabeth." Anne envisaged the pain and humiliation Jessica may have to go through before feeling overcome with exhaustion herself.

Jessica

Chapter 41

Jessica had been secretly listening to her mother and aunt as they talked on the verandah. They were unaware that she had already thought about what she would do to make sure she was believed. She had discussed it with Dr Quade. She knew the risks but believed she would be strong enough to get through the trial and have a judge believe her. Just as she was thinking about Anthony, she felt her phone vibrate in her pocket. She realised with a cold shiver that it was him. This was the time he usually came home to be with her after school, while her mother was at work. She thought that now was as good a time as any to try out the new App on her phone.

"Hi, Anthony," she said, trying not to sound any different than usual.

Anthony greeted her smoothly, "Hi, Jessica, your Aunty Elizabeth just called to say you and your Mum are over there. I missed you after school today, I just wanted you to know."

"Sorry, Anthony, it was Mum's idea and I had no control over it. I couldn't actually tell her that you and I have a thing going on, while she's at the office, can I?"

Slightly taken back, but trying to ignore Jessica's curt response, he replied, "I suppose not, but I still miss you."

"That's because I'm always there for you. Mum and I don't usually dare to change our routines, do we?"

"I'm not happy that she did that today." Anthony sounded disappointed, but then he said with more enthusiasm, "Elizabeth told me not to say anything, but I know that you are all there planning my fiftieth birthday party aren't you?"

"Yes we are, but it's a supposed to be a surprise." *God bless Elizabeth with her excuses*, Jessica thought to herself. She played along with Elizabeth's ruse. "Please don't tell Mum you know, or Elizabeth and I will be in trouble."

Anthony sounded a little petulant. "I waited all day to come home to be with you and now you aren't here. You know how much I need you, Jessica."

Jessica looked at her phone. He was calling from his mobile, which was perfect for her plan. She knew what she had to get him to say on the phone, and she had practised her part of the dialogue so many times in her head. She needed to get him to say what he had been doing to her and then maybe she could get him to confess to the police so that they would not have to go to court. She knew this was worth a try.

Trying to sound as relaxed as she could, Jessica continued, "Anthony, do you really think what you do with me is right?"

"What we do is natural and loving. I love you and I love your mother."

"I really didn't understand what was happening when you started this with me and I trusted you when you told me what you did to me was okay. I was only thirteen when you started touching me. Now you're having sex with me three times a week. I was too young when you started doing things to me and I'm only fifteen-years-old now. It's wrong for us to keep doing this to Mum, especially when you're her husband."

Anthony was shocked at Jessica's outburst and tried to convince her, "Jessica, it's not wrong. It's beautiful and it completes what we have as a family. I love your mother and I love you. It would hurt her if she knew, so we can't say anything to her. You don't want to hurt her, do you? Our lives are perfect now, we are a family and we have such a good life."

"But, Anthony, what we do is wrong, and you shouldn't have started having sex with me, when I was only thirteen-years-old. I didn't understand what you were doing. I know now that it's all wrong and we should stop this."

"Jessica, please don't be silly. I make you feel good and you make me feel good. There's nothing bad about that. When you come home, we'll talk about it and we'll work this out."

"What if I don't want to do this anymore? What if I won't do this anymore with you? I've met a boy my age that I really like. I want to be normal, like my friends, and go to parties with kids from school and have a boyfriend and you won't let me do that."

Anthony was getting angry, "We have a perfect life, and nothing is going to change, Jessica. You will do as you have been and that's that. You don't want your mother's perfect world to change, do you? She wouldn't cope. You don't need another male in your life and I won't have it. Your mum agrees with me about that. No boyfriends."

"Anthony, the last time you talked about boyfriends with me and Mum was a year ago and you were already having sex with me. She agreed I was too young to go out to parties and have a boyfriend then, but you didn't ask her if I was too young to be having sex with you, did you? How old do I have to be before I can have a boyfriend?"

Anthony quickly changed tack. "Jessica, just calm down, we have a beautiful home and a good life. Your Mum is happy and she has no stress, not like she used to have. I give her everything she wants. You want your Mum to be happy, don't you? When you come home we'll all be happy again. I miss you both already. Come home soon."

Jessica hung up the phone. She had tried to convince him it was wrong and to stop, but in her heart, she knew he would not. She had bought and installed the App on her phone after her friend had told her about how she had used it to record a call with a guy she was seeing and then played the call back to another girl who did not believe she had been dating him. It turned out he had had similar conversations with both of them, back to back on the same day.

Jessica didn't know if the police could use the recording in court, but at least she had some proof that she was not making everything up when no doubt Anthony would accuse her of doing so. Having proof of what he said to her made her feel so much better.

Katrina

Chapter 42

Katrina lay on the lounge of her family room. She was crying and staring out of the glass doors to the pool. She knew it was because she was already emotionally drained by the separation with Geoffrey, that the incident of having an unknown intruder in her home had caused her to feel completely overwhelmed. She realised she was extremely stressed and that this was starting to affect her badly.

Recently, she had been forgetting where she had parked her car and even watching the news made her cry if someone was hurt in any way. Yesterday, after dropping the kids to preschool, she sat in her car and could not stop crying until one of the other mothers noticed her and came to her aid. She knew it was not normal and she knew she had to help herself for the sake of her children.

Katrina just did not feel safe in her home anymore, even though she had the alarm checked and turned on at night. She was anxious being alone during the day with the children, and she woke up with the slightest sound in the night. The police had found no explanation for the man being in her home or the fact that he took off after seeing Mick. After speaking to her parents, she agreed that although she did not really want to leave her home, it was time she thought about moving. It made sense to move into a secure apartment so she and the children could feel safe, at least until she was able to settle herself down emotionally. Looking around her home, she reflected on how happy they had been when she married Geoffrey and moved into his beautiful house. But now, as her father had said today, her marriage was over and she had to face reality.

"Moving on and moving out, was the first step she had to take to get on with her life," he said. She knew her father was right and she was grateful he was there to support her.

Katrina allowed herself to cry until there were no tears left. Exhausted, but satisfied that she had processed her decision, she pulled herself together to call Geoffrey to let him know. She picked up the phone and was determined to talk to him calmly and sensibly, but when he answered, her voice wavered. "Hi, it's Katrina can we talk?"

Geoffrey knew she would call and was pleased with how distressed she sounded.

"What's up honey is something wrong?" he asked, assuming the role of a caring husband. It was such a surprise to hear Geoffrey sounding concerned again that Katrina was taken aback.

"Yes, it is, I'm really worried about us being here in the house by ourselves." In her heart, she felt torn as she was saying it. One part of her was hoping that he would say he would come back home so they could be a family again and keep them safe, and the other part of her wanted to move on.

Instead, Geoffrey made his calculated move. "I've been worried about that for a while, Katrina. Remember I did suggest you look at an apartment with security."

Geoffrey had manipulated Katrina so well that, although her heart sank at his reply, she played right into his hands. "Dad and Mum have suggested an apartment that's for sale in their building with three bedrooms. Could I have a look at that for the kids and me to move into?"

Bingo! Geoffrey thought. He put that idea in her parents' heads a month ago. The apartment would cost him nothing compared to what the house was worth. He would have her out and he would be back in the house in no time at all.

"Of course, Katrina. Get your dad to sort it out with the agent and let me know the details before someone else snaps it up. I just want you and the kids to be safe. You know I still love you all."

Then Geoffrey played his masterstroke, speaking tenderly as he reeled in the catch, "Maybe, we can work things out if we really try. I like the idea of you having something in your own name that you own outright. That's something you deserve, darling."

Although she felt Geoffrey had been a monster in the last six months, Katrina remembered why she fell in love with him. He was being so kind and caring that it seemed impossible he had done such hurtful things. He had said the words that she so longed to hear, that he loved her and that maybe they could work things out. For the first time in a long time, she felt that maybe things would work out after all. Geoffrey could make her feel like a princess, at times, and that was how she felt right now.

The apartment would be a haven for her and the children until they were back together. After the children had grown up, maybe they could sell the house and use the apartment as their base, like her parents did, and travel most of the time. They had talked about that and Geoffrey had obviously not forgotten.

With those thoughts in her head, Katrina said, "Thank you, Geoffrey. I'll call Dad now. He'll be very happy when I tell him you said it was OK."

"Just get him to call me after he has the paperwork from the agent and I'll fix up the rest." Then, as an afterthought, he said, "Also Katrina, you should look at furniture for the unit, don't you think? It may be nicer for you to have new furniture that suits the apartment rather than the furniture that was made for the house. It would definitely be too big for a unit." Geoffrey was so pleased with himself; that was a brainwave. She would think he was doing her a great kindness in letting her get new furniture but in reality, she had no idea what the furniture in the house and the artwork was worth. He wanted to keep it that way.

Katrina thought Geoffrey's suggestion about the furniture was so sweet. The furniture in the house had been made or bought especially for the house and would be too big and strange in the unit. "That's such a good idea, Geoffrey. Are you sure?"

"Yes, of course I am, Katrina. Why don't you call Alison? She has some great furniture where she works now."

Katrina smiled for the first time in months. She had thought Geoffrey did not pay attention to anything she said about her friends, but obviously he did. Alison had started a new job with a furniture importer a month ago and had sent them brochures of all the imported furniture they were bringing into stock.

"That's a good idea," she agreed. "I'll call her and see if she can help me. But what will we do about the house, Geoffrey?"

"Don't you worry about that, honey. I'll sort out the apartment with the ban, so you can have that straight away and I can move into the house to look after it, until we work out things between us. I like the idea of us having the house and a apartment which could always be an investment."

Geoffrey knew that after he moved back into the house and she and the children had moved into the apartment, the game would be over. Once Katrina knew he was never coming home, she would surrender like a tortured animal, and agree to settle on any basis.

After finishing the call with Katrina, Geoffrey felt happier than he had been in months. Although Amber excited him sexually, she was not a challenge for him and did nothing for him mentally. He had by chance met another woman the other day that he was attracted to. She was the new accounts manager at his stockbroker's firm and he was going to start getting much more interested in his share portfolio.

Katrina

Chapter 43

After calling her father and telling him that Geoffrey had agreed she should buy the unit, he got into action quickly to secure it for her. He had put the agent's number into his phone the week before when he and his wife had attended the first open inspection. They knew the apartment would be perfect for Katrina and the kids and they had sent photos from their phone to her as they inspected it. It did not take him long, being a former real estate agent, to close the deal on a price.

Katrina was in the car with her father on the way to see the apartment. The agent was meeting them there with a copy of the contract. Her father was the rock of her life and she knew that he had been worried about her and the girls since Geoffrey left them.

"I'm really excited about this. I know it's going to be perfect for me and the kids, but it's also going to be so nice to be near you and Mum. I think it's amazing that Geoffrey is doing this for us. He told me yesterday that he still loves us Dad."

Her father stared straight ahead and kept driving. She looked at his face and could see he was trying very hard not to comment.

"Dad, really it's going to be great."

Her father pulled the car over to the side of the road, then turned and spoke to her.

"Katrina, your mother and I think that moving into the apartment is a great idea for you and the kids. We will be so relieved when you are closer to us, secure and safe, and we can help you more. Right now, you're very vulnerable, and I know that you want Geoffrey to come home, but darling you need to face the fact that he may not.

Your mother and I are convinced he won't be back and that he's already moved on. Look, he's doing the right thing by getting you this unit, but don't be mistaken. He's also going to look after himself and move back into the house. It was his house and he wants it back."

Katrina looked over at her father. She realised that what he was saying was true, but she just did not want to face the truth. As her psychologist had told her, her head knew it but her heart did not want to believe it.

Katrina surprised her father by holding his hand, and with tears in her eyes said, "I know, Dad. I know, and I knew that you and mum knew too. In my head, I realised but my heart has taken some time to catch up. I still hope that maybe, just maybe he will come home to us, but I know that's just a fantasy. I need to get a home where the kids and I feel safe and something I can cope with. The apartment will be perfect and that is all we need."

"Katrina, please don't think I'm encouraging you to see a lawyer, but you realise that you could get more from Geoffrey by way of a property settlement than just this apartment don't you? He is a wealthy man."

"Yes, Dad I do. But what I also realise is that I would have to fight him for it and I don't want that. This way, he'll be kind with the extra's like the furniture and he even mentioned putting money in my bank account for the kids and a holiday. I know it's better for both me and the kids to keep Geoffrey happy."

Her father looked like he was going to cry, and he reached over and hugged her.

"Honey, I'm so relieved. I didn't care if you and the girls came to live with your mother and me, and you got nothing from that bastard. I just don't want you to accept this because you think it will encourage him to come home to you."

Her father almost regretted what he had said when he saw the pain in her eyes.

He apologised, "Sorry honey but a man who leaves my beautiful daughter and his kids is a stupid bastard. I don't care about money, but I do care if he thinks he has outsmarted you. If you've decided this is what you want, and all you need, then your mother and I are here for anything and everything else."

"Thank you, Dad. I want to behave and act in a way that I can live with. Maybe I won't get what I'm legally entitled to, but I know doing it this way I will be able to move on without Geoffrey getting angry or scary."

"You know that he'll ask you to sign a property settlement, Katrina, and when he does you know that you should make sure he looks after you and agrees to pay the kids' expenses and maintenance until you can go back to work. I've been looking around for a lawyer to help you and I have the name of a lady that I think would give you the right advice. When you're ready, can we go and see her?"

Katrina smiled at her father. "Thanks for looking after me, Dad. Sure. When we sort out the apartment and the move, then we'll focus on that."

"That's a relief, darling." He started the car and pulled back onto the road. "Now let's go get you a new home so you and the kids can start a peaceful life."

Katrina felt the security and comfort with her father that she had felt since she was a little girl. She reflected on what this might mean for her children.

"Dad, do you think Geoffrey will try to be a good father to the children? I don't know what I would have done without you?"

"I don't know what happened to Geoffrey to make him the way he is, but we can only hope that he's good to the kids. Whatever he can't give them emotionally honey, we are here for them. They will have all my love, yours and your mother's and that's enough for any child. Whatever Geoffrey gives them will be a bonus. I think he'll try with them. I really do. Especially when he realises what he's lost in you."

"Thanks Dad. You're amazing. I know I'll get through this with you and Mum supporting me and the children will be fine if I'm fine."

Anthony

Chapter 44

After Jessica's phone call, Anthony knew something was wrong. Jessica had never spoken to him like that before, especially not on the phone. What they had between them was something they had enjoyed for nearly two years now and she had stopped questioning it a long time ago. When he first started developing an attraction to her, it surprised him. The first time he saw her get out of the shower, he was overcome with desire and had to walk away until he could decide what to do. After things developed, he was convinced that she would never tell Anne. He knew it was wrong of him to tell her not to tell Anne, but it was better not to hurt her mother. He and Jessica had developed something very special. When she got home, he would convince her that everything was fine.

He wondered if it was the boy at school who was getting in the way. He knew that, one day, she would be interested in boys and that she would be going to school formals and dances, so he might lose her then. He was not ready for that to happen yet though. She was still his for a while longer and no pimply faced, goofy, testosterone driven teenager was going to get his hands on her.

Just thinking about Jessica made him feel good. He loved her as much as he loved her mother, only differently. He would grow old with Anne and they would be happy forever. Jessica would leave them one day and he knew that. He did not know if he would need another girl to replace her, but when the time came he would work that out. The one good thing about having an office was that his staff were always trying to get work for their kids in the school holidays and they were very happy if the kids got along with the boss.

Laughing at himself, Anthony decided that Jessica was just being unnecessarily distracted and that he would remove the pest boyfriend ASAP. He was sure it would not take much to scare him away. He had done it before without her even knowing it.

Jessica

Chapter 45

Anne and Elizabeth drove Jessica to school and walked with her into Dr Quade's office, where two detectives were waiting with him.

"The detectives have said I can be present if you would like me to be there when you talk to them. Would you like that?" Dr Quade asked.

"Yes, I would like that," Jessica replied, then turning to her mother, she checked, "Is that okay, Mum? Can you and Elizabeth wait outside, please? I would feel more comfortable with Dr Quade, as he already knows everything I have to say."

"Whatever you want darling. We will wait outside," Anne said as she gave Jessica an encouraging smile as she and Elizabeth headed to the door. Jessica sat down in a chair across from the detectives. She had thought about this day for months, but now it had arrived she was unsure if she could do it.

It was almost as if they knew what she was feeling, as one of the female detectives came over and said, "Jessica, we know this is hard for you and we're so sorry this happened, but it wasn't your fault. The school psychologist has told us what you told him, but we need to hear from you - in your own words everything that happened between you and your step-father. Take as long as you like. Then we can help you Jessica, and we really want to make sure you're safe."

Jessica sat up straight and looked them both in the eyes. Even if they thought less of her when she had finished, she needed to tell them everything. "It started after Mum had been dating Anthony for a couple of months. When we saw him, he was always really kind to me. I used to go to his place with Mum and I liked helping him around his house.

Mum used to say to me how lucky I was that he was so nice to me and how lucky she was to have met someone that loved us both. Mum and Anthony got married and we moved into his house full time.

"Mum was still working for Anthony after they got married and she got promoted as a sales representative. She was so excited about the promotion but told Anthony she couldn't do the job, as she couldn't leave me alone. He told her that he would look after me and that she needed to do something for herself. So, when Mum had to go away for work for a couple of days, I was left alone with Anthony.

The first morning I was there, I was having a shower. As I finished rinsing the shampoo out of my hair, I saw him standing in front of the shower looking at me. I screamed when I saw someone there. When I realised it was Anthony, I didn't know what to do. I just stood there. Eventually he moved, and I got out and got dressed. When I went into the kitchen to have breakfast, he said nothing about it, so I didn't either. I thought maybe he had accidently walked in and was embarrassed.

That night when I went to bed, he suddenly appeared and got in beside me and lay next to me. I just froze and didn't know what to say. He said to me that he really liked us spending time together, "just the two of us", and then he put his arm over me and lay there for a while. I just stared at the ceiling until he got up and left, after kissing me on the forehead and saying that he loved me.

The next day, after I came home from school sport as usual, I went to have a shower. I went to lock the door in the bathroom and he suddenly appeared and opened it and told me not to be silly. He told me to leave the door open and to get undressed and get into the shower. He watched me the whole time and when I was finished, he told me to get dry and then to come into his bedroom. I was scared, and I didn't know what to do. I said I had to do my homework, but he grabbed me saying, 'Don't be silly, Jessica! We are just going to talk for a little while. You can do your homework later.'

We went into his room. He held my hand and took me over to the bed and pulled me down next to him. I could smell my Mum on the pillows and I told him. When I said that, he looked at me and got a weird look in his eyes. I thought he was angry with me and I went to get up, but he reached over and pulled me back onto the bed. He said it did smell like my Mum and that I smelled like her too. He said that

159

sometimes, when he looked at me, all he could see was my mother and while she was away, he longed for her and that I needed to help him when he missed her.

I asked him what he meant. He told me to just lie with him and relax. At first, we just lay there, with him holding my hand. Then he put his hand on my leg and started to rub my thigh. I thought he was just patting me, like Mum does, and he closed his eyes and I thought he might fall asleep. But, suddenly, he sat up and he told me to take off my dressing gown. He had that weird look in his eyes again and I froze. Then he undid my dressing gown and pulled it open. He started touching me everywhere with his fingers just sliding them up and down my chest and then my hips. He kept telling me how soft my skin was and how beautiful I was. He asked me if I liked him touching me, and I said it felt strange. He said he liked touching me and then he put my hand on top of his pants. He told me to feel how hard he had become from touching me and he said that this was how men showed their love. He showed me with his hands how he wanted me to touch him.

This happened every time Mum had to go away for work. I dreaded it. I pleaded with Mum to change her job back, so she didn't have to travel anymore, but he kept telling her I was being selfish. I hated it, but I was too scared to tell Mum and by now I felt so ashamed and embarrassed that I couldn't tell anyone.

I was never allowed to have friends over or to go to friends' parties or sleepovers. When I begged Anthony and Mum, Mum would try to convince Anthony, but he would never agree. When I cried, Mum would say Anthony was just trying so hard to be a good father to me. She said so many people had told her that when they saw us together it was amazing how committed he was to me as a father and how we looked so close.

Anthony liked to have little secrets between him, me and Mum. He had a photo of Mum on one side of his wallet and me, when I was thirteen in my school uniform on the other. Mum thought it was so sweet that every time he opened his wallet, he would see both of us. What Mum didn't know, is that Anthony told me he would masturbate over my photo, when I was at school. He said to me that he never used Mum's photo to do that, just mine.

I don't know why, but I just couldn't tell Mum about anything because she seemed so happy. Anthony kept telling me that if I told her, it would upset her for no reason. I didn't want to upset Mum. I thought I didn't count and that if Mum was happy, then I should be too.

I thought no one could tell that I was miserable. I would cry in the shower and into my pillow, at night. I started to eat alone, in the school library at lunchtime, because I gave up trying to have friends. The lives of all the other girls were just so different from mine; I felt weird trying to talk to them. They were all talking about boys and especially about David, the hottest guy at school. I knew David liked me. We talked sometimes, on the bus.

"One day, he walked me home, but when Anthony saw him he told him to leave. He warned David never to speak to me again on the bus or anywhere else, or he would tell the school and his parents. I didn't want David to get into trouble, so I just avoided him after that.

"When I went to see Dr Quade, at first, even though he told me I could tell him anything and that it would be confidential, I just couldn't open up. For some reason, yesterday, I eventually let go and told him everything. I'm actually amazed that I told him, but I felt so relieved to have finally gotten it off my chest. I'd been going to see Dr Quade for a few months but yesterday, yes, I told him." Detective Brown sat close to Jessica, her arm firmly encircling the young girl's trembling shoulders. Detective Smith said, "It's a very brave thing you're doing, Jessica, and we will be here to support you. There will be a number of procedures to go through, both legal and medical."

Jessica was quite calm as she said, "I'm ready for it." Then she drew a deep breath and said, "I have to tell you that yesterday I spoke to Anthony.

Dr Quade was taken aback, "You called him?"

Jessica shook her head. "No, he called me. Anyway, I tried to get him to see that what he had been doing was wrong and to stop it, but it didn't work."

"So, he knows that you have reported him?" Detective Smith interjected, in a concerned voice.

"No, he doesn't," Jessica assured the detective, "I didn't tell him that. I just wanted to see if I could avoid all of this. My friend got an App to record a guy she was dating who was also dating another girl, to catch him out. I have a new phone and I bought and downloaded the App. When Anthony called, the App recorded the conversation on my phone. I just wanted to see if he would apologise to me and say he was sorry. He wasn't sorry and as usual, he didn't see he was doing anything wrong. At least I know that I tried to get him to stop."

The detective asked Jessica if she could play the recorded conversation. Jessica took her phone from her handbag. She pressed several buttons and then handed the phone to Detective Smith, instructing, "Just press 'play', it's on speakerphone."

The room was silent as they listened to the recorded conversation. After it came to an end, Detective Smith said, "I need to take this phone into the station and have our guys record this call, Jessica. We don't want to lose it."

"Can you use that recorded call as evidence?" asked Dr Quade. Detective Brown had been taking notes throughout the interview but looked up from her notepad to explain "Not normally, objections are usually made against recordings, when they are done without consent, but as Jessica is a minor, we'll have a go at it. In any event, this will be very helpful in negotiations, at the very least. In children's cases, sometimes different rules can apply. This may also be very useful to get a confession out of Anthony and that would avoid a lot of unnecessary pain for Jessica and her family."

Detective Smith then spoke to Jessica and said, "Well done, Jessica. We'll let you go home and we will prepare the papers to charge Anthony. We'll let your mother and Dr Quade know exactly how everything goes."

"Thank you." Jessica sighed with relief, adding, "I didn't want this, I just wanted it to stop."

"We know, Jessica," the detectives replied, in one voice, as they gathered their files together, bringing the interview to an end. Detective Smith hugged Jessica and said, "Please call me anytime you want to. Here's my card with my mobile number on it. I was a victim of child abuse and I know what you're going through. Helping children like you is why I became a police officer." As they looked into each other's eyes the bond between Detective Smith and Jessica had been firmly established.

Dr Quade returned with Anne and Elizabeth, to whom he was saying, "Well, I'm glad that is over. Jessica did very well. I'm sure she will be exhausted. You can take her home, now. I'll leave it to Jessica to tell you what went on in the interview."

"Thank you, Dr Quade," Anne replied. In a loving gesture she took Jessica's hand and guided her out of the room. She said, "Let's go home."

Dr Quade turned back to the detectives and said, "I know you know how to do your job, but you need to get his wallet. It will surely have his DNA on it and inside he has a photo of Jessica at just thirteen years of age, which will be serious evidence for you." The detectives reassured the doctor that they had already noted the need to obtain Anthony's wallet and the photo as soon as possible.

Elizabeth

Chapter 46

Elizabeth went into her home office and telephoned Sarah Walters. An efficient receptionist put her call through to Sarah's secretary, Kate.

Elizabeth explained that her sister Anne's husband was about to be charged with child sexual abuse of her niece. She also told Kate that the police suggested that Anne needed urgent family law advice to protect her position.

Kate knew that if the police were involved already, it was serious. She made an appointment with Sarah for the following day at 6 p.m.

Elizabeth felt a huge sense of relief and expressed her gratitude to Sarah and Kate who replied, "I'm sure that Sarah will be able to help Anne."

Kate knew that Sarah would be back to the office from the family court shortly as it was approaching 4.30 p.m. While she waited, she added Anne to her appointments for tomorrow.

As Sarah walked into her office she saw Kate sitting at her desk and looking worried. "What's wrong?" she asked, as she hung up her jacket.

Kate looked up quite startled that she had not noticed Sarah walking in. She sprang from Sarah's chair and stood next to the desk. Sarah smiled and after sitting down waited for Kate to explain.

"Elizabeth, your yoga teacher called and she asked to see you with her sister, Anne Shaw. You acted for her years ago. Anne's young daughter has been sexually abused by her new husband and the police advised Anne to get urgent family law advice because the criminal case may affect her family law rights," Kate said. Sarah could see that Kate had been emotionally affected by the call.

"Of course, I'll see them," Sarah said.

"I'm sorry Sarah, I just get so upset by these types of cases. Elizabeth sounded so upset. I just can't imagine what they're all going through. That's all. I looked through your diary for the next two weeks and couldn't fit them in except tomorrow at 6 p.m. I hope that's okay?"

"Sometimes this job is tough, and we must tackle cases that we wish we didn't have to. I assume they've already been to the police?"

"I'm so sorry, yes they have. The police recommended that Anne get family law advice. Why would Anne's family law rights be affected by the criminal case? How could that be?"

Sarah was impressed with the police. "Well, I must say it was sensible of them to suggest Anne get advice before the criminal proceedings commence. You see, if Anne is seeking a property settlement but some of the same evidence is to be used in the criminal proceedings, which would be the case in this situation, then Anthony's lawyers could ask for the family law case to be stayed until the criminal case is finalised, as it takes priority."

"So, any case Anne had in the family court could be put aside to be dealt with after the criminal trial which could take years to finish?"

"Yes, that's right and during that period Anne would be left in limbo financially, if none of the assets and/or bank accounts are in her name, unless we could get some interim orders. Anthony's side would utilise as much money as possible to pay for his legal defence, and transfer as much of his assets as they could away from him."

Sarah could see that Kate still looked concerned, even though she was walking back to her desk. Sarah called out to her, "Kate, are you sure you're okay?"

Kate turned back and, with tears in her eyes, said, "I just find these cases so hard, I'm sorry. The case you did last year with those two little girls and their stepfather still causes me to lose sleep sometimes. It was just so unfair what he did to those children and then he even had the hide to report you to the Law Society. I saw you go through hell for six months from your own supervising body because he alleged you advised the mother to breach the Court Orders and not to hand the girls over to him on their next due visit with him, and he alleged that was a breach of your legal ethics. It was just all so unfair and somehow it's all coming back to me and upsetting me."

Sarah got up from her desk, walked over to Kate and put her arms around her. She forgot how hard their cases were to deal with sometimes and she felt terrible that it was affecting Kate this way.

As she let go of Kate, Sarah said, "These cases are hard and sometimes very difficult. I had to put my practising certificate on the line last time because, technically, advising a client to breach Federal Court Orders is a breach of my ethics. However, there's a loophole if someone is in danger of harm and those girls were. I would do it again because that's why I became a lawyer, Kate, to help people. Going out of our comfort zone is what we need to do to be good at what we do. If we didn't help these families, Kate, what would they do?"

Sarah waited for Kate's reaction and saw her words had had the desired effect. Kate had a resolute look in her eyes and she was back on track. She said to Sarah, "You are so right", then she walked back to her desk and went straight back to work.

Anthony

Chapter 47

When the police arrived at Anthony's office the next day, he was shocked. His secretary told him that the police had requested to see him immediately.

Two detectives walked into the room. They both had a look in their eyes that could not be described as friendly. The older detective said flatly, "Mr Shaw, we are here to arrest you. You have a right to an attorney and anything you say could be held..." Before he had finished, Anthony was spluttering, "A right to what? Am I being arrested? This must be a joke, you can't be serious! What are you arresting me for?"

"Mr Shaw," the detective said, "we have a warrant for your arrest. We have had to come to your office, but as a courtesy, because your staff are present and able to hear this, we will not go into the details of the charges yet. I am sure you would prefer us to read you the charges in a private place, in the presence of your lawyer. You should call your lawyer and ask them to meet us at the Sutton Forest Police Station."

"I'll call him now," Anthony said, picking up his phone. "Rupert," Anthony said, "the police have arrived at my office and are arresting me. They are taking me to Sutton Forest Police Station. Can you meet me there?"

"Put them on the phone please," Rupert responded.

The detective doing all the talking informed Rupert that they were taking Anthony to the police station.

Rupert said he would meet them there and then asked, "What are the charges?"

"There are several charges for child sexual abuse against his step-daughter, Jessica."

"Don't ask him anything without me present. This must be a terrible mistake, officers, as I know he adores that child and her mother."

Anthony was shocked but understood the implication of what the detective was saying. He buzzed his secretary on the intercom and said, "Sharon, please call Brian and ask him to go to the Sutton Forest Police Station urgently." Anthony did nothing without his business manager.

"Of course," she replied.

The detectives then escorted Anthony out of the office and into the waiting police car, which was being driven by a male police officer.

Sharon called Brian on his mobile and said, "Brian, the police have just come into the office and arrested Anthony. He told me to call you and tell you to meet him at Sutton Forest Police Station."

"What the fuck is this about Sharon?" Brian asked.

"I have no idea. The police just came in and arrested him. Anthony called Rupert Showers and he's meeting him at the police station too."

Once he was in the car, Anthony asked what the charges were. The detective told him, "They are charges for the sexual abuse of a child, being your step-daughter Jessica, Mr Shaw."

Anthony looked at the detective sitting next to him and stated coldly, "My relationship with Jessica is none of anybody's business."

"She is fifteen and she is your step-daughter," the detective replied.

"It's none of your fucking business," Anthony snapped.

What man responds to such allegations with that reply, the detective pondered. He had seen a lot, but nothing as callous as Anthony's reaction.

Anthony displayed a cold composure in the car on the trip to the police station. Inside, he was far from composed. He still could not believe that Jessica had told someone about their relationship. He thought he had made her feel special and had given her and her mother a life they never would have had without him. He would fix this. He would convince Anne and the police that Jessica was just a troubled teenager who needed attention and that he would forgive her for being so ridiculous. Jessica could ruin everything when it was all just about to be perfect.

He started to think about what he could do to make them stop this from going any further. He loved the life he had and he did not understand why anyone would want to ruin it. They both loved him, and he loved them, so why not? Why was this happening?

Amber

Chapter 48

Amber arrived at the restaurant with her best friend, Sally. Geoffrey had asked her to bring Sally along to meet his mate who was suddenly single after his wife called him from Aspen to say she was leaving him. He was rich, pissed off and lonely. Geoffrey said his mate was really cut up, especially because the other guy had been their family ski instructor for ten years. Amber knew Sally needed a new "wallet" since her last boyfriend had gone back to his wife and they would be a good couple for them to have fun with. She knew that if he was a friend of Geoffrey's, then he would be loaded and very generous.

They had spent all morning at Amber's getting ready for Sally to meet her new man and she looked hot. Amber made a wolf whistle as Sally did a twirl and then said, "Hun, he needs someone to take him to heaven and help him forget his wife. He needs to say to himself, after you fuck him, 'What the fuck was I upset about?' Get ready to catch him quickly Sally, because if you don't someone else will. Single men in this town are as rare as pink diamonds and more valuable. If you play it right, you'll get both." Amber laughed and held up her newly decorated right hand with a sparkling ring.

As the women walked into the restaurant, Amber spotted Geoffrey sitting at his usual table, but he was alone. Amber could tell by the look on his face that he was horny. He had dangerous roving eyes that undressed a woman as they approached him. It made her worry about him, but she also enjoyed the game, as she walked towards him.

As they neared the table, Amber noticed that Geoffrey could not take his eyes off Sally. She was not surprised, as Sally was wearing a dress that was so low cut her large breasts were almost bouncing out with every step she took. As she looked again at Sally, Amber started to regret helping her as much as she had. Geoffrey stood up as they reached the table. Amber made a point of walking straight up to him and kissing him passionately but the whole time he was kissing her he was staring at Sally.

"You look fucking hot!" he said to Sally. He motioned Sally to come and sit next to him. As she sat down, he openly ogled her breasts before leaning forward and running a finger down her cleavage. Sally giggled but Amber sat frozen, staring at the scene before her.

Geoffrey said, "My friend just called and had to cancel, Sally, so it looks like it's just us. Can't say I'm upset about that, are you?"

Sally was disappointed that Geoffrey's mate hadn't turned up, but she was enjoying Geoffrey flirting with her. The way he looked at her was turning her on. He was almost devouring her with his eyes. The tingle she felt when his finger ran down her chest took her breath away. His touch was gentle and sensual, and she did not want him to stop when he did.

Amber was irritated, and she showed it. She suddenly spat out, "He's not coming? We spent all morning getting ready, Geoffrey!"

Geoffrey dragged his eyes away from Sally for an instant to look at Amber and delighted in what he saw. She was angry, jealous and off balance. This was going to be even more fun than he had thought. He looked at Sally, who had turned to putty and was looking at him like she wanted it. He ran a finger down her cleavage again.

She giggled like a school girl, "That tickles, Geoffrey". Amber grabbed Geoffrey's hand and flung it away from Sally, screaming, "What the fuck are you doing?"

Geoffrey stared at Amber with a piercing glare as he said, "Sally has gone to all the trouble of looking fucking hot and I can't go ignoring her, can I? I mean, I'm just a man and you can't have her come in looking like that and not expect me to feel like this, can you?"

Amber sat back and realised what a fool she had been. Geoffrey had flirted in front of her before, but not with one of her friends. She was hurt and angry with Sally and she was furious with Geoffrey. She could see that they had clicked instantly. Sally was already lost in Geoffrey's attention and Geoffrey was clearly about to take her. Amber could not believe she had done this to herself as it was unfolding before her eyes like a tsunami.

The waiter came over and Geoffrey asked him to pour the girls a glass of champagne. Amber grabbed hers and skulled the first glass before he had finished pouring Sally's. She then raised her glass and asked the waiter to refill it. Geoffrey laughed at Amber which humiliated her.

"Just relax, Amber. We're all going to have a fun time, honey."

Geoffrey took the menu, called the waiter over and ordered the seafood platter and another bottle of champagne. "Are you good with seafood, Sally?" a considerate Geoffrey asked while he ran his hand up her thigh, lingering for a moment before moving it up to the top of her leg and resting it there.

"I love seafood," Sally whispered as she began to blush. Sally could see Amber was upset and she felt bad about that, but she did not know what to do as this was not what they had planned. She felt nervous about the whole situation and pulled back from Geoffrey.

"What's up?" Geoffrey asked.

"I just need a smoke. I'll be back in a minute." She reached for her handbag and started to walk outside.

Geoffrey jumped up from the table and called after her, "Wait Sally, I'm coming to have a smoke with you."

Amber shook her head. "You don't smoke, Geoffrey".

"I do whatever I fucking want Amber, and I think you should come outside with us," Geoffrey said as he slid his hand behind Amber's neck, twisting her hair in his fingers and lifting her up and yanking her towards him. "I saw the look you were giving the waiter and I'm not going to leave you here to flirt with him, you slut." He grabbed Amber's hand and followed Sally towards the lobby. Amber had to run to keep up with him.

As they reached the lobby, Geoffrey stopped Sally, placing a hand on her arm. He looked at them both and with a wide smile suggested, "Let's just go to our suite, girls. Sally can have a smoke there and I'll have the seafood and champagne brought up. That way we can all just relax."

Geoffrey noticed Sally looking nervously at Amber and said, "Amber wants you to come upstairs." He turned to Amber and, his eyes piercing into her, demanded, "Don't you Amber?"

Amber crumbled and asked in a pitiful whine, "Why are you doing this, Geoffrey? Sally's my friend."

A large grin appeared across Geoffrey's face as he responded, "Because that's what friends are for, Amber. Now be nice to Sally and let's all go up and play."

Geoffrey clenched Amber's arm in a vice like grip but made gestures to suggest that he was just guiding her to the lift.

The grim expression on Amber's face revealed he was hurting her and she tried to resist but Geoffrey was too strong.

He called out cheerfully, "Let's go girls," as he pulled Amber into the lift, with Sally following, a knowing smile playing at the corners of her mouth.

They walked to his suite, where they were greeted in the sitting room by a butler, who handed them each a glass of champagne. Geoffrey said, "Thanks Jeff," then took a few gulps as he walked over and stood behind Sally. Sally was playing up to Geoffrey's attention. She sipped her champagne and remained standing expectantly in front of him. After fondling the nape of her neck, Geoffrey undid the zipper of Sally's dress so that it dropped to the floor. He fixed his eyes on her panties.

His eyes glinting with mischief and hot with desire, Geoffrey looked first at Sally then turned to Amber and said, "That's fucking hot!" Amber stood motionless. She was furious that they were her panties turning Geoffrey on. Geoffrey knew they were Amber's and he could see the anger exploding through her. The butler remained stone-faced and continued to top up their champagne glasses as though this was all perfectly normal. Geoffrey took Sally's hand and began to walk her towards the bedroom.

Over his shoulder, he called to Amber, "Come here, Amber!" He gripped her arm again and said in a threatening voice, "I'm going to make love to Sally and you're going to video it."

Amber stood horrified in the corner of the room as she watched Geoffrey lead Sally to the bed. He told her to undress him. He turned to Amber to check she was recording them and seeing that she was not, he yelled, "I told you to video this, Amber. What the fuck are you doing!"

Sally started to undress him as he had instructed her to do. She was undoing the buttons on his shirt as she slowly ran her tongue down his chest. Geoffrey was watching Amber and enjoying her agony.

"Come closer," he ordered Amber and he saw her look like a startled rabbit, scared and not sure which way to move. Sally had taken off his shirt and moved onto undoing his pants. She was taking her time and teasing him whilst torturing Amber at the same time. As Amber moved closer, Geoffrey called out to her, "Give me a kiss darling," and as Sally moved towards him, he grabbed her hair in his hand and twisted it tightly as he kissed her passionately.

This spurred Sally on. She gently pushed against his shoulders indicating with her eyes where she wanted to turn her attention to. Geoffrey let her hair go as Sally slid down to pull his pants off. As soon as his pants were off Sally jumped on top of him straddling him immediately whilst enjoying his full attention. Having forgotten Amber was in the room, out of the corner of her eye Sally noticed Amber was watching blankly and yelled at her, "Get back to filming."

Geoffrey laughed at the scene between the two women. Seeing that Amber was frozen he mocked, "Do what Sally told you Amber - keep filming."

Amber picked up her phone and stood videoing. She obediently did so over an hour until they had finished. Finally, Sally and Geoffrey collapsed exhausted on the bed and they fell into a post coital sleep. Amber sank down onto the lounge. She felt angry and humiliated, but at the same time she felt sad and depressed. She walked over to the table and picked up the opened bottle of champagne and a champagne glass and took it back to the lounge. She lay back down, poured herself a glass of champagne and took two Xanax. She was going to keep drinking until she fell asleep too.

Anthony

Chapter 49

The police arrived at the station with Anthony. They showed him into an interview room to wait until his lawyer arrived. He used his mobile phone to call Rupert, and without disguising the urgency said, "Rupert, how far away are you?"

"I'm just parking. Don't say anything. Don't answer any of their questions until I get there," Rupert replied, detecting panic in Anthony's voice. He hoped Anthony would not lose his cool and say something stupid.

Anthony grew heated, "I'm in an interview room and they're leaving me alone. I just want you to fucking get here and get me out!"

"Mate, I'll be there in a few minutes!" Rupert assured him. "Don't say anything and don't be a smartass. Do as I say and I will get you out of there as quickly as I can."

Although he had an enormous ego, Rupert Showers was the most famous criminal lawyer in Sydney. He had always been a gruff, hard and aggressive legal advocate, an approach that attracted elite clients but also bridged the gap between the law and ordinary people. Rupert possessed the art of hypnotising both judges and juries. He was one of the most instinctual lawyers, who was prepared to represent his clients without fear or favour.

Detectives Smith and Brown sat outside the interview room, looking in at Anthony. They were sitting with Sergeant McGrath, who was overseeing the case, and a police prosecutor named David Bell, who had been asked to brief them on the interview.

"So, what's this case about and who's his lawyer?" asked the police prosecutor.

Detective Smith answered, "Child sexual abuse allegations by his step-daughter for the last eighteen months from the age of thirteen to fifteen."

"Any chance the kid is making it up?"

The two detectives replied, almost in unison, with a decisive, "No."

Detective Brown outlined the facts of the matter, "We were contacted by the school and they notified the mother. The victim confided in the school psychologist, who had suspected for some months that there was abuse taking place. He had worked on gaining the girl's trust, so that she would tell him. It was the school and not the victim that notified the mother and the police."

The prosecutor turned to the detectives and asked to see the victim's statement. Detective Smith handed him the statement and watched his face as he read it.

The detective observed the details of the charges were affecting the prosecutor as he read the statement; his face revealed his emotional response. "It never gets any easier dealing with this stuff, does it?"

The prosecutor looked up at the detectives and replied, "No, but more importantly, how is the girl?"

The detectives looked at each other and shook their heads, then Detective Smith replied, "She's quite together, Mr Bell. She was obviously emotional and upset when she gave us her statement. She says she got to the stage where she just couldn't stand going home any more to the abuse. She told a friend who told the school, and then the school psychologist became involved."

The prosecutor nodded sympathetically while the detective spoke of the victim, then said, "Rupert Showers is a very good lawyer. He'll fight hard for this guy, who's very wealthy. But, money doesn't buy everything and if he is guilty we will do our best to put him away. What money can buy is a good legal team, who will resort to every delay tactic, not only to keep their guy out on bail but to distort the victim's story. Our best result for this girl would be to try and get a plea bargain with this guy, with a confession, and get him to agree to time in a psychiatric facility. I would hate seeing such a young girl, who has already gone through so much, have to go through a three to five-year trial, be accused of everything under the sun and then risk this germ getting off."

Just at that moment, Rupert Showers walked into the police station and announced, in his usual booming tones, "I'm here to see Anthony Shaw."

"Here we go, the show begins," Sergeant McGrath said under his breath before directing the detectives, "Ladies, take your seats!"

He then turned to Rupert and said, "Good afternoon, Mr Showers, we will show you to your client, Mr Shaw. Here is the charge sheet, containing the four charges against Mr Shaw, so far."

Rupert entered the room and shut the door. A look of relief swept across Anthony's face. Rupert sat down and read the charge sheet. He looked at Anthony and said, "Okay, we can get started. You have been charged with several counts of child sexual assault against your step-daughter Jessica. They include sexual penetration and oral intercourse for a period of eighteen months, starting from the age of thirteen until two weeks ago."

"Yes, I know," Anthony replied. "They gave me a copy of it, when they came to arrest me. This is bullshit. There's no way Jessica would have told them any of this and what the fuck is this child sexual assault crap! Jessica's not a child. She's fifteen-years-old."

Most of the time, Rupert enjoyed his job and although, at times, he did not like his clients, he did not think they deserved to go to jail. But, having worked in criminal law now for over thirty years, Rupert knew that in ninety-five per cent of his cases, if his client was guilty. That was even before they started telling him lies which did not add up. Anthony was as guilty as the day was long. Acting for child abusers was the only part of Rupert's job that he had difficulty with at times. It was probably the reason he drank so much or maybe that was just another excuse, as his wife would say. Easy for her, when she lived with all the benefits that his successful career offered them, like a multi-million dollar a year income and the fame and notoriety of being a famous criminal lawyer's wife.

As Rupert sat reflecting on his client's position, Anthony suddenly blurted out to him, "It's no one's fucking business how Anne, Jessica and I live our lives and love each other. We are a happy family. All families are different and no one has the right to judge us."

Rupert got up and paced the floor. He could not believe Anthony's behaviour. No innocent man would react like this with the allegations made against him. An innocent man would be shattered. Rupert's conflict was whether he should coach Anthony to act normally, because the prosecutor would pick up on his response and destroy him with it, or just let Anthony sink himself.

Rupert calmly looked directly at Anthony as he said slowly and precisely, "If you confess to me that you did these things to Jessica, then I can't act for you, except to plead guilty and try and get you the best plea deal I can. I can only defend you with a not guilty plea, if you tell me you didn't do these things to Jessica."

An astonished Anthony burst out with the question, "Are you kidding me, Rupert? This is family stuff they are talking about here. This is nobody else's business but Jessica's, Anne's and mine. How can I be arrested for this?"

Rupert addressed himself very clearly to Anthony. "Are you telling me that what has been alleged is true and that Anne knew about it? Remember, Anthony, if you say yes, I can't run a defence for you that you are innocent of what you have been charged with."

Anthony replied, "How am I supposed to explain myself to you Rupert, if you say that you can't defend me? I'm not going to go to jail for this. I love my family and they love me. I live in a highly sexual household and that's how we roll. What we do is our business and no one else's."

Rupert looked Anthony in the eye and said in a serious tone, "Anthony, I need to get this clear. Are you telling me you did not have sexual relations with Jessica?"

Anthony asserted loudly, "What I am telling you is that it was not sexual abuse."

Rupert decided to bring the meeting to an end. He had to get Anthony out on bail and work out what he should do after that. He said, "Anthony, I'm going to tell the police you wish to defend the charges and we will be applying for bail. We will see if they oppose. I'm sure that if you put up the bail and hand in your passport, we will be able to negotiate that. After we get out of here, we can meet and work out what we're going to do from that point on."

Anthony look confused, clearly uncertain of the process, but replied, "Okay, just get me out of here. Agree to what you must, regarding bail. I can get hold of money for a bond, if that's needed. Just fix this!"

"Ok, you need to be patient and let me go and talk to the prosecutor. Don't say anything, don't get smart. Just wait Anthony."

"Yes, I get it," Anthony replied.

Rupert walked out to the detectives and told them that Anthony would be defending the charges and that he wanted to sort out bail conditions immediately. He asked to see the prosecutor. Detective Smith took Rupert to another interview room to wait until the prosecutor was brought in.

David Bell entered the room and Rupert stood up. The two men were not friends, but they had a mutual respect, having been on the opposite sides of cases frequently.

"What can I do for you, Rupert?" asked David.

Rupert did not seem his usual aggressive self; he was anxious and concerned, which surprised David. For once, he thought he may be seeing a human side to Rupert.

"David," replied Rupert, "I'm going to apply for Anthony Shaw to get bail so we can get him out of here today. I don't think I will be acting for him in the long run though. I know all of the parties involved and I need time to think about that. There's no way I would feel comfortable cross-examining Anne or Jessica because I know them, albeit through Anthony."

David sensed that Rupert was trying to get out of the case because he knew Anthony was guilty and he was clearly feeling for the victim. He thought it was now or never to try and get a plea bargain started, so he decided to put a deal to Rupert, "Mate, I'm sure we can work a deal for bail on the usual conditions in a case like this, with the money your guy has. I know you are saying that your guy wants to defend this case at this stage, but I would like to see a plea bargain, involving an admission and time in a mental facility. I'm going to do you a favour and let you listen to a phone recording between your client and the victim which took place yesterday. After you listen to it, you may want to reconsider your client's plea."

Trying not to look concerned Rupert replied, "Can't see how you will get the recording into evidence but I'll listen to it anyway."

"Be my guest," David replied, as he handed Rupert Jessica's mobile phone. Rupert was good, his face did not change at all while listening to the recording. At the end, he simply handed the phone back to David.

David stated clearly, "Don't get me wrong, I want to see the germ in jail and the key thrown away. I'm just trying to protect a young girl, who has already been through enough from going through a trial that could last three to five years and inevitably involve you or some other bastards attacking her in the witness stand. This recording will get in and he will go down."

Rupert would usually have jumped up and shouted at David to jam any such deal and to put his recording where it belonged, but today he sat staring at the desk as he said, "Look, David, let's sort out the bail and let me think about your offer. You know it's something I normally react well to and it may not be in my hands for much longer but give me a few days to get back to you on it."

Now David knew that Rupert not only thought Anthony was guilty but was almost feeling guilty about it himself. He had never seen Rupert like this and he knew he needed to let Rupert work on Anthony and see what he could come up with.

David nodded. "I'll go talk to my supervisor and come back with some bail conditions. If he hasn't got his passport with him, you'll need to get someone to go and get it now, before we release him and finalise the bond etc. Can he come up with two million dollars?"

Rupert bit back. "Are you kidding? Who is going to ask for that?" David backed down a little. "Okay then, one million, a passport and reporting in twice a day. The security needs to be set up, before we let him out and hand the passport over. Any day he doesn't report in twice, he will be back in here."

"Go get it approved," Rupert said, his distaste for the matter palpable.

Anthony sat in the interview room. He could not believe what was happening to his life. First Peter had appeared in his life again and now Jessica was doing this to him; all of this when he had done nothing wrong. He had given Jessica the same attention and love that Peter had given him, when he was the same age, except he would never leave her. Not like Peter left him. He would never leave Anne either, whereas Peter had also left his sister.

It had been perfect up till now. All three of them, Anthony, Jessica and Anne, had been together and have been able to love and enjoy each other, without hurting anyone. Anthony could not believe Jessica was now saying that she did not want him. They were inseparable and everyone knew it. He was the world's most loving and dedicated husband and stepfather. Surely everyone would see that, once he had spoken to Jessica and sorted this out? Anthony stood up as Rupert re-entered the room.

Rupert sat at the table and placed his folders neatly in front of him and looked at Anthony, who was staring intently at him. He told Anthony the deal that had been struck.

"They will give you bail, Anthony, at one million dollars, and you must surrender your passport and report to the police station twice every day. Who do you need to contact to arrange the funds to be transferred?"

Anthony was unsettled by the terms of bail and said, ashen-faced, "I'll call Brian, my business manager to chase him up. He's already on his way here." He reached into his jacket pocket for his phone, with a hand that would not stop shaking.

Rupert said, with a degree of gravity in his voice, "Anthony, the prosecutor has just offered a plea bargain and I suggest you seriously think about taking the offer. If you plead guilty to the charges they will give you one year in a mental institution or until you are declared safe to leave the facility. On the evidence they have, you should consider accepting this offer."

"Why should I plead guilty when all I did was love my family?" protested Anthony.

Rupert replied in a matter of fact tone, in light of the offence, "Because your stepdaughter was thirteen years old when you apparently started loving her in a way that the law regards as illegal and as child sexual abuse. The penalties range from ten to sixteen years and with the new law just introduced, which allows the terms for each charge to be added together, you could face sixteen years behind bars."

Anthony was still resistant. "If they think they have such a good case, why are they offering me a deal?"

Rupert's patience was wearing thin. "They are offering you a deal because the prosecutor doesn't want Jessica to have to endure a trial. He thinks she's been through enough. He indicated that all Jessica wants is for you to admit what you did to her and for you to agree to get help for it. She doesn't want to see you go to jail but is prepared to testify if you will not admit everything that you did to her and that it was wrong."

Anthony's resistance to his offence switched to an attack on Jessica. "Who will believe her over me? She's just a soft kid, who you could easily break down in the witness box. I think I'll take my chances in court."

Rupert had seen a lot in his career, but this man was different. First, he claimed he loved this girl that he had sexually molested for years and now he was willing to have her humiliated in court and possibly destroyed for life. Rupert knew it was time to reveal to Anthony the damning recording evidence. "Anthony, the prosecution have a phone recording of you admitting what you did to Jessica. The recording is apparently recent."

"That's impossible!" Anthony shouted. "I don't know what you're talking about! Have you heard it?"

"You apparently spoke to Jessica on her mobile phone and admitted what you had done to her. She recorded the conversation."

"Isn't it illegal to record phone calls without the other person's knowledge?"

"They'll try and get the recording in on the basis she is a minor. The fact is, once we even start objecting to the admission of the recording, your guilt is already starting to become apparent."

Anthony started pacing the room and his professed love for Jessica now disappeared behind abuse and threats. "The fucking little bitch. I'm not letting her get away with this."

"Look, Anthony, let's just look at the facts." Rupert tried to calm him before advising him of his best option. "There are serious criminal allegations of child sexual assault that have been made against you and you may serve up to sixteen years in a maximum security prison if you go to trial. The prosecution has a phone recording, in which you confirm the offences with Jessica. There is an offer on the table for you to spend one year in a mental facility with bond of one million, on the basis you confess to the allegations and seek medical treatment. I strongly recommend you take the offer and take it quickly before they retract it, which they can do at any time."

Anthony stopped his frantic pacing and turned to face Rupert. "You could make millions running this trial for me. Why are you throwing that away? Why are you being so quick to get rid of my case?"

Rupert held Anthony's gaze and replied, "I'm a very busy lawyer, Anthony. If I'm not running your case, I will be running someone else's.

I don't need to run cases for the hell of it. My job is to get you the best result possible and, in your case, it's the plea bargain. However, the decision is yours. What I can tell you is that I have run more child sexual abuse defence cases than any other lawyer in town and the story that Jessica is telling is very solid. This isn't a case where a mother has made the accusations on behalf of a young child, in the middle of a family law case, to tip the scales on her side, or where the alleged victim has told her friends and/or her mother. Jessica had been watched by the school psychologist at the request of the school principal because they were concerned about her and she confided in him - someone neutral, at arm's length, a professional and at the school. I'm telling you that this will be a difficult case to win on just those grounds. If you choose not to accept the plea bargain, I will run your case and it will cost you millions of dollars. I can make life hell for this child and her mother in the interim and I can delay for years any family law matter your ex wants to bring. I can do all of that and I may even win this case for you. It makes no difference to my life, but it could make a hell of a difference to yours if you go to jail for five to ten years instead of taking this offer. But it's all up to you."

Anthony appeared to back down and asked, "How much time have I got to think about the offer?"

"They said they want an answer within forty-eight hours."

Anthony sat down, put his head in his hands and said in a muffled voice, "Okay, I'll think about it." The thought of making Anne and Jessica's life hell right now was sounding good to him.

Rupert gathered his files and briefcase together and headed for the door. He turned to address Anthony with finality, "I'll go and let the prosecutor know you're considering the offer and I'll finish sorting out the papers for bail. Once your accountant arrives with your passport and finishes the bond, we can get you out of here."

Amber

Chapter 50

It was a week since Geoffrey left on his business trip to Singapore. Amber was surprised at how exhausted she had been after he had left. But now he was due home, she was excited to be seeing him again and she knew she needed to get ready for him. Amber was already on her way to the hairdresser for her appointment. She had to make sure she looked perfect. She looked awful and felt it. She was a nervous wreck in the last few weeks before he left and while he was away she had hardly got out of bed. Ordering room service and not seeing anyone for a week had been a much-needed holiday for her.

Before he left, Geoffrey told her she was becoming impossible and she knew she had been driving him away with her mood swings. The more she tried to please him the more she drove him away. The day before he left, Geoffrey handed her a bottle of Valium and a bottle of Xanax saying, "Take what you need darling. There's no need to ever feel stressed." She had started taking Xanax like Tic Tacs. Geoffrey had an old school friend who was a pharmacist and he would give Geoffrey any prescription drugs he wanted in exchange for Geoffrey picking up his restaurant tab each month.

Geoffrey had told her he was on a business trip, but she knew what he got up to there. She needed him to want her again, like he used to. If she lost him, she knew she had lost everything.

She had not realised just how in love with him she had become, and the thought of life without him was just something she could not bear.

She also missed Sally. She and Geoffrey had been the two closest people to her in her life and now they were both more interested in each other than in her. Sally was the one she usually turned to when she was stressed or down, but since Geoffrey had started having sex with her, her friendship with Sally had ended. Sally made Amber feel like she was the third wheel, even though she was the one living with Geoffrey. The arrangement had gone from an occasional amusement to a daily event and she hated it. She was heartbroken that Sally did not care. Sally knew Amber was in love with Geoffrey, but since Geoffrey had been taking Sally shopping with Amber and buying both of them whatever they wanted, she knew Sally was not going to walk away from Geoffrey easily. Everything had changed, and Amber just could not work out how it had happened or how she could change it back again.

Her life with Geoffrey had gone from being perfect to being unbearable. Instead of enjoying Geoffrey's obsessive love for her and being spoilt and pampered, Amber felt tortured by him. Although she felt humiliated and depressed, she had no alternative anymore. She had given up her flat and her job and had been living off an allowance Geoffrey had been giving her since she moved into his hotel with him. If she left Geoffrey, she would be homeless and without any income. She had no life to go back to, let alone the tragic life she once had.

Amber had also booked the beautician after her hairdressing appointment. She was going to look perfect for Geoffrey when he got home today.

Amber had been secretly plotting against Sally and she knew she would get her time for revenge. Every time she filmed Sally and Geoffrey, she had zoomed in on Sally. When they watched the replay, the stupid bitch had not noticed that Geoffrey could never really be identified, whereas all of Sally could be seen, especially her face and genitals. When she was ready, Amber was going to put the videos on the sex website Pornhub. She knew Geoffrey wouldn't give a fuck about it, but it would really upset Sally. Amber knew Geoffrey would like the fact that Amber had plotted her revenge, especially if it ruined Sally's life.

On the way to the beauty salon, Amber went to send a text to Geoffrey but realised it would not be delivered because he was still on the plane. She missed the constant texting and phone calls between them and she started to cry. She knew Geoffrey had his divorce on his mind and she hated his wife, Katrina the bitch. The stress of the divorce was doing his head in and she knew he missed his house and wanted it back. Katrina could cost him millions, not to mention that she knew all the drama was probably stressing him out. Maybe when he fixed up the shit with Katrina things would improve.

None of this was Geoffrey's fault. It was just because of what he was going through, she kept telling herself.

Amber

Chapter 51

It was 6 p.m. and Amber knew Geoffrey would have landed by now. She was ready for his return and wanted him home. The suite looked amazing. She had filled the room with candles and flowers and arranged four bottles of champagne on ice in the hotel's most amazing ice bucket, in the centre of the room. She had missed Geoffrey so much that she was physically aching for him.

Amber sent a text to Geoffrey's driver asking him if he had arrived, hoping he would respond. A few seconds later, she received a text from Geoffrey, "I'm nearly at the hotel. Hope you are ready for me babe X." Amber was so happy and relieved that he had replied and wanted to see her. She opened a bottle of champagne and poured herself a glass. She was now ready to celebrate.

Geoffrey walked through the door a few minutes later. He called out Amber's name and she ran towards him. He leaned down and wrapped her up in his arms and kissed her passionately. In a sudden movement he ripped off her flimsy silk dress revealing her black lace lingerie underneath. Amber saw the glint in his eyes and was pleased with herself for all the trouble she had gone to. Geoffrey smiled at her and he knelt on the floor at the end of the bed whilst spreading her legs apart with his hands. Using his teeth, he swiftly unclipped the studs on her lace lingerie between her legs. They made love and he was as passionate and hungry as when they first met. Afterwards, they lay in bed, drinking champagne and laughing until they made love again. She fell asleep in his arms, as happy as she had ever been in her life.

When Amber woke up the following morning, Geoffrey had left the bed. She thought he may have been in the bathroom but when she called out his name there was no answer. She walked through the suite but he was gone. She found her mobile phone and saw he had left her a text message, "Gone for a run and coffee with Paul. Be back soon X". She smiled with relief. She walked back to the bathroom and started to run a bath. She would get ready for him when he returned. She wanted more of him already. She was ecstatic; she had him back.

Out of the corner of her eye, Amber noticed Geoffrey's briefcase on the table. She knew she should not look in it, but she was unable to resist. Geoffrey usually brought back a present for her when he went away and she could tell, from their lovemaking last night, that he had missed her. Amber had to see if he had bought her something. She unclicked the catch but to her disappointment there were no presents inside; conspicuously missing was the piece of jewellery she had been expecting. She felt a bump at the side of the bag and she unzipped it. She found a bundle of printed emails. Geoffrey liked to print important emails, especially if they were long. She wondered if they were about his property settlement with his ex and she sat down and began to read them slowly, all six of them. Amber felt tears streaming down her face. Things had started to make sense.

Amber learnt from the emails that about three months ago, Geoffrey had met a woman who was in Sydney doing a photo shoot. Erica had been at lunch at one of Geoffrey's favourite restaurants where he apparently did his "send a bottle of champagne over to her table" trick.

Looking at the dates and piecing together the timeline, Amber remembered it had actually happened while she was having lunch with Geoffrey. She was so angry with him when the woman walked up to their table to thank him for the champagne. It was one of Geoffrey's little peccadillos. He had told Amber at the time, because she was annoyed, that he was just looking for another girl for them to have a threesome with and laughed it off. Amber continued to dissect the emails and they indicated that Geoffrey and Erica had met up every week or so since. Erica's emails were full of her love and adoration for him, expressing how beautiful he made her feel. She had quoted some of the words he had spoken to her and Amber recognised the same things he had said to her. She felt gutted, stupid and completely heartbroken. Everything Amber had said to Geoffrey was heartfelt.

Everything Geoffrey had said to her, he had said to Erica and, she realised, probably to every other woman he had ever been with. She thought about how passionate he had been with her the night before. How could he do that if he had been with Erica for the past week? Erica's last email was dated the day before he had flown home. She said she could not wait to meet his children and spend time with him and his family as his future wife.

Amber reached for her handbag, pulled a bottle from it and popped two Valium tablets. She went to the ice bucket, took out a bottle of champagne and poured herself a glass of bubbles. It was only 8 a.m. and she was drinking. *What the fuck else can I do? How am I supposed to cope with this sober?*

Amber picked up her phone and sat in the lounge. She googled Erica Blom and realised it was a huge mistake. Erica looked far sexier in the lingerie shots online than when Amber saw her in the restaurant. She had the most amazing figure Amber had ever seen. Amber realised why Geoffrey had been making comments about her needing her breasts redone. Erica had the best set of boobs Amber had ever seen, and even worse, they looked natural. Amber was feeling confused and angry. She hated this woman. She hated her intensely. Amber knew it was Geoffrey she should hate but it was Erica that she wanted to slap right now. Her emotions were plunging from anger to distress. She wanted revenge and she was determined to get it.

Amber poured herself another glass of champagne while ruminating on how she was going to get this woman. She seized upon an idea. She picked up her phone and found the videos she had recorded of her threesomes with Geoffrey. She walked over to the desk where Erica's emails lay open and noted Erica's email address. Amber forwarded the last video she had recorded of Geoffrey with her and Sally having a threesome to Erica, with an accompanying note, "Geoffrey told us you were the worst fuck he ever had. He couldn't wait to come home to us, loser!"

The satisfaction of picturing Erica reading the email and then watching the video cheered up Amber, and she set about getting ready for Geoffrey's return. She went to the bathroom and ran a bath. She stepped in and lay in the bath with her bottle of champagne and her Valium tablets on the ledge next to her. Her new- found cheer was only fleeting, however, and she began to feel sick and pathetic. There she was last night, thinking everything was perfect again but it was all a sham. Geoffrey had just used her, like he was using this other woman. He did not love Erica and Amber knew he did not love her either.

Amber wondered what cruel fucked up mind made him do this destructive push/pull to her. She had put up with more than anyone could ask. She had become a pathetic wreck, doing whatever he made her do. She felt used, stupid and dirty. She had been an idiot. The pain in her chest was so intense she thought she was having a heart attack. She reached for the bottle of Valium and saw she had already taken four or had it been six already? She did not care; she had to blot the unhappiness from her mind and relax before Geoffrey came home. Amber popped another two tablets with another glass of champagne and sank into the warm water.

Shortly afterwards, Amber felt the veil of drug and alcohol induced sedation descend upon her. It was the relief she had been waiting for. She closed her eyes, waiting for her thoughts to be blocked. She hoped she had the strength to forgive Geoffrey and not to confront him with Erica's emails. She knew if she confronted him, he would be finished with her. *How had I not seen it? How had he kept the affair from me?*

Amber felt herself go numb and realised the Valium had kicked in hard and that perhaps she had taken too many. She tried to pull herself up, but the effort was beyond her. Her body was limp and uncooperative. Amber knew she was in trouble. She reached out her hand to release the bath plug but she only managed to push it slightly ajar. She could hear the water trickling out slowly and she hoped it would be enough before she lapsed into unconsciousness.

Geoffrey sat in the coffee shop and wondered whether Amber had woken up yet. He pictured her going through his briefcase, as she always did when he came back from a trip and finding the emails from Erica that he had written himself. They were so romantic, they would drive Amber to the edge - he knew it. Stupid bitch was too smart for her own good and it was going to come back to bite her. The fact that Amber had not sent him a text message yet told him she had found the emails. She always woke up early and it was now 9 a.m. The hotel had not called him to say she was screaming or smashing things, so he assumed she had either started drinking and taking pills or she had left the hotel to go and cry with one of her girlfriends. Either way, it would not be long until she cracked. He decided to order another coffee before going back to see what state she was in.

Geoffrey was enjoying the hot bitterness of his long black. He thought he should perhaps take someone back to the hotel with him, just in case Amber had gone nuts reading Erica's emails. As good luck would have it, he received a text from Sally, asking, "You back yet? Miss me?"

He picked up the phone and called her, telling her to meet him at the suite. She said she was on her way. Sally and Geoffrey arrived at the hotel at the same time and wasted no time getting friendly in the lift, on the way up to the suite. Geoffrey opened the door and called out to Amber, "Hey honey, I'm home and I have a surprise for you. Sally is here!" Sally started to laugh, knowing Amber would be furious.

Geoffrey knew just how to wind Amber up and although Amber was one of her friends, Sally found it funny to watch how quickly it worked. Geoffrey continued to call out to Amber as he looked for her. He walked into the bathroom and called out, "Sally, quick come in here!"

Geoffrey was on his knees, leaning over Amber's body in the bath. He felt for her pulse. She was clearly unconscious; her head slumped to one side and white froth at the corners of her mouth. Geoffrey saw the pills at the side of the bath and the empty bottle of champagne. A look of pure hatred clouded his eyes, because of the nuisance Amber had caused him.

"Fucking stupid bitch has overdosed in the bath. She has a pulse, call an ambulance!" Sally did as he asked. Geoffrey left the bathroom and crossed the sitting room to the desk, where the emails lay. He picked them up, folded them and put them in his blazer pocket.

Sally called out to him. "The ambulance is on its way, but they said it could take about fifteen minutes so we have to keep checking her pulse and call if anything changes."

Geoffrey and Sally both went back into the bathroom, where Geoffrey knelt down and felt for Amber's pulse again. He looked over at Sally, clearly irritated with the situation, and said, "She's still alive, I can't believe she was this stupid. Go and get us a champagne for fuck sake."

Sally walked into the loungeroom and poured them both a glass of champagne, ironically from the ice bucket that Amber had organised for her and Geoffrey. She handed a glass to Geoffrey but was so unnerved by the scene that she spilt her own glass down her cleavage. "I'll get it", Geoffrey said and lunged at her breasts, playfully licking up the champagne. Both of them started laughing and Geoffrey threw Sally up on the vanity saying, "Well if the ambulance is going to take fifteen minutes there's no reason why I should be rude and not attend to your needs, while we keep an eye on Amber!"

Geoffrey pulled up Sally's skirt and saw she was naked underneath. Sally gave a mock apology, "Sorry I forgot my undies, but you did say to come as quickly as I could."

Geoffrey was delighted and undid his pants while pushing her back on the vanity. Sally wrapped her legs around him with equal enthusiasm and they completely forgot about the unconscious Amber until shortly thereafter, the paramedics bounded into the bathroom.

Peter

Chapter 52

When Peter reached his office after finishing up for the day in court, he looked at his watch, which flashed 1.20 p.m. He remembered Sarah saying that one of the bonuses of his job was getting paid a full day's rate even though most of his cases settled by half way through the day. It was one of those days today and he was going to enjoy having the rest of the day off.

Unlike Sarah, his clients required fewer appointments. They were mostly all in jail and accordingly, had restricted demands. That was the way he liked his life. It was Friday afternoon. He would return a couple of phone calls and then go to the pub to meet up with other barristers who had finished early for the day for a late lunch and a few drinks. As he walked into reception and proceeded to the lift, he had already decided which calls he needed to return from the text messages sent by his secretary, Kim, who had been working from home.

Peter loved working alone in the office, even though he liked Kim. It was just that she was so eager to be of assistance to him that sometimes he found it hard to get anything done with her there. It was a small office and she always seemed to be right next to him when he was on the phone, which was difficult sometimes, especially when he was arranging a date with a woman. As a solution, he encouraged Kim to work from home two afternoons a week. Modern technology now allowed this to happen and it worked beautifully. It meant he could get what he needed to do in ten minutes and be out most Fridays by 1.30 p.m.

Knowing he would have the place to himself today, Peter headed straight to his desk, sat down and picked up the phone to return his phone messages. After he finished his last call to his client Jim Hall, who was currently a guest of Long Bay Jail pending his trial, Peter snatched up his keys to head to the pub. As he opened his office door, a man wearing a balaclava barged in, grabbed him and pushed him back inside. Before he could speak, the man punched him in the face and Peter fell to the floor. The attacker kicked him repeatedly sending sharp pains through his body with accompanying cracking sounds. Peter groaned with pain and writhed on the floor. The man kicked him again, this time full-throttle in the chest. Peter struggled to breathe, and he could taste blood in his mouth.

Despite the pain, he had a sudden memory flash of what the forensic examiner had once told him during the post mortem of a rape victim, "You know, if victims only didn't try to fight back they would more times than not survive the physical attack. The best thing to do is to pretend you're dead so they stop attacking you."

Knowing he had no alternative, Peter closed his eyes and lay still while the attacker kicked him several more times to his stomach, chest, and head whilst muttering to himself over and over again, "Fuck you Peter, why did you do this to me". Instinctively, Peter threw his hands in front of his face, before he remembered that he should not have moved. He felt another kick to his jaw and to his arm and was sure it snapped. He went limp, closed his eyes and concentrated on not making a sound or moving until it stopped. Peter then heard the man moving away from him.

Peter heard the man smashing his furniture and throwing things all over the office before he returned and Peter felt his breath on his face when he heard the man say to him, "Look what you made me do." At that instant Peter realised who had attacked him. He heard the door slam shut and he blacked out.

Peter was still on the floor when he stirred. An almost unbearable pain was shooting through his body. It was difficult to breathe and he had no idea how long he had been out of it. He knew he needed help. He tried to open his eyes, but they were glued shut. He had a slither of vision, which was blurry and limited peripherally. He tried to move his arms and legs, but that caused shooting pains throughout his body. He spat the blood out of his mouth and ran his tongue over his teeth, realising some were missing. He was relieved to find he could open and close his right hand, and although it hurt, he reached painstakingly down to his inside jacket pocket, hoping to feel his phone. He sighed with relief when he felt the familiar shape.

Peter held the phone in front of his face but could not see clearly enough. He tried to recall the positioning on the screen. He swiped along the bottom and then touched the screen bottom left, where he knew the phone icon was, hoping that something would happen. He touched the screen again, hoping to dial someone, anyone. For what seemed an eternity, nothing happened. He repeated the swiping and touching actions, more deliberately this time, and he heard a ringing sound. When the call was answered, he was relieved to hear a voice that he recognised, it was his secretary, Kim.

"Hi Peter, what's up?"

"Kim, I…" Peter tried to speak but the blood pooling in his mouth and sliding down his throat reduced his voice to a gurgle.

"Peter are you okay?" Kim asked, panic rising in her throat.

Peter spat some of the blood from his mouth, sucked in some air and managed to whisper, "I was attacked." Exhausted by the effort to speak, Peter dropped the phone and blacked out again.

Sarah

Chapter 53

Sarah was on the phone, when Kate came in to her office to tell her Geoffrey Pemberton was on the other line. Sarah was baffled but put her other call on hold, and asked Kate what he wanted. Kate informed her that he was being asked by the police to go with them to the police station for routine questioning. Apparently, he had found his girlfriend Amber unconscious in the bath, in his hotel room. From what Geoffrey had said to Kate, he seemed to think that Sarah could explain to the police how crazy Amber was and that she was capable of overdosing on drugs and alcohol.

Sarah sat for a moment assessing her position before making the decision as to whether to take the call or not. She reasoned with herself that Geoffrey was not a client, she did not like him at all and did not need to help. However, she did know that Amber was crazy. When she reminded Sarah that she had acted for Amber's ex-husband in her family law matter, she recalled what Amber had put him through.

Kate saw Sarah's hesitation about taking the call and said she would place the call on hold until she was ready. Of course, Geoffrey abused her when he was advised he was being placed on hold again, but she hit the button before he had finished his last set of obscenities.

Sarah ended her other call and buzzed Kate to put Geoffrey's call through. Kate waited with interest to hear what had happened. When she saw from her phone that Sarah had hung up, she walked into her office and Sarah told her with some concern, "He asked me to go to the police station with him because Amber was found unconscious in the bath at his hotel room, a couple of hours ago, and has subsequently died in hospital. He said the police are making noises that he killed her or assisted her in killing herself."

"Seriously?" Kate was surprised. "Why would he ask you to go to the police station? And, why would you go when you don't act for him?"

Sarah stood up and walked over to her window; something she did when she was mulling over something. She stared out at the harbour and replied, "Because it's the right thing to do." *Although I know Geoffrey is an appalling human being, I also know that Amber was as capable of suicide as any other borderline personality I have dealt with in my life. Geoffrey knows that I acted for Amber's ex-husband and that I know how dysfunctional she is.*

"I agreed to help him; to speak to the police about what I know about Amber, but only if he agrees to retain Rupert Showers. I want Rupert at the police station as well. This is not my field and I don't want Geoffrey Pemberton accusing me of damaging his case. At the same time, I told him that I'll agree to him retaining me to act for him in his family law case, but only on the basis that he will settle with his wife reasonably and do the best parenting plan possible in the interests of his children."

Kate was impressed. "Only you could have thought of that, Sarah. I don't know how you thought of it, but if you can do it, it'll at least make a positive ending out of a terrible situation."

"I won't be able to get him to be generous, but if his wife knows what she wants I will do my best to get him to agree to it. I'm more interested about the kids being protected than anything else."

"How will you do that?"

"I'll make sure they are protected in the consent orders and that any concerns be addressed by a stipulated counsellor. I just have to try to make sure that his wife has some help keeping him in line," Sarah replied. "I'll call Rupert from the car on the way to the police station to check if he's free to act for him."

As soon as she pulled out of the car park Sarah called Rupert, but the call went straight to his message bank. She left a message regarding Geoffrey and asked if he could return her call as she was on the way to the police station.

Rupert called back within minutes and sounded nonplussed, "I've acted for Geoffrey Pemberton before, very successfully, so I'm wondering why he called you before me if he has been arrested."

"He's had criminal issues in the past?" Sarah asked, surprised by the news.

"Just a few, nothing really serious. More recently, a couple of assaults in pubs with guys and a girl who accused him of assault when he claimed it was consensual rough sex. A few years ago, I acted for him where an ex- girlfriend of his was found dead, hanging in her bedroom, a couple of months after they had broken up. The police questioned him but no charges were laid in that case. The girl had a history of mental illness, which Geoffrey knew about; in fact, he described as a complete 'fruit cake'. Her family and friends knew about her mental instability too and were apparently not surprised when she was found. What I did find interesting, though, was when I asked Geoffrey why he had got involved with the girl when he knew she was nuts. He said, 'Rupert, all the great fucks are nuts, nuttier the better. If you don't know that mate, you don't know what you're missing out on.' Anyway, enough of his history, what's Geoffrey's problem today?" Rupert asked.

Sarah was shocked by what Rupert had just told her. She had not seen it coming, particularly the bit about another ex- girlfriend who had killed herself. "You still there, Sarah?" Rupert asked.

"Sorry Rupert, I'm just a little shocked at his history. He's been taken in by the police for questioning about a girlfriend of his, who was found unconscious in the bath of his hotel room. She later died in hospital. He says he thinks she overdosed. The woman was an ex-wife of a client of mine and I had a big win against her. Strangely enough, she brought in her new boyfriend, Geoffrey, not long ago, to see me about his family law matter with his wife. Then today, I had a call from Geoffrey asking me to go to the police station to say that I knew how crazy Amber was," Sarah replied.

"Was she?"

Sarah drew a deep breath then said, "Look, she was no angel and I'm sure she had borderline personality disorder, but I'm feeling quite odd about the repetition of dead girlfriends in his life."

"Sarah, let me give Geoffrey a call now. If we need you, I'll let you know. Quite frankly, Geoffrey going on the defence about her mental condition before charges are laid by the police won't help him. Leave this to me and I'll let you know if we need you. Otherwise, I'll send him back to you to clean up his family law matter."

Sarah slowed down and pulled her car over to the side of the road. She said, "I would rather never speak to him again if possible, Rupert. If you can take care of this, I'll go back to my office and hope I don't have to get involved any further."

"I understand Sarah," Rupert replied. "Best you leave the bad boys to me."

Sarah sighed, then responded, "I wish Rupert," as she ended the call.

Peter

Chapter 54

The police arrived at Peter's office before the ambulance. The door was open and Peter was lying on the floor in the reception area. Constable Stanton, a seasoned policeman, leaned over Peter and checked his pulse.

"He's a mess but he's alive," he determined. Glancing up to see the ambulance officers walk in, he said to them, "He has a pulse." Kim ran in and saw Peter lying on the floor, covered in blood, with paramedics attending to him. On his other side, she knelt and started to cry when she saw how badly he was hurt. She leaned over his face and whispered, "Peter I'm here, it's Kim".

Although Peter could hear everything, he was unable to move. He was panic stricken that he might be paralysed. He was relieved to hear Kim's and the paramedic's voices when they had arrived.

Kim felt a hand on her shoulder and looked up to see Constable Stanton, who asked, "Are you his partner?"

"No, I'm his PA. He called me, and I called the ambulance and police and then came straight here."

The constable said, "I'm amazed he could make a call. It certainly saved his life. If he had been left here much longer he would have bled to death."

Kim shook her head, her eyes glistening with tears. "I just don't know who would want to do this to Peter or why even?"

The paramedics continued to work intensively on Peter. One raised his head to ask Kim, "Miss, do you know if he's on any regular medication or if he's allergic to anything?"

"No, he's not. As his PA, I know just about everything about him. His name is Peter and he…" Unable to restrain her emotions any longer, Kim burst out crying.

Constable Stanton walked towards Kim and comforted her by putting an arm across her shoulders. He knew he had to take her away from Peter, so the paramedics could work on him, so he walked her into the adjoining room and closed the door.

The constable tried to settle the distressed PA. He said, "Peter's alive. Let the paramedics do their job and please help me do mine, so we can try to work out what has happened."

Kim walked towards one of the chairs and sat down. The constable sat in Peter's chair behind his desk and said, "So that we can try and piece together what happened, Kim, please tell us what went on today at the office and anything else that may help us to work out who did this to Peter."

Kim had dropped her head into her hands and was rocking back and forth, submitting finally to shock. At the Constable's appeal for help, however, she composed herself and focused on providing as much information as she could before saying, "Peter is a lawyer who does mainly criminal law and he's a lovely, kind man. He helps just about everyone and sometimes for nothing. Most of the time, I think he gets taken for a ride by people. He has a pretty regular routine, coming into the office usually by 8 a.m. and leaving between 4 p.m. and 5 p.m. most days to go to the gym. He has a daughter named Chloe and is a great dad."

Upon mentioning Chloe, Kim's emotions began to over- take her again. She stopped abruptly, pulled out a tissue and wiped her eyes. Then she leant forward and asked, "He'll be okay, won't he?"

"Please Kim, keep going," the constable said. "How old is Chloe? Is Peter married or in a relationship? Is there someone we should call?"

"He's divorced. We should call his ex-wife, Sarah Walters. They have a daughter, Chloe." "The lawyer Sarah Walters?" "Yes."

One of the paramedics popped his head inside the door to let the Constable know they were leaving. Kim asked the para- medic, "Will Peter be okay?"

"We're doing our best. We've stabilised him as much as we can. He's lost a lot of blood, most likely from suffering blows to his head and body. He has several fractures. It's internal bleeding and damage that will be the danger. We won't know any more until they look at him in emergency."

Kim looked back at Constable Stanton and asked, "Can I go now please, Constable? I'd like to go to the hospital, in case Peter wakes up. I can call Sarah, his ex-wife and let her know?"

Constable Stanton nodded but put up a hand to indicate he was not quite finished, "Can you please give me Sarah's phone number and yours, and then you can go. By the way," the constable looked inquisitively at Kim, "I hope he knows how much you care about him."

Kim dropped her eyes to the floor, then in a sheepish manner asked, "Is it that obvious, Constable? I don't think Peter has been as observant as you about my feelings towards him."

"No, it's just my job to pick up on these things," the Constable said, aware of her embarrassment then added, "Maybe this is the time to let him know". *That is, if he makes it*, he thought.

When she walked out onto the street, the paramedics were loading Peter into the back of the ambulance. They closed the back doors, the sirens pealed, and the ambulance sped off. Kim stared after it, with a lump in her throat.

Peter

Chapter 55

As he lay in the hospital bed, Peter heard everything through a foggy haze in his head but he was still unable to move and fearing that he was paralysed. He could hear the doctors discussing whether he should be alert by now. With great relief he found he could feel someone touching his arm.

"Can you hear me Peter? If you can hear me, you're in hospital and I'm your doctor. You've had an accident and you are in the emergency department. We're taking care of you. Kim is here. Your eyes have been badly bruised, so you won't able to open them when you wake up, but don't panic, your eyes are fine. You have broken ribs, a fractured cheekbone and a broken nose. You've been in surgery for a punctured lung, but the operation was successful. You don't look pretty, right now, and when you wake up, you'll be sore, but you'll be okay. You'll feel very tired because you've been sedated. I'm going to let you rest and I'll be back tonight to check on you again."

Peter heard, "broken ribs", "fractured" something. He became aware of someone holding his hand. Another voice was piercing the fog in his brain, which was starting to clear.

"Hi Peter, it's Kim. The doctor told me you might be able to hear me, so I thought I'd try and let you know everything will be okay. I called Sarah to tell her about the accident. She is on her way to the hospital. The doctor said you'll be here for a while. I'll stay here, in case you need anything. I've diverted the office phone to my mobile, so I have everything under control." Under her breath, Kim uttered, *I love you.*

Peter began to have flashes of someone attacking him. It started to fall into place. What was burning in his mind was Anthony's voice saying to him as he kicked him repeatedly, "Fuck you, Peter. Why did you do that to me Peter?"

He knew that Anthony would have been upset when he shut down all contact with him thirty years ago, but he could not have imagined that Anthony could still be angry with him all these years later. He remembered seeing Anthony the other day in the coffee shop and there seemed no indication that he was angry or revengeful.

Peter knew that he could not tell anyone that his attacker was Anthony. He did not want to have to explain to Sarah or anyone else what had happened between them, even though it was so long ago and none of their business anyway.

Anthony

Chapter 56

It had been the worst forty-eight hours of his life and the only thing that had released the seething anger inside him was bashing the fuck out of Peter. He smiled at the thought of him lying on the ground, covered in blood. The prick had gone down like a rag doll and had not even tried to fight back. He wondered if he was dead, but then he knew Peter could not tell the police or anyone else that he had done it, even if he had survived. Peter would try to take this secret to his grave. There was one little problem for Peter; Anthony was going to make sure that everyone knew what Peter had done to him.

Safely back home, sitting alone at the large mahogany desk in his study, Anthony wondered how he could avoid the phone call he knew he had to make. He stared at the photographs of Anne and Jessica on his desk and struggled once more to accept that they had turned on him like this. Why Jessica had decided to ruin their perfect lives in their perfect home would never make sense to him.

In the last two days, he had listened to the advice of his lawyer and business advisor, which was to accept the plea deal the prosecutor had offered him and to do it within the forty-eight-hour period they had given him. Anthony was shocked and confused that none of them believed he would be able to success- fully defend the charges made against him by Jessica. After deciding that time had run out for him to delay the decision, he phoned his lawyer.

Rupert picked up the phone and heard Anthony's voice. Anthony was calmer now but still defiant and attempting to set his own terms. "I have decided to take the offer, Rupert. If the trial lasted a few years

I couldn't stand it, let alone the millions of dollars I would waste. The only condition I want is that the terms of the settlement are strictly confidential. I don't want it to be public."

"The prosecution will seek a guilty plea for you to accept the offer, Anthony, and this is a criminal matter not a commercial matter. An agreement with the Crown will be a conviction and on your record."

Anthony, still trying to bend things his way, replied, "Can't you say it's a private matter or that it was a mental health issue? I read all the time about people getting off charges for that or at least keeping it confidential on that basis."

"I know the law can be confusing but you need to trust that I am giving you the best advice in your case. People charged with criminal offences can be found by the courts, at times, to be criminally insane but that is when it's found that they don't know what they are doing. In your case, Jessica has stated she believed you knew what you were doing."

"Why does all of this depend on what Jessica believes?" "The plea offer has been made by the prosecutor on the basis that Jessica says you have some distorted view that what you did was not inappropriate, let alone illegal behaviour. Jessica therefore believes that if you admit what you did and admit that you now see it was wrong, she will consent to you getting psychological help to rewire your thinking. But Jessica isn't prepared to accept that you won't say what you did to her was wrong and against the law."

Rupert heard the penny finally drop for his client as Anthony clarified, "So are you saying that it's a good offer for me and to just accept it, get the year out of the way and get on with my life after that?"

Rupert felt like breathing a sigh of relief but confined his response to professional objectivity. "That's a very practical way of looking at it, Anthony."

Anthony, to Rupert's dismay, remained unpersuaded. "I'll have to think about that then. That's different and I'm not sure if I can agree to that."

Rupert persisted. "I understand that it's not as good as just getting off the charges but there is no chance of that. The Crown is going to proceed with the case and it looks to me that if it goes to hearing, it would be a jury case rather than just a decision made by a judge.

The time and money you spend will be painful, as will likely losing and spending time in jail. That's a risk I would not want to take if I were in your shoes."

It was clear to Rupert that the enormity of the charges had still not sunken in with Anthony and that he was struggling to come to terms with the situation.

"Can I just talk to Anne and Jessica? I'm sure I can get them to come to their senses."

Rupert felt like throwing the phone against the wall but instead, he painstakingly reminded Anthony of his bail conditions. "Anthony, the last time you spoke to Jessica she recorded your call on an app and gave it to the police. Apart from that, you are on bail and part of your bail condition is that you are not to speak to, attempt to contact in any way or go near them. I understand you're still in shock, so take another day to think about this but remember this deal involves you spending no jail time, which I can't guarantee if we do go to trial."

"You sound like you're sure I'll go to jail."

"I will always tell a client when I think they could possibly get a jail term. I would say five out of ten times in my cases it doesn't happen, but that's because I'm good at my job and not because the case may not have warranted it. When my clients are considering an offer from the Crown, I will tell you if the offer is as good a result as I may be able to get you. Otherwise, if you spend millions on a defence and still get sent to jail, you may think I have deceived you."

"So, there is honour amongst thieves. Is that what you're trying to say?"

"I suppose, as a lawyer, I have been called worse," Rupert replied.

"I'll get back to you tomorrow," Anthony said, ending the conversation abruptly.

Sarah

Chapter 57

Relieved that Peter was in a stable condition at the hospital and being well cared for by the doctors, Sarah left the hospital to go back to the office. Of course, Kim insisted on staying in attendance. It had been an eventful day starting with Geoffrey Pemberton's situation which she was relieved she had extricated herself from, and then the attack on Peter. Still reeling with shock Sarah knew she had to go back to her office for her afternoon appointments. Her last appointment of the day was Anne Shaw, and she knew it was going to be a long and difficult conference.

Sarah sat at her desk opposite Anne and Elizabeth. She opened the folder containing the material on Anthony's financial affairs that Elizabeth had compiled. The police had notified them once Anthony arrived at the police station so that Anne and Jessica could go to the house and pick up some of their personal belongings. While they were packing, Elizabeth had gone through Anthony's paperwork and computer, to find what she could on his finances. Although Anthony kept most of his paperwork at his office, in his desk drawers, Elizabeth found several bank account statements and rental statements from properties he owned.

Elizabeth told Sarah, "The police have told us that they're hoping Anthony will accept the plea deal they offered him. They said this would mean that he would plead guilty to the charges and agree to at least a year in a psychiatric hospital. They told us this would save Jessica the awful stress and trauma of having to go through a trial."

Sarah was genuinely relieved for them. "That's very good news. The trial process would have been difficult for all of you, especially Jessica and there's never a guarantee that justice will be done. Getting a result and ending this part of the problem will allow Jessica to start to heal."

"Thanks Sarah. We appreciate your support and feel so grateful. Now this part looks like it may be out of the way, would you agree with me that Anne now needs a property settlement so that she and Jessica can get on with their lives? Everything, the house, car and credit cards are all in Anthony's name. Since the charges, his business advisor, Brian, has cancelled the cards and frozen the bank accounts. It's as though they have been punished when he's the one guilty of the wrong doing."

Sarah felt the women's pain, as she always did when she sat across from her clients, observing them, while their world was falling apart. She felt for Anne. The woman had placed her love and faith in a man, who had not only abused that trust, both emotionally and financially, but he had done the incomprehensible and sexually abused her daughter. Now Anne not only had to deal with grieving the loss of her relationship, but also the guilt and shame she felt as a mother from somehow failing to protect her daughter. The pain she must be feeling now was just incomprehensible.

As far as Anthony was concerned, Sarah was always dumbfounded that any man could act this way towards a woman and a child, who he had mistreated. She thought to herself, *Why was this man not on his knees, begging forgiveness from both of them, rather than trying to destroy them?* She had spoken to her psychiatrist friend, Trent, about it and he had said that paedophiles believed that their victims enjoyed what they did to them just as much as they did. He also said that some people demonised those they hurt, to justify hurting them. In their minds, the victims deserved the treatment and they would never see it differently.

Sarah addressed Anne and provided her with the best counsel she could muster, "Anne, I'm so sorry about what you and your daughter have been through. I can't even begin to imagine your pain. However, for me to protect you both now we need to be very clinical about this situation. As part of the plea deal that has been offered to Anthony, he will be going to an institution and no doubt his affairs will be controlled by his accountant or other guardian. We need to try and sort this out as quickly as we can. It's best for you if Anthony accepts the plea deal because if the case were to go to trial, he could ask for the family law case to be stayed until the criminal proceedings were finalised. A protracted litigious family court case would allow them time to move assets and funds to reduce the asset pool and that will make it a lot harder for me to get you a fair settlement. I would suggest that we put a very reasonable offer to Anthony's lawyers, which they will recognise as a good deal for them and it will be the best thing for you. That's the best way to get this sorted out quickly, so you and Jessica can move on with your lives."

Anne was puzzled and asked, "What do you mean by 'move his assets and funds', Sarah?"

"The people looking after Anthony's affairs will try and reduce his asset pool to give you the least they can," Sarah explained. "To do that they may even start to try and hide assets and/or move or sell assets and get rid of the money. If they start doing that, all we can do is try to get court orders to stop them but that takes time and money and it's always harder to claw back assets that are gone. You and Jessica have had enough emotional pain and drama. I really recommend we try and get you the best settlement that we can. That means you may not get the amount of money you would get if you went to hearing but it will finalise this aspect of your life, without any further stress and as soon as possible."

Anne was concentrating on what Sarah was saying. She asked what Sarah thought she could get as a settlement.

Sarah replied, "On the figures you have given me, which Elizabeth has done a very good job of putting together, I would estimate that if you received a payment of two million dollars, your car and other personal possessions, that would be a very good result for him and a result that would allow you to rent or buy a home and pay Jessica's school fees."

Anne was surprised as she asked, "Do you really think he would agree to that?"

Sarah was relieved that Anne seemed pleased with the suggested amount and that her pain had not caused her to seek revenge financially.

"You are entitled to that, Anne. Anthony is a very wealthy man and has tens of millions of dollars that we know about. I would be very surprised if there was not more money hidden in places that would be very difficult to find. If his legal team doesn't press him to accept this settlement, then Anthony has other intentions, and/ or they have intentions to milk him for all he's worth in legal fees before they let him go."

"Their intentions?" quizzed Anne.

"Sometimes, people want to settle their affairs reasonably and expeditiously. Other times, they want to draw things out and make things as hard as they can for the other person. I don't know which way Anthony, or his team, will want to deal with this yet, but we need to prepare for them playing hard."

Seeing Anne's face fall in anticipation of the difficult road ahead, Elizabeth put a comforting arm around her. "If Jessica and I could have a home and I could pay her school fees until she finished school that would be fine for us. The only other major expense I would like is to be able to pay for Jessica to continue having therapy as frequently and for as long as she needs it," Anne said.

Sarah was struck by Anne's modest expectations and hoped Anthony and his lawyers appreciated it. "Well, Anne," she said, "I'll start trying to sort this out with Anthony's lawyers and I'll get back to you and Elizabeth shortly. In the meantime, I agree that you and Jessica should both get counselling to help you through this. Now, do you have any money in a bank account in your name solely, that Anthony can't get access to?"

"I have a bank account in my own name but there's not much in it. Most of our money is in a joint bank account which both Anthony and I have access to."

"How much is in the account now? Do you know?" Sarah pressed her.

"It varies because both Anthony and I pay bills from it, but it usually has about fifty to a hundred thousand dollars in it."

Sarah was relieved to hear there was ready cash available to Anne but she instructed with some urgency, "Anne, you should withdraw all of that money straight away into the bank account that is in your name only."

"Really?" Anne asked then added, "I feel funny about doing that. I've never transferred money to myself before, only to pay bills."

"I hope I'm wrong, but just in case, move what you can to your bank account. I suspect that money will soon be moved out of the joint bank account into his or someone else's bank account and you will be left with nothing."

Elizabeth, who had sat back and listened while Anne and Sarah discussed Anne's options, realised the importance of Sarah's advice. "You need to listen to Sarah and do what she tells you, Anne. I can look after you and Jessica but you should still have your own money for your security and Jessica's. That is what you are entitled to."

Elizabeth then turned to Sarah. "Thanks Sarah. We really do appreciate this. I'll make sure Anne transfers some money to herself. Also, I would like to pay for Anne's fees until she gets her settlement."

"I've known you for over ten years, Elizabeth. We can sort paying the fees out after I have sorted out the settlement. Kate will arrange the retainer agreement, as we are required to have that completed, but there's no problem with paying later. That's the least of our worries right now."

Once they had left, mulling over the interview, Sarah felt some concern. She really hoped Anne would do as she advised her. Ready cash in a joint bank account was always the first thing that was moved by smart accountants and lawyers. If they did not get a settlement done it may take years for Anne to get any cash out of Anthony. She may already be too late.

Anthony

Chapter 58

Anthony had been sure that bashing Peter would be the remedy for his pent-up anger but instead it had intensified his memories of him. They continued to infiltrate his mind every hour of the day and at night he found himself waking up after having a nightmare about what had happened between them. He thought he had buried that part of his life, but it had resurfaced powerfully, and it was torturing him. After grappling with what could be done to stop the pain, he decided to confront his sister with the reality of what had happened to him all those years ago.

Anthony had not seen Madeline for many years, for several reasons - the most insignificant being that it was a three-hour drive to her home. As he drove along her street, he recognised her house from the photos she had emailed him over the years. He got out of his car and walked up to the front door. He hesitated, as he realised that confrontation could disrupt her world like it had his, and he almost decided to leave before he pressed the doorbell.

Over the last twenty years, he had pretty much ignored Madeline's pleas to come for dinners and visits. He had avoided her as much as possible, but he would read the emails she sent every couple of months. Because of this, he knew she was married with twin boys, who would now be about two years old. She had been very excited when she received his email advising he was coming to see her today.

Anthony heard both the pounding on the floor of the children running towards the door and their excited voices. His sister was not far behind them and the door opened to reveal Madeline, holding the wiggling little boys in her arms.

"Hi, Anthony, we're so happy to see you!" The twins wiggled out of her arms and beamed up at Anthony. He crouched down and extended his arms. To his delight, the twins rushed straight into them. Anthony picked them up and squeezed them, which produced squeals of laughter from the boys. He threw them into the air to cries of, "More!" but finally set them both down and followed his sister into the kitchen.

Anthony could smell the same aromas that had graced his mother's kitchen, during his childhood. His mother and sister were always cooking. The smell of roasting chicken was most prevalent, but soon the aroma of newly baked cookies and cakes also filled his nostrils and his mind with memories. His life had been idyllic as a child, until Peter had ruined it all.

Madeline called the twins, who were holding on, steadfast, to Anthony's legs. She picked them up, despite their vociferous protests, and put them into their playpen in the living room in front of the television, which was, sensibly, suspended from a wall.

"Would you like a glass of wine, Anthony?" Madeline asked, adding as a persuader, "I'm having one."

"I'd love one," he accepted. Then Anthony began to explain himself to her, "Sis, I know I haven't been in contact or to see you for a while and I'm sorry about that."

"That's okay. You're here now."

Madeline poured two glasses of white wine which she had already set out for his arrival. As she walked towards him and landed him a glass she said, "Tell me about your life. Are you in a relationship or married, Anthony? Do you have any children?"

"Yes Maddie, I'm married, and I have a step-daughter. I'll talk about them later. I came here today because I saw someone, by chance, the other day and he reminded me of you and how close we were. It stirred something up in me again that I had buried and unfortunately when I buried it I had to bury you with it."

"We were once so close and then you just disappeared. Hearing you call me Maddie again has brought a tear to my eye. It's been so long since you called me that," she said, with a tinge of wistfulness that made Anthony feel sad. "What was it Anthony? Who did you see the other day?"

"It was Peter," Anthony said, in a flat tone. "It was the first time I had seen him, since you two broke up and he disappeared."

"Good heavens, Anthony! I'm so surprised you even remember him. Did he come up to you or did you recognise him? It was, what almost thirty years ago that I dated him?"

"We didn't talk, I just saw him in a coffee shop where I was having breakfast. I knew it was him as soon as he walked in."

Madeline looked at her brother and became concerned. His demeanour had suddenly changed, and he looked sad and haunted. She was trying to recall if she had ever heard Anthony mentioning Peter after she and Peter had broken up, but she could not.

Madeline asked, "Why are you looking so sad? There was really nothing much between Peter and me. In fact, I often wondered why we ever went out for those six months. He seemed interested at first but after a while, I thought he had a better time playing pool with you and Dad. I was sixteen, Peter was eighteen and you were twelve. Even then, Mum and Dad would say he had to go home or stay the night, if he slept in your room. Do you remember we could never get you guys up in the morning because you had been playing Xbox all night?"

"That's what he told you we did, Maddie, but you, Mum and Dad never asked me what we did. Nobody ever asked me if I wanted him to sleep in my room or if I had a problem with it."

Madeline was puzzled but attempted to rationalise, "Anthony, you were only twelve at the time. You always seemed so in awe of Peter and you never said you didn't like him there. What did you do all night, then, if it wasn't playing Xbox?"

Anthony agreed, "I was in awe of him. I thought he was the best friend I had." Then, in a rush of anger he added, "That was until I found out, a couple of years later, that he was just a fucking paedophile, who had groomed and trained me to fulfil his fucking sick fantasies."

Madeline reeled back and her hands flew to her face in shock. She remembered the boys together, when she would go into Anthony's room to wake them up in the morning. They would always look so tired that she ended up going back to her room. Now, thinking about it, she realised that Anthony never said a word. It was always Peter that spoke.

"Anthony." With a gentle touch she reached out and stroked his arm and said, "I'm so sorry. I can't believe that happened to you and that

Mum, Dad and I allowed it to happen, because we suggested he sleep in your room."

Anthony stood up and walked over to Madeline. He put his hand on her shoulder and assured her, "It wasn't your fault, Maddie. I used to like it. That's the hard part. I actually liked it because he told me it was natural and that boys learned about sex by first doing it to each other and then later to girls. At the time, of course, you and I were both victims."

Madeline was white with shock and despair. She asked, fearful of the reply, "Anthony, what did he do to you?"

Anthony saw Madeline was very fragile from what he had told her and knew she would not be able to deal with the truth. He knew, because when he was at school he had told the school counsellor, and even she had started to cry. The school counsellor had continued having sessions with him, but as he did not want his parents to know what had happened, she agreed to his request and did not tell them.

Anthony tried to dismiss Madeline's fears by saying, "We just played around a bit, that's all. He told me he had to practice kissing and cuddling with me so he would know how to do it with you."

Madeline stared at Anthony and the tears that had been welling in her eyes now spilt down her cheeks. "What a sick man!" she exclaimed through her tears. "I'm sorry, but what a sick person."

"As I got older I realised what a sick creep he was. I'm probably very lucky that I was in some kind of fantasy and I thought what was happening was normal and all boys did it. Anyway, when I saw him the other day, I froze and I've had this anger building up inside me ever since. I've been obsessing about him and I just felt I needed to tell you what happened so I can get it all out of my head."

Madeline nodded. "I'm so glad you told me, Anthony. Do you think we should report him for what he did to you?"

Anthony shook his head, "I don't want that in my life. I want as few people as possible to know about it. I don't want Mum and Dad to ever know and they would be dragged into it, if it went to court. Please leave this with me and I'll work out how to deal with it Maddie."

Madeline nodded, then turning her head on one side, her eyes piercing his, she asked, "Why did you tell me now?"

"Because I realised that secretly, during those months, I was trying to keep Peter to myself and take him from you. After you two broke up and I never saw him again, I hated you and that was why. I was heartbroken and felt deserted by Peter, but I didn't understand why. Now I know why I've distanced myself from you. It's because of the guilt I felt from loving him and then hating you for losing him. I just want us to be close again and now I think we can be."

Madeline hugged him with a mixture of sadness and relief. "All I can say Anthony, is that I'm so sorry for what happened and that I'm glad you're back in my life now."

Anthony kept from his sister that because Peter had initiated him into sex, he was damaged for the rest of his life. After Peter left him, he tried to become attracted to girls, during his school life, but he never felt the same attraction or ecstasy as he had felt with Peter. The only way he could feel anything was by being with girls that were way younger than he was. He was attracted to girls and boys aged between eleven to sixteen years old. The way he got close to those kids as he got older was by dating their mothers. All of this was Peter's fault. He started the problem and now Anthony could not stop. He wondered if Peter cared about what he had done and if he would ever pay for it.

As he paused and thought about the mess he was in, Madeline was looking at the confused look on his face. She asked, "Anthony what are you thinking?"

Anthony looked at his sister with sadness. He realised she really cared about him. He could not bring himself to discuss his damaged sexual needs but he decided to tell Madeline about the charges he was facing. "I've had allegations made against me by my step-daughter and the police have charged me."

Madeline gasped in shock, "What are you going to do?"

"I'm going to defend the charges. The police have offered me a plea deal and my lawyer is advising me to take it. I told him I'm thinking about it, but I made up my mind on the way here and I've decided I'm not going to plead guilty to something I don't believe was wrong. I don't want to discuss it any further than that, but I just thought that you should know."

Madeline put her arms around her brother and said, "I'll always support you. You know that don't you? If you need me or want my support, I'll be there for you."

Anthony hugged her back and replied, "Thank you, Maddie. I have to go now. I'll let you know how things go."

As Anthony started walking towards the front door Madeline said, "Wait Anthony, please let me get the twins so they can say goodbye to you." She lifted them out of the playpen and they ran towards him to say goodbye. He hugged them both then he walked towards the front door and left.

Anthony was not sure how he felt about what had just happened. He thought it would make him feel better telling Madeline about the truth about him and Peter and how he had been neglected by both her and his parents, but he found he just felt emptier and more confused. He could feel the anger inside him building up again as he thought about Peter and then Jessica and Anne - all the people who had used and abused him. He decided the only way he was going to deal with his anger was to get revenge against them all. He reminded himself, *Revenge is best served cold.*

Jane

Chapter 59

Jane was excited, but not as much as the girls were. Brett had surprised her by coming home from his business trip and telling her that he was taking her and the girls on a holiday for five days to Hayman Island. He said he wanted to celebrate his successful business trip with them and he had booked a private plane and villa at a resort.

Jane was doing her final check of the house and all their bags. She heard Brett telling the girls they were going to fly in their new "family plane" and how much fun they were going to have. He had already told Jane that his company had the use of a private jet and he had use of it for the trip.

Jane heard the intercom buzz and Brett called out, "That'll be the hire car. Are we ready girls?" The girls ran excitedly to Brett and held his hands as they walked with him to the car.

The hire car pulled up to an area of the airport Jane had never been to before. Brett got out of the car and directed the girls towards the plane. "This way to our family plane girls," he said and led the girls to the plane, holding their hands.

Jane feel odd in the private jet. The flight attendants greeted them with champagne and juice for the girls. Shortly after taking off they were served large platters of fruit and cheese, followed by cakes and ice cream, especially for the girls. The flight was amazing and the kids were so excited it was hard to keep them in their seats. When the plane landed, the crew led them off the plane to a private helicopter to the resort.

Once they arrived at their villa, the girls squealed and upon seeing the pool they asked Brett if they could go swimming. Brett surprised

Jane by saying, "Yes," and telling them he would go in with them. Jane could not remember the last time he had gone swimming with his daughters.

Jane was in their suite unpacking when Brett walked up to her and handed her a box. She opened it and gasped, then said, "Brett, this is the most beautiful ring I've ever seen."

Brett placed the ring on Jane's left hand, kissed her gently and said, "I love you, Jane. I know I haven't shown it as much as I should have lately, but I'll try harder from now on." Then he ran out of the room to the girls who were at the pool gate yelling for him to come outside. Brett took off his clothes and jumped into the plunge pool in his underwear, bringing delighted squeals from the girls.

Jane noticed that Brett had left his phone on the table and that it was turned off. Brett never had his phone turned off. He would always answer the phone, even in the middle of the night. She was not sure if this was a good or bad sign.

She looked through the French doors and saw Brett playing in the pool with the girls. He seemed genuinely happy and Jane started to relax. She held up her left hand admiring her new ring and wondered why she had been so worried. She looked out again and saw the girls jumping on Brett, who was throwing them in the water.

Jane walked back into the bedroom and returned to her unpacking. She was starting to undo the zipper on Brett's bag when he walked into the room with the girls. They were all drip- ping wet and laughing. He said, "What are you doing?" He went over to Jane and put his hand on his bag.

"I was just unpacking, honey. I finished my bag and thought I'd start unpacking yours and hanging your clothes up."

Brett picked up his bag from the bed and placed it on the floor. "Don't you worry about that, honey, I'll do that later. Why don't you just relax? We're on holidays. I can unpack later."

The girls had walked into the bathroom and called out, "Can we have a spa bath? It's the biggest spa in the world and it's in your bathroom, Mummy. Can you come and see?"

The girls grabbed Jane's hand and took her into the bath- room. "Of course, you can." Jane leaned over, turned the taps on and poured in the bubble bath that was next to the towels.

While the girls were happily splashing away Jane walked back into the bedroom. Brett had not heard her walk in because of the noise of the girls playing. Jane noticed him fussing about with his bag. She saw him unzip and then rezip the inside of the top of the bag and then flick it back to finish unpacking the remainder of the contents.

He turned around and saw Jane, "Are you sneaking up on me?"

"No, darling, I just put the girls in the bath and thought maybe we could have a glass of wine on the balcony. The butler left a bottle in an ice-bucket with glasses on the table, while you were in the pool."

"I love this place already," he said. "I'll be out on the balcony in a minute. I'm just about finished here. See you out there."

Jane sat down at the table on the balcony and poured herself a glass of wine. She looked back at the bedroom to see if Brett was on his way and saw him reflected in the mirror in the bedroom. He was zipping up his bag and pushing it back under the bed. He then picked up his mobile, turned it on and listened to his messages. Jane saw him smile before he turned the phone off and put it down before heading out to the verandah. Jane turned her back towards him before he could see that she had been watching him.

Brett put his arms around her and kissed her on the side of her neck. He knew that was her favourite spot to be kissed and when she giggled he chuckled, "You're so easy to get Jane, seriously." Smiling, he then kissed her on the forehead before saying to her, "Now, where's my glass of wine darling?"

Anthony

Chapter 60

In his office, Anthony sat and tortured himself by thinking about what Jess and Anne were trying to do to him. He had come so close to agreeing to the plea deal suggested by Rupert Showers. Rupert would be furious when he told him he was not going to take the plea deal. After he heard that the little bitch had recorded him he had decided they could all go to hell. He had loved and trusted Jessica, but she had abused that love by taping their phone call to trap him. *Fuck her, and fuck Anne,* he thought. He was going to spend every dollar proving Jessica was a lying slut, just as his lawyers told him he could. He knew that Jessica had enjoyed the sex. The little bitch had loved it and now she was trying to get out of it by blaming him. He would see how she liked being cross-examined in court. The stupid little bitch had no idea what she would have to go through to prove her case. She thought he would let her carry on with her new boyfriend and because he would not allow that, she turned on him. Well, he was going to turn on her and her mother.

He would make sure they got nothing. He had just spoken to his secretary and Brian his business manager, who were at that moment arranging to have Anne's car repossessed and the locks changed on the house. He was also notifying the security company so that Anne and Jessica would not be able to get back into the house if they tried. He would cut off her credit cards right now and empty their joint bank accounts. She would feel what it was like to be broke again. If they were going to cross him, he owed them nothing and they were going to suffer.

A smile spread across his face when he thought about Jessica having to go back to a public school. Served her right for betraying him. Anthony suddenly felt gutted. The thought of betrayal brought Peter back into his head and those feelings returned. Peter would pay again too. Anthony had already started arranging that. Peter needed to know he had ruined his childhood and his life, until he met Anne. At the thought of his wonderful life since meeting her, Anthony felt broken. He realised that everything he had achieved was all for nothing. No one had ever loved him, and no one would ever stay with him. He tortured himself saying over and over again in his head, *Why did I ever kid myself they would? It was the lifestyle they wanted, not me.*

His business manager, Brian, walked into his office to tell him he had some good news from the new lawyer he had found. The lawyer had told him that if Anthony defended the case, then any family law proceedings would have to be deferred until after the criminal case was heard.

"What does that mean to me?" Anthony wanted to know.

"It means that while the court case is going on with the police and Jessica, the case in the Family Court is stopped. That way, they can't get the Family Court to give them any money or make any orders until after the criminal case is finalised. That gives us time to get rid of all your assets or hide as much as we can and have the cars and house sold, the bank accounts closed, credit cards cut off and school fees stopped."

Anthony felt far more cheerful. "Now that's really good news. Why didn't Rupert tell me about that strategy?"

Brian dismissed Rupert with a wave of the hand, then he smacked the desk and said, "I told you Anthony, my guy is the best. He's the toughest prick in town and Jessica and Anne won't know what hit them. They'll be begging for mercy and pleading to drop the charges before you know it."

Anthony felt pumped up from the power that money can bring as he stretched out his long frame in his leather chair and put his feet up on his expansive mahogany desk. He was feeling quite satisfied with himself and regaining his confidence. Through an enormous grin he said, "Let the games begin!"

Rupert

Chapter 61

Rupert had just seen the message on his desk, but before Rupert had time to dial Anthony's number, his phone rang. His secretary announced that Anthony was calling again, and she was putting the call through to him.

"Rupert, you can tell the police to jam their plea offer. I'm not going to admit anything, and I'm not going to accept their plea bargain. Tell them that if they won't drop the charges, we're going to trial and I'll wipe the floor with Jessica."

Rupert was stunned by Anthony's unexpected decision, but the heavy silence that ensued only provoked Anthony to shout. "Rupert, are you fucking listening to me?"

Rupert was stung into retaliation. In his most arrogant courtroom voice, Rupert boomed down the phone, "Anthony, you do not yell and swear at me, do you hear? I am a senior counsel and you need me right now, so if you can't treat me with respect then I won't represent you."

Anthony went on the attack. "Come off your fucking high horse, Rupert. I've researched you and I know you act for the scum of the earth. Don't try and make out that my swearing is something new to your world of drug dealers, stand over men, rapists and murderers. Are you telling me none of them swear, for fuck's sake?"

"Not to me they don't and if you don't change your attitude right now, I'm going to cease acting for you, immediately." He could hear Anthony laughing hysterically on the other end of the phone. *The guy is clearly insane*, Rupert thought. Anthony really did not understand that the only reason the prosecution had offered the plea deal was because

Rupert was acting for him. If he ceased to act, Rupert was sure they would withdraw their offer.

"You go fuck yourself, Rupert. There are thousands of lawyers out there and I've been given a list of the top five criminal lawyers, all of whom are biting at the bit to take my case. You're sacked." The line went dead.

Good luck, Rupert thought, He was relieved as he realised he had just dodged a bullet. Anthony would be impossible to act for as a client. If Rupert could not get him to accept his advice and behave civilly, then it would be impossible to get him to behave for the judge and the jury. The prosecution was going to be unhappy with the news, as it meant that Jessica would have to go to trial, but Rupert was confident they would indeed wipe the floor with him. On the evidence they had and with the newly appointed crown prosecutor, Senior Counsel Fiona Lane, who Rupert knew would be given the case, Anthony would be going on a long holiday, care of the Crown, for quite a few years.

He picked up his phone and called the Crown Solicitor's office to advise them of Anthony's decision. They were very surprised and immediately confirmed that, as Rupert had ceased to act, the deal was off. Rupert told them he would be following the trial with great interest. He told the Crown Solicitor that Sarah Walters had contacted him to advise that she was acting for the wife in the family law matter and that she wanted to put a settlement offer to Anthony, with their consent. The Crown Solicitor had no issue with that. Both Rupert and Sarah knew that if Sarah could not get Anne a deal now, the family law case would be deferred until after the criminal proceedings by Anthony's legal team and all his assets would disappear by the time of the criminal trial.

After discussions with Sarah and the Crown Solicitor's office, it was agreed that if they could get Anthony's new lawyer to agree to an expedited trial, it would be in everyone's interests. That way, instead of taking three years to get to hearing they could do it in a year.

The most interesting part for everyone was who Anthony's new legal team would be. Rupert could not help but wonder who was on the list of top five criminal lawyers, when Rupert could only name two at the most that he would even rate next to himself. More than likely, Anthony had retained a B grade firm who had pandered to his wallet and fluffed up his ego, making him feel confident and important. They would take millions of dollars from him and then smile as he was led off to jail at the end of the hearing. Rupert's sole concern was that B grade lawyers had a habit of playing dirty because their clients liked it and he hoped that Jessica could cope with it.

Rupert decided to call Sarah and give her the heads up. The earlier she knew, the better it would be for her client.

Sarah answered her mobile, "Hi Rupert, how are you?"

Rupert marvelled that Sarah always answered her mobile when she was such a busy practitioner and was always on top of every case.

"I'm fine but I'm calling about Anthony Shaw." "What's happened?"

"He sacked me and is going to use someone else to act for him, but he didn't tell me who it is. He's not accepting the plea bargain and will be defending the charges. I just thought you should know."

Sarah frowned and took a deep breath before replying, "Thanks for that, Rupert. I was hoping that we could settle that one. I know how badly it can go with a guy like that who has a few years up his sleeve to lose his assets when the family law case is stayed during his criminal trial."

Rupert smiled to himself. As usual, Sarah knew exactly what the state of play was. He warned her, "I'm afraid he won't be playing nice, so good luck with it. I'm sure he'll put to the court that bail cost him one million dollars and he'll need a few more million for his defence, so the family law matter will have to wait until his case is done."

Sarah nodded in agreement. "I get it. Luckily, my client can stay with her sister and I'm sure she'll manage. Thanks for the heads up."

"My pleasure," Rupert said. "If I hear anything else, I'll let you know."

Sarah interjected before Rupert could hang up, "Do you think I could get the Crown and Anthony to agree to an expedited criminal hearing if I had my client agree to stay her family law matter without seeking interim spousal and child support?"

"The Crown would, but Anthony's legal team will say they can't get the case ready in time, and they'll be wanting to drag out a case like this for as long as they can, so they can charge him millions. I think his strategy would be to bleed her dry and make her suffer, so what would be in that for him, and what would that achieve for Anne with no maintenance as well?"

Sarah paused and Rupert was not sure if she had hung up as he asked, "Sarah, you still there?"

"Sorry Rupert, the angle just came to me." Rupert was intrigued. "What do you mean?"

"If I can get Anthony to believe that his criminal lawyers are dragging this out to milk him for millions, then maybe he'll agree to the expedited hearing. Psychopaths have to be in control and if he thinks he's being had, then he'll want to take control back."

"Okay, so how are you going to do that?"

"I don't know yet, but I think chances are I may need your help. Once I've worked it out, I'll let you know."

"Please do," Rupert replied.

Sarah knew she had to call Anne, before Anne received a call from the Crown Solicitor's office. Sarah had hoped that things would not go this way. She poured herself a glass of wine first, then made the call.

"Hi Anne, it's Sarah. I've just had news from Anthony's lawyer that Anthony isn't going to accept the plea deal and that he's going to defend the charges against him. I'm sorry to have to tell you this, but I thought it was best to come from me first. I'm sure the Crown Solicitor's office will call you soon to let you know the same thing." She spoke clearly and slowly, conscious that Anne needed to take it all in.

There was only silence at the end of the line, so Sarah tried to offer some encouragement. "I know this isn't what we were hoping for, but we'll get through this, Anne. We'll all help Jessica get through the trial, if she wishes to proceed with the charges against Anthony."

When Anne finally spoke, Sarah sensed the betrayal and the disappointment in her voice. "I'm just so disappointed in Anthony. Why does he want to do this to her? He knows what he did and if he just admitted it, we could all get on with our lives and he could get help."

"We can't control his decisions and he'll be now be influenced by his family and legal team. We'll just need to brace ourselves for the journey ahead for Jessica and help her through it. The other disappointing factor is that I doubt he will now agree to a family law settlement and, in that case, he can ask that any family law proceedings are stayed until after the criminal trial is heard. Criminal proceedings are always given precedent. We can ask for orders for urgent maintenance and support but having regard to the bail paid in the sum of one million dollars and his upcoming legal fees, I'm sure he'll say he can't afford any further commitments. In fact, I'm sure that even if we had interim orders made, pending the criminal trial, he would just breach them and not pay." "We can live with Elizabeth for as long as we need to; she's able to support us. I've already spoken to the school principal and she said that Jessica could apply for a scholarship they're working on for next year. They've just been so understanding and helpful."

Sarah was relieved that Anne and Jessica would be able to manage with such support. "I'll go ahead and prepare the application in your case with the family court, because we need to do our best to protect your position there. If it's deferred because of the criminal trial proceeding, we'll deal with that then. I'm sure the Crown Solicitor's office will contact you shortly and let you know how they'll be proceeding and what they'll want from you and Jessica. Let me know at any time if you need my help."

"Thanks, Sarah," Anne said. "I know you'll do the best you can for us. I know we'll get through this and we're very lucky to have so much support. It means a lot to me. This is a nightmare and I still hope I'll wake up and it'll go away, but I know it won't.

"Sarah expressed her sympathy for Anne and Jessica and asked if she could help in any other way.

"You've done more than enough. We'll be okay. I'll go now and tell Jessica what's happened. She'll probably deal with it better than me. My sister will tell me it's worked out for the best and we'll get on with it. Please don't worry."

Sarah tried to work out in her mind how she should proceed with Anne's case. She needed to apply for orders on an urgent basis in the family court, even before the criminal charges were commenced so that she could at least ask for some support for Anne and Jessica. But did Anne and Jessica need the stress and trauma of a family court case while they were preparing for a criminal trial?

After a lot of reflection, Sarah decided to go ahead and prepare the case for interim orders and see how it went. If things did get complicated, she could have the case adjourned until after the criminal case. She felt that if she did not get on the attack, Anthony would see this as weakness on Anne's part and feel he had a victory.

The ring tone on Sarah's phone broke into her thoughts. It was Anne again. "Sarah, a man just knocked on my door. He said he is from a hire purchase company and said he's come to take my car. When I told him that my husband gave me the car for my birthday, he said Anthony obviously didn't tell me it was leased and that he was just letting me know as a matter of courtesy that he was taking it. He pointed to my car, which was already on the back of a tow truck."

Oh dear, just what I thought would happen. "I'm sorry that's happened. I was just about to prepare an application to the court and Anthony's stunt will give us a basis on which to file an urgent application. I suspect he's cancelled your credit cards and closed your joint bank accounts, so you had better check before you try to use them. Did you manage to transfer any money from your joint account into your name, like we discussed in our last conference?"

"I only transferred $10,000 even though you told me to transfer everything that was there. I just didn't feel right about it. I could have taken $50,000.00, but I didn't."

"I suspect if you look now, it'll all be gone. At least you managed to get $10,000."

Sarah could hear Anne crying into the phone as she said, "I've got to go now, Sarah. I'll call you tomorrow. This is just unbelievable, I'm sorry."

Before Anne hung up, Sarah heard Elizabeth in the back- ground. She was saying that it was just a car and that Anne could use her car. Anne was so lucky to have her sister's calming influence and support right now. As Sarah and Rupert had suspected, Anthony was going to play dirty and put pressure on Anne and Jessica to withdraw the charges.

While she was still fuming over Anthony and his lawyers' tactics, Sarah's phone rang again. "Hi Sarah, it's Elizabeth. I'm sorry Anne was so upset."

"I know this must be just awful for her."

"I'm just calling to say I can look after Anne and Jessica for as long as this takes. I have money and a good business. They'll be perfectly fine. There's no need for you to worry about that."

"It's wonderful that they have your support, Elizabeth," Sarah said. I'll file the family law case but as we can see, Anthony is going to give as little as he can and take back as much as he can. This won't be easy. We'll get an order in the end, but after his legal fees and whatever his family can transfer, I suspect there won't be much left."

Elizabeth understood, "We can only do our best for Anne. Whatever happens, they can always live with me and I can take care of them. I love them, and they're all the family I have."

"Thanks for calling Elizabeth. Anne's so lucky to have you."

Jane

Chapter 62

The next morning at the resort, Jane woke up to the girls jumping on the bed beside her. They had come in with Brett, who was holding a tray of scrambled eggs, toast and tea. Pleased with themselves at the surprise they had thought up, the girls told her, "Mummy, we ordered you breakfast in bed with Daddy."

"Good morning, darling," Brett said. "The girls and I wanted to surprise you with breakfast in bed."

"Thank you, my beautiful girls, and Daddy. This is a lovely surprise."

Brett came over to Jane, kissed her on the cheek, then put down the tray on the bed. He said, "Now you enjoy your breakfast while the girls and I go to the gym."

"You're taking the girls to the gym?"

"Well actually I'm going to the gym and the girls are going to kids' club. The butler brought in the kids' club itinerary this morning and they want to do the early morning kids' gym class."

Brett ushered the girls along. "Come on girls, we need to go now or we will be late."

"Bye Mummy," the girls yelled as they ran out the door with Brett, holding his hands.

Jane was enjoying the quiet time eating her breakfast, finishing her tea and reading the papers. In her relaxed mood she could not decide whether she should go for a swim or just sunbake by the pool. She pushed the tray aside and walked into the wardrobe to find something to wear. Without any real reason, she had an overwhelming urge to look inside Brett's bag, which she had seen him push under the bed, the day before. She walked over and pulled it out. She paused, rethinking her decision, when she noticed a slight bulge in the top of the bag. It was where the inside zipper was. She opened the zipper section and she found tucked into the bottom corner a red satin G-string. It was not hers. She reached further and found an envelope. It was a travel itinerary from last week when Brett was away working. The itinerary was for Brett and Ms Catherine Forrester. They had flown to and from Brisbane and had stayed at the Versace Hotel on the Gold Coast. There was only one room booked and it was a suite.

Jane put the envelope and the panties back in the bag and pushed the bag back under the bed. She knew she was about to burst out crying, so she got into the shower and cried. Jane had only been in the shower a few minutes when she heard Brett.

"Hi Darling", he called out, "I'm back. The girls were having fun, so I left them at kids' club, so we could have some time together." Jane called back, "Hi honey, that's fantastic. Let's go for a swim."

She stepped out of the shower and had a good look at herself in the mirror. With years of practice she had developed the art of shower crying. Somehow the water helped stop her eyes going puffy and red.

Brett walked in and kissed her. He had already put on his swimmers. "I'll meet you in the water, honey. Take your time." Jane did not know what to do. She needed to stay calm, but she also needed to know what was going on. She went down to the beach and dived into the waves. Brett was waving to her as she swam out towards him.

As she got closer to him Jane yelled out playfully, "I'll race you," and she just kept swimming.

She turned at one stage when she heard Brett yelling, "Jane what are doing? Where are you swimming to?" Jane stopped and lay on her back in the water. For a moment she had even forgotten that Brett was there until she heard him splashing up towards her and yelling loudly at her, "Jane what the fuck has gotten into you? You've taken us out a mile. Are you crazy?"

Jane turned until she was facing him in the water. He was still swimming towards her and was about five metres away when she yelled out to him, "Who's Catherine Forrester?"

Brett stopped swimming where he was and started to tread water. He said nothing.

Jane asked again. "Who's Catherine Forrester Brett?"

Brett replied nervously, "What the fuck are you talking about, Jane? Have you gone mad?"

Jane cried angrily, "I know you were away last week with her and I want to know why. What's going on?"

Brett looked confused. "Jane, stop this. We're having a wonderful time. The kids are so happy. I don't know why you're talking about this person and I don't know who she is. Why are you trying to ruin this holiday for us?"

Jane swam towards him, close enough to stare into his eyes. He looked tired and agitated. She said, "If you talk to me about this then we can sort it out, but if you continue to lie to me then this is all a lie and we're over."

Brett punched the water and shouted, "Fuck it, Jane. Just stop it. You're ruining everything for nothing."

Jane was so angry she wanted to hit him. She dived under the water for what seemed an eternity, until she could not hold her breath any longer. She surfaced and started swimming back to shore. She got out of the water and walked past the Villa to the hotel pool where she thought she would find the girls. Luckily, they were there with the other kids from kids' club. She knew if she saw them she would calm down. She sat on a pool lounge directly opposite them and they saw her and waved. Jane waved back and lay down on the lounge. She knew she needed to get herself together. She knew that if she allowed her emotions to process what was happening to her family right now that she would not be able to cope. She felt a little calmer and thought about the appointment she had made for a consultation with Sarah Walters on her pro bono day. It was supposed to have been tomorrow, but she cancelled when Brett surprised her with the trip. She now realised with some irony that her gut feeling had been right.

Sarah

Chapter 63

It had been a hard thing for Sarah to ask of Anne, but to achieve what she wanted today Sarah had to get her to do it. With Rupert's help, Sarah had managed to arrange a meeting at her offices with the Crown Prosecutor, Anthony and his legal team and Anne. Sarah had insisted that Anne and Anthony not be forced to be in the meeting room at the same time unless they were both comfortable with that. All parties had agreed, however, that at the beginning of the meeting, both Anne and Anthony be in separate meeting rooms and that the lawyers for both sides and the Crown initially meet together.

After making sure that Anne was settled with Elizabeth in a separate room, Sarah walked to the boardroom to greet the Crown Prosecutor and Anthony's legal team. Sarah opened the meeting quickly.

"Thank you for all coming today. I'll get straight to my point and that is that I wish to inform you both that I have filed an application in the Family Court to commence proceedings for urgent maintenance and a final property settlement."

Anthony's barrister responded loudly, "Well we would like to thank you for that, Sarah. It was just what we were hoping for, as the reason your client and her daughter have come up with these ridiculous charges is now evident."

"How so?" asked the prosecutor.

"Cleary the allegations were concocted in the hope that our client would offer to come here to settle today in exchange for withdrawing the allegations. I am right, aren't I?"

"No, you're not. That's not the purpose of the meeting today. In fact, it's the opposite if that's possible. We have advised you we are filing for interim orders, so we can try and reach agreement on whether the case may be expedited. If your client and the Crown agree to expedite the matter to hearing within the shortest time possible of six to eight months, then we will agree to adjourn our application in the Family Court until after the criminal case and that will save your client time, money and the trouble of that interim application."

"I would agree to that," the Crown responded. "We can have our case ready in that time and this is a case that should be dealt with quickly and not dragged out."

"You have to be kidding," Anthony's barrister responded. "Why would we advise our client to agree to that? That's not enough time for us to prepare his case and we can drag out the interim hearing in the Family Court for at least three to four months, so you're wasting your time here with this angle. Now if you want us to let you know what offer we would be prepared to make to your client, if her daughter dropped the allegations, that may be another story."

"Are you offering a bribe?" Sarah asked.

"Of course not. What we're offering is a property settlement in exchange for your client agreeing that her daughter withdraw the allegations."

The prosecutor stood up from the board table and said, "If your client wants to make his wife an offer in relation to their property settlement that's fine. But to make it conditional on her daughter withdrawing charges is firstly unenforceable as against his wife and the Crown; and it's totally unethical."

Sarah asked Anthony's barrister, "Does your client know about this?"

"He thought this was what this meeting was for."

"Does he want to come into the meeting?" Sarah asked. "Yes, he does. In fact, he would like to meet you and he would also like to see Anne."

"Well I'm sorry to say Anne doesn't want to see him, but I'm happy enough for him to come into the meeting. Why don't you bring him in?"

"He'll be disappointed that Anne won't be in here, but I'll go and ask him."

Sarah was hoping on the one hand that Anthony would not come into the meeting, but on the other hand she knew her only chance of getting what she wanted for Anne was if he did. She was getting nowhere with his barrister.

There was a knock on the door and Anthony walked into the boardroom. He was an impressive man who, despite the situation he found himself in, looked self- assured and confident. He followed his barrister to the other side of the table and was introduced to Sarah.

"Anthony, this is Sarah Walters, the lawyer acting for Anne."

Anthony reached across the table to shake hands but Sarah ignored his hand and just nodded in response. She said to him, "Mr Shaw, I spoke to your barrister about an offer that we would like to make to you regarding expediting the criminal hearing against you. He indicated you wouldn't accept it and that you had a perception that we were here today because my client was seeking a settlement offer from you."

Anthony looked confused and said, "Well that's what they told me they thought you were going to do today. I didn't know what you had called this meeting for."

Sarah knew Anthony had just thrown his legal team under the bus in front of the prosecutor and that they did not like it. She seized the moment. "We wanted to advise you, that on behalf of Anne, we have filed an application in the Family Court for urgent maintenance and a final property settlement. We would agree to adjourn those matters if you and the Crown agreed to have the hearing for the criminal proceedings heard as quickly as possible, which we are told could be in six to eight months' time."

"But what if I just offered Anne a deal if she and Jessica dropped the charges?" Anthony sounded confused.

"Part of the property settlement with Anne can't have anything to do with Jessica dropping the charges," Sarah replied.

Sarah watched as Anthony took in what she had just said. She could see he was trying to work out a way to buy his way out of the situation which would work for everyone. Looking frustrated, he asked his barrister, "So how do we make this work?"

Anthony's barrister was flustered by what Sarah had said and told Anthony. "Look, you're innocent so let's just tell them to jam their offer and run your case. We shouldn't agree to have the hearing expedited because that only helps them."

Sarah spoke directly to Anthony. "Expediting the criminal case helps everyone Anthony, especially you. We'll agree to an adjournment of the family law case, which you would otherwise have to apply for to the Family Court to do, and your criminal case will be over in six to eight months instead of years. If you are innocent, wouldn't you want this over as quickly and cost effectively as possible?"

Anthony's barrister was angry with Sarah. "How dare you speak directly to my client. You will put your questions to me. We are here to advise our client what is best for him, not you."

Anthony ignored his barrister, which pleased Sarah and asked Sarah directly, "What do you mean as effectively as possible?"

"Well, either you can have a long drawn out criminal case that takes years to run and your legal team will charge you millions of dollars per year, or we can have this case dealt with in six to eight months. If you're innocent that would save you years and millions of dollars."

"Could the case take years?" Anthony asked his barrister. "Of course, and it should, as do most criminal cases of this nature, because we need to prepare, get witness statements, and have an interim hearing to decide on what evidence is admissible and what isn't. If you want to win, things can't be rushed."

The prosecutor, who now saw where Sarah was going, saw her opportunity and said, "The Crown can have its case ready in time, but I understand the defence is usually not forced to work this hard and efficiently, cutting costs and time to have their case ready."

Seeing he had a problem Anthony's barrister stood up and said, "We need to have time to speak to our client privately." He gestured to Anthony to leave the room.

Anthony remained at the table, looked up at his barrister and asked, "How much extra would my costs be if the hearing went on for two to three years as opposed to what they are suggesting?"

"Some cases can go on for up to five years if the defence team strings things out," said Sarah.

"Why can't we do this in six to eight months if the prosecutor can? I want this over with."

"Let's go outside and talk," the barrister replied, annoyed that Anthony had not followed his lead to leave the room.

Anthony turned to Sarah and said, "I'm going to agree to this expedition of the trial. I want you to ask Anne and Jessica what they want in exchange for dropping the charges all together. There must be a way to sort this out if we agree on that. The prosecution can't run their case if Jessica won't testify, and Anne and Jessica will end up with nothing if they go on with this." Anthony stood up and walked out of the room.

Jane

Chapter 64

Jane lay on the lounge by the hotel pool watching the girls. She felt like her life had been turned upside down. A wave of emotions swept over her but the one thing she knew was clear was that her marriage had been a lie. She had suspected at times that there were other women, but she always talked herself out of it. She realised now that she should have got the significance of what those women they bumped into in Ireland had said, about being newlyweds. Her head started spinning when she felt Brett's heavy hand on her shoulder.

He sounded flustered, "What are you doing, Jane? Why are you doing this when we've been so happy on this trip? Why are you trying to make yourself unhappy again, darling?"

Seeing Brett play the role of the concerned husband, Jane thought that any idle observer would think she was being a difficult wife. But the bastard had been having an affair, which she had discovered, and this was how he dealt with it, by telling her that she was ruining everything.

Brett's wheedling voice cut into her thoughts. "Jane, stop this. Look at the girls, they're so happy. Don't let these little stories in your head convince you to sabotage our marriage. I'm going to get us some cocktails, darling, and we're going to sit here and watch our girls and have a beautiful day."

He continued to prattle on, painting a picture of himself as father and husband of the year, while Jane seethed inside. "At lunchtime, the staff have organised a chef to do a picnic at our Villa with the kids. It was their idea and they made up the menu with the chef this morning. Honey, please don't upset the girls, they're so excited about this. I'm going to get our drinks now."

Jane was furious. She saw that he was turning the whole affair around and putting the blame on her. She realised he had her over a barrel though, because she would not upset the girls. She had to stay, and she and Brett had to look happy together.

Brett came back with the drinks and handed her a Pina Colada. Jane made things clear to him, "I don't want to upset the girls because they're having a lovely holiday with you. But you must know that you can't expect me to get over your affair by just telling me that it's my imagination. Brett, confess to me, tell me everything and then maybe we can work through it and I can get over it. I need to understand how and why it happened."

Brett spat his cocktail out as he burst out laughing. He said, his face a study in innocence, "Confess to what, Sarah? Nothing happened."

"Okay Brett, then our relationship has to end. I can't do this anymore. You're obviously leading another life that doesn't include the kids and me. For so many years you convinced me that I was just insecure, but it was my intuition that was causing me to be stressed about our relationship and I was right."

Brett paced up and down in front of the lounge chairs, occasionally waving and smiling to the girls in the pool. He finally stopped in his tracks, looked into Jane's eyes and said, "You know what, Jane? When we get home, if you want to end our relationship, you can do that. But let's just leave it until we get home, okay? We're in paradise and even if you don't like me, you can still have a good time here for the kids' sake."

Jane had the sudden realisation that she had been play acting the whole time they were married. She had been pretending their marriage was okay to keep up the façade of a happy family. She understood now that that was what Brett wanted, the perfect front to achieve his professional ambitions. He had always said that they gave management positions to the guys who had the whole package - the happy wife and kids, the lovely home, so they could devote themselves to their career.

Jane was too exhausted to care, so she agreed to do what he wanted. "Okay Brett, why not? I've been doing this for thirteen-years now, so what's another week. But when we get home, will you introduce me to Catherine Forrester?"

Brett laughed and with a puzzled frown said, "Catherine who? Believe me Jane, if there were a Catherine there won't be one now." He moved to the lounge next to Jane's, kissed her lightly on the forehead, took a sip of his cocktail, picked up his book and started reading, looking like the ideal husband and father.

Jane

Chapter 65

For ten minutes, Jane maintained her calm and composure, so that Brett would not suspect what she was about to do. She got up from her pool lounge and said to Brett, "Please look after the girls until they've had enough. I'm going back to the room." To her relief, Brett did not ask her why. He just nodded his head which was still buried in his book and sank further into the sun lounge, his drink in hand.

As she walked toward their room, Jane started to cry. Luckily, she was wearing sunglasses so it was not obvious to the happy holidaymakers she passed on her way. She knew what she had to do and she was going to do it. Their marriage had been a lie but she could not understand why he had not only been lying to her but deluding himself. *Why had he insisted that they move to a new house when he was seeing another woman? Why take her and the girls on this holiday?*

Jane found the travel documents in Brett's briefcase and called the travel agent. She called the airline and changed the flight back for herself and the girls to that afternoon. She then grabbed their suitcases and started to pack. As Jane looked through the bathroom cabinet to pack her toiletries she found Brett's phone. He had tried to hide it. She looked at the screen and saw three new messages from someone called Lisa.

"How has she taken it honey?"

"Honey I miss you so much x"

"Babe I miss your body. Come back to me now."

Jane took a screen shot of his phone and Lisa's phone number and then put the phone back into the cabinet. She was dumbfounded.

In only a couple of days, she had found out about not only one but two other women in Brett's life. Firstly, Catherine and now Lisa.

Jane finished packing and changed as they all walked back in. Jane hugged the girls and said, "Girls please change into the new dresses on your beds". Brett noticed the packed bags lined up near the front door of the Villa. His face looked like thunder.

"What's going on Jane?" he demanded. He swung around and grabbed her arm. "Do you think you're leaving with the girls?"

Jane knew she had to be strong. "We're leaving Brett. I don't think it, I know it." Just there was a knock on the door. Brett opened it. It was the bell boy. He collected the bags and told Jane her car had arrived.

Jane went to help the girls finish getting dressed. They were squealing with delight about their new dresses. Brett walked in to see the girls twirling in the mirror and Jane grabbing her handbag to leave.

Brett glared at Jane and said, "So, are you going to wait for me to pack and leave too?"

Jane took the girls' hands, looked him straight in the eye and said, "Goodbye Brett." She would not falter. She would be strong for her girls. Jane took them out of their villa and headed to the driveway at the front of the hotel. She smiled as the girls pointed to the stretch Hummer limousine that was parked right at the front.

When the driver opened the door and said, "Hello ladies," to the girls, they stood open mouthed. Jane laughed and told them to jump into the car. At that moment, she felt a hand on her shoulder; it was Brett.

Jane said to the girls, "I'll be just a minute," and she stepped a few metres away to speak to Brett.

He grabbed her arm and pressed so hard that she winced in pain but he did not release his grip. He said, "I have tried Jane, but this is it. I'm not putting up with any more of your fucking dramas. I've met someone else and I want you to out of my life. It's just lucky isn't it, Jane, that you've already signed the papers."

Jane wanted to slap him but willed herself to remain calm.

The limousine driver, who was watching the scene came closer and called out, "Mrs Elliott, is everything OK?"

"Yes, it is. I'll be there shortly," Jane replied.

Brett was put off by the approach of the driver so he let go of Jane's arm, but he could not let go of his anger as he snarled, "And one of the first conditions of our divorce is that you change your surname. My fiancé and I are getting married as soon as the divorce comes through, so you are no longer my wife or Mrs fucking anything. I'll get the girls for half the time and I don't ever want to see or speak to you again. Goodbye Jane," Brett walked away, almost frothing at the mouth.

Jane opened the door of the Hummer and was relieved to find that the girls were wearing headphones and watching the music clip on the screen that the driver had put on. She slumped into her seat, thankful to be away from him. Jane felt that the man she had thought she had loved and who had loved her had gone. It was as though someone else had invaded his body. Her partner had vanished and, in his place, stood a monster, who was seeking to erase her from his life, as his wife and the mother of his children. *What did I do to make him treat me like this? Like I was a cancer to be cut out and disposed of? Discarded like outdated furniture so that he could get on with the excitement of a new look and beginning?* She did not realise that the girls had been yelling out to her until the driver touched her on the arm. She turned around and smiled and waved at them. She knew she had to put aside her anger and hurt now and just get on with parenting her girls.

She noticed that the driver kept glancing back at the girls as they were singing and enjoying the music and he was smiling. Her eyes glistened with tears and she wondered why it was him and not Brett sitting there smiling at her girls. It occurred to her that Brett had not looked at their girls like that in a long time. *How blind I've been!*

Brett

Chapter 66

Brett felt a huge surge of relief as he walked away from Jane. He knew he had to pretend to be upset about her leaving with the kids, but the truth was he had had enough of playing the game. The fact she was now leaving him suited him perfectly and the timing could not have been better. It was going to make it easier for him to be tough on her.

As he walked back to the Villa the anger started to well up inside and he realised Jane deserved everything that was coming to her. She always played the bloody great mother role but she did not even bother to think that perhaps he needed some attention as well. The girls had become her main priority and not him. He stopped coming home from work for dinner because it was like eating in a childcare centre. Long gone were the days when they sat, just the two of them, drinking wine and laughing and ending up in bed, unable to keep their hands off each other.

Reflecting on the last couple of years, Brett realised that Jane must have seen his disenchantment with their life. When she told him that she was pregnant with twins, all those years ago, he realised straight away he had to do something. There was no way he was dealing with that sort of chaos. Two kids were bad enough but four was going to be nuts. It had been pretty easy to slip a Stilnox into the tea he brought her in bed every morning when she was suffering from morning sickness. When she got up to go down and make the kids breakfast, he could see she was a bit wobbly. All he had to do was give her a soft nudge at the top of the stairs.

What he had not predicted was her depression after losing the twins. Also, the timing had not been right for him to leave her and the kids.

The firm was making him an equity partner and he knew that the guys would not offer it to him if he was not "happily married."

Brett poured himself a glass of wine and sat and thought about the sudden turn of events. He was angry and frustrated that Jane had placed him in this position. He was shocked she had actually had the balls to leave him. It was not like her and it occurred to him that it had been a while since he checked her emails or mobile phone to see if anything was going on. He turned on his lap-top and logged into Jane's email account. Scrolling through the boring ones, mostly from the kids school and family, he almost missed the one single email that was a red light. It was from the office of Sarah Walters confirming an appointment. Brett saw the appointment was for tomorrow when they were supposed to still be here. Jane was now obviously returning to keep her appointment. This must have initiated her dramatic exit, which he now thought may have been planned the whole time, so she could expose his affair to take him to the cleaners.

Brett knew he had to proceed with the back-up plan he had thought out over the last months. He would wait a couple of days before he flew home and by that time it would be all done. The deceptive bitch would get everything that was coming to her. If she wanted to try and set aside the deal they had, then he had no choice. He would not let Jane ruin everything he had worked for and was entitled to.

All he had to do was to fix this, was to make two phone calls and then he would go back to relaxing by the pool. The first call was to Lisa, to get her to catch the first flight over. She might as well replace Jane immediately. Now that Jane had left him, he was relieved of all possible guilt. The second call was to his mate the plumber. He and his mate had been waiting for the right opportunity, and now that Jane had gone home early, it was the perfect time to have the fridge sorted.

Sarah

Chapter 67

Sarah was just about to get into her car to head to the office when her phone rang.

"Good morning, Kate."

"Sarah, you obviously haven't heard the news, have you?" "No, I'm just getting into the car, why?"

"Sarah, it's been all over the news that the body of a forty-year-old woman and her two children were found in a home in Vaucluse."

"That's awful."

Kate could see that Sarah had not made the connection and explained.

"There was a woman called Jane Elliott who called about a week ago to make an appointment for one of your pro bono consultations. She had heard you on the radio discussing financial agreements. She said that she had signed a financial agreement but hadn't seen a lawyer, like you said was necessary for it to be binding. She said she looked up our website and saw you gave free consultations on certain days. When she said that, Sarah, I must tell you it worried me, but I told her that you would be able to give her all the advice she needed and I squeezed her in for tomorrow's list. She rang and cancelled a few days later because she said her husband had booked a surprise holiday. Sarah, I've got a bad feeling about this. I just know in my bones this is her."

"Kate, this is awful news and I know how upset you must be, but we can't jump to conclusions. There's nothing more you can do." "They're calling it an accident, 'a technical issue', they said in the radio reports, but Sarah can you see if you can get someone to check what actually happened?"

Sarah understood Kate's concern. "I'll call Rupert Showers and see what he knows or what he can find out. Rupert's always up to date with anything in the news. I'll be able to tell you everything the police are prepared to release. Don't worry."

"Thanks, Sarah. I don't know why I feel weird about this."

Sarah said, "Okay, I get it. Leave it to me and I'll see you at the office shortly, Kate." Sarah scooped up her laptop, bag and keys and headed to her car.

Kate would have to wait for Sarah to get the information from Rupert before she jumped to any more conclusions. He would know more than anyone whether the woman's death was suspicious or not and her identity.

Sarah

Chapter 68

Sarah turned the car radio on to find the woman's death was the lead story on the news. There was some further commentary on the ages of the deceased woman's children and a statement from her husband, who was apparently away on a business trip, asking that their privacy be respected during such an emotional time. Sarah was not sure if she had a preconceived prejudice against the man, but she thought he sounded insincere. He seemed far too composed for a man who had just lost his wife and two children.

Sarah called Rupert. He answered on the second ring, "To what do I owe this pleasure, Sarah?"

"Hi Rupert, I was calling to ask about the woman and children found deceased in their home in Vaucluse, this morning."

"Was she someone you knew?" Rupert asked in a concerned tone.

"No, she wasn't officially, but Kate just told me that a woman fitting her description made an appointment about a week ago and then had to cancel."

"Sarah, I don't know a lot at this stage, but I'm told it does look like an accident and they all died in their sleep. At this stage it looks as though there was a gas leak from a fridge in the kitchen. It was a huge commercial style glass door fridge with its own gas system, which had become faulty. Apparently, they only recently moved into the home and because the fridge had been left unused for some time, the gas leak had gone undetected."

Sarah was listening and processing what Rupert was saying without comment.

"Are you still there?"

"Yes, I'm here. I don't know. I have no reason to say this, but really, it sounds a little odd."

Rupert made no comment on Sarah's remark but added, "Well the husband is usually one of the first people interviewed by the police, as you know, but he was apparently away on business and is on his way back now. If I hear anything else on the grapevine, I'll let you know."

"Thanks Rupert. I really appreciate it. Any chance you know her name?"

"It hasn't been released to the media yet, but her name is Jane Elliott."

Rupert heard Sarah gasp and asked, "So it was your lady?" "Yes," she said.

Sarah pulled into the car park under her building and caught the lift to her offices. The doors opened, and Sarah strode out. As soon as she arrived in her office, through her private entry Kate came in with her iPad and showed Sarah the leading story.

Daily Newspaper

A Mother and two children found dead by a family friend at their home in Sydney's exclusive Eastern suburbs.

The bodies of a forty- year- old- woman and her two children were found in their eastern suburbs home by the cleaner yesterday morning. The woman's husband had been away on business and was returning today after being notified by police. Neighbour's were gathering at the house to pay their respects.

They described the deceased as being a quiet but friendly woman who was happily married and a doting mother who adored her daughters. The little girls were described as sweet, shy and polite. Police say there are no suspicious circumstances at this stage, but that they are continuing with their enquiries. Police have stated that it appears that the cause of the deaths was a technical issue with a gas leak at the home. The woman had been alone with her children at the Vaucluse property at the time.

***

After reading the article, Sarah began to think that Kate's concern was well founded. She looked up at Kate and said, "I can see what you mean, Kate. If the couple had been happily married, why would the wife have been asked to sign a financial agreement recently?"

Kate was relieved that Sarah could now see she was not overreacting. She nodded agreement and said, "It doesn't make sense. I could feel her confusion over the phone, Sarah. She knew something wasn't quite right."

"I rang Rupert and he confirmed the woman's name was Jane Elliott."

Kate sighed. She felt a real sadness for the woman. "I just feel I could have or should have done more for her than I did. I know that's crazy because I didn't even know her but that's how I feel."

"I'm sorry Kate."

Kate nodded at Sarah. She knew she understood. "Thank you. I'll go back to work now. I've done all I can and that makes me feel better somehow."

Sarah sat in her office going over what she had said in her radio interview on financial agreements. She hoped that she had not created any issues for this woman by imparting the information that she had in that segment. Sarah did not want to discuss it with Kate, but she had had a case, earlier in her career, where a husband killed his wife after Sarah had given him advice about what she would be entitled to in their property settlement. The man had obtained criminal law advice and worked out he would get about four to seven years in jail for murdering his wife whereas it would take him more than fifteen years to make back the assets he would have to give his wife in the divorce. He killed her because it was more convenient financially for him. In that case, the husband almost got away with the murder after he dumped her body in the harbour and tied it down with concrete blocks. Unfortunately for him, he dumped her where a local dive school went and the body was discovered within days. Sarah was subpoenaed to give evidence in the case and it was an experience that took her many years to get over. She hoped that she and Kate were wrong about this case, but the more she thought about it, the worse she felt.

Brett

Chapter 69

Brett and Lisa were having a late champagne breakfast on the terrace of the Villa when Brett got the call from the police about Jane and the girls. He was feeling very hung over after having had a long romantic dinner with several bottles of wine and then spending the rest of the night and most of the morning devouring Lisa's voluptuous body. He stood up and walked away from the table when he took the call, pacing up and down the room as the police informed him of what had happened.

Lisa was watching him and noticed his face change as he was talking on the phone. Whatever he was talking about, he was pleased with the result, so she knew it was nothing to do with the office. His time there was about to come to an end now that she had given the partners more than enough material for them to sever Brett from the partnership, effective immediately.

Lisa poured herself another glass of French champagne and while finishing her omelette, she thought about how much she had enjoyed this job. Brett had been fun to be with and he was great in bed. She was going to miss him, but a job was job and this one was over. She looked up and wondered what was taking Brett so long, when he appeared on the terrace.

"Sorry about that, darling," he said as he leaned over to kiss her and then grab his champagne. He threw it down in one gulp. "I needed that. That was a heavy phone call", he fell into the chair beside her.

"Brett are you going to tell me what it was about?"

Brett stared straight ahead and said, as though he could not believe it, "Jane and the girls were just found dead at home by the cleaner. The police have apparently been trying to call me for a couple of hours and it's now all over the news."

Lisa gasped, "Oh no, your family are dead?"

Brett chastised himself during the phone call from the police for having forgotten to cancel the cleaner. He had hoped that Jane and the girls would not be found for a couple of days so that he and Lisa could finish their holiday together before their bodies were found.

Although he appeared to be shocked and upset, Lisa had the feeling that Brett was pleased with the news.

Brett then went on, "Apparently they were gassed in their sleep by the refrigerator in the kitchen. It was faulty."

Lisa let out a long sigh and she felt a wave of nausea overcome her. She closed her eyes and leaned forward onto the table, resting her head on her arms.

"Are you okay, what's wrong?" Brett asked.

Lisa raised her head and spat out, "What's wrong? Your wife and kids died while I'm here with you at a resort. That's what wrong!"

Brett knelt on the ground and put one hand on Lisa's leg and with the other, he stroked her cheek. He said, "Darling, this is nothing to do with us; it was an accident. As bad as it is, it means we are free to be together with no complications. Don't you see that?"

Even though Lisa knew Brett was a terrible husband, she had not anticipated any of this. She knew she had to get herself out of there before she told him what she thought of him and blew her gig.

"You need to go back now, right?" she said.

Brett smiled. "Yes, I do. I've just booked us on the next flight back. We have to leave the hotel in half an hour to catch the 1 p.m. flight."

Lisa was relieved to hear she could leave soon. She stood up and said, "I'll go have a quick shower and pack then."

Brett thought she was upset about the end to their trip. He said, "I'm sorry honey, I know this is awful. You do that and I will get through some calls I have to make."

Lisa picked up her mobile phone and once she was safely locked in the bathroom she sent a text to both Ian and Tim, Brett's partners. "Did you hear about Jane and the girls dying in their home overnight? Apparently gassed by a leaking fridge? I heard Brett talking to some guy on his mobile last night about 'fixing the fridge' at the house. We are booked on the 1 p.m. flight back to Sydney."

After she sent the message, she deleted it, as was her usual practice.

Brett

Chapter 70

The flight back from Hamilton Island had been on time. Under the circumstances, Brett and Lisa agreed that they should fly commercial and not take the company's private plane. They agreed to sit separately and leave the plane separately, just in case any media were waiting at the airport. Brett was the first person off the plane. He headed straight to the baggage carousel without looking back for Lisa. As he waited for his luggage, he was surprised to see his partners, Tim and Ian, walking towards him but greeted them happily, forgetting to play the role of the sad and shocked husband that he had put on for Lisa. "Hey guys, what are you doing here?"

Ian was the first to speak. "We heard the news about Jane and the girls and thought we should be here for you mate." Brett, realised he had dropped his guard. He was trying to regain his composure when he felt a hand on his shoulder and saw Lisa standing next to him with her bag. Ian and Tim were staring at him with a "Please explain" look. Before he could say anything two policemen walked up. Ian indicated Brett to the policemen and said, "That's him." Brett was confused and asked Ian. "What's this about?"

Ian remained silent, but one of the police officers said, "You can come with us voluntarily or we can arrest you, Brett. Which one will it be?"

"Are you the officer who called me this morning and asked me to come in and see you about my wife and daughters?"

"It's most certainly about your wife and daughters. We now know what happened and it was no accident. Lisa informed Ian and Tim about your phone call to your friend Adrian Cooper and he's already at the station."

Brett had forgotten that his mobile was a work phone and his office had access to all his phone records. He looked nervous and his gaze darted from Lisa to Ian and Tim. Seeing only disdain on their faces, his shoulders dropped. He said in a resigned tone, "I want to call my lawyer." The officers led him towards the police car waiting at the exit of the airport terminal.

Ian, Tim and Lisa were subdued in the car as they followed the police to the police station. The police had already taken Ian's and Tim's statements but now they needed Lisa's. Their plan to find a way to throw Brett out of the partnership had led to them exposing Brett's involvement in the murder of his wife and daughters. They all lamented that they had not had any idea he could do something like this and how bad they felt about it. Lisa was taking it the worst, but that was understandable as she had become intimate with the man. The only good result had been that in uncovering Brett's deviousness, they had also found the "handyman" who had been asked to tamper with the fridge. Both had now been arrested upon evidence that they would find impossible to refute. The police had Brett's phone records and a confession from the guy he had hired to tamper with the gas line to the fridge.

Sarah

Chapter 71

It was the third week into the trial at the District Court of the Police v Shaw regarding the charges relating to Jessica. Sarah had been extremely surprised when she was served with a subpoena by Anthony's legal team to appear as a witness. The police prosecutor was unable to shed any further light on it either, which concerned her.

At the court it was business as usual with crowds of lawyers, barristers, police and the general public making their way through security. It was a strange day for Sarah. Instead of being in the court room, sitting behind the bar table, she was outside the court room waiting to be called in. She was feeling vulnerable, which she did not enjoy. *Yet another experience she could now relate to with her clients*, she thought. The court officer called out Sarah's name and then escorted her to be sworn in. As Sarah sat in the stand, she tried to read the faces of the members of the jury, which she observed was made up of seven women and five men. They were all looking at her trying to do the same thing. The jury had the advantage over Sarah though, as they had been sitting in on this case for three weeks now. She could see they were comfortable with their role; all of them had notepads in their laps and pens in their hands. She could already tell which one of them would be the foreman; the efficient, professional looking fifty-something woman in the front row, at the far end, dressed in a suit. She would dominate all jury discussions and try to convince the other jury members of her views. She was most likely in a secretarial or public relations role, Sarah thought, definitely wanting to milk her new-found importance for all it was worth.

After she was sworn in, the defence counsel stood up to ask Sarah her first question. "Ms Walters, you are a lawyer who practices mainly in the area of family law, aren't you?"

"Yes, I am."

"You are a very well-known and successful family law lawyer, aren't you Ms Walters? In fact, you are a media identity known as a legal expert and commentator in the field of family law."

The prosecutor objected. "Is that your question, Mr Thomas?"

"Ms Walters, your work in the media involves commenting on family law in news and current affairs programmes, doesn't it? Such as your article yesterday about the family law case involving grandparents applying for the right to see their grandchildren after their father went to jail and, oh yes, my favourite, the couple who spent $700,000.00 in legal fees fighting over who got the best sheep in their divorce."

"Yes, Mr Thomas that's correct. I comment for the newspapers, on radio and on television about family law matters and I also provide legal advice."

"Anne Shaw, the mother of the victim came to see you, Ms Walters, to obtain legal advice in relation to her separation from the defendant?"

The prosecutor stood up before Sarah could answer. "For the court record your Honour, Ms Shaw has waived her claim of privilege in relation to the legal advice received from Ms Walters. Ms Shaw has no objection to the court hearing the evidence of her family law lawyer in response to this question."

"Thank you," replied the defence counsel, looking extremely surprised with the waiver of privilege by Anne. He looked like the cat that was about to pounce on and swallow the canary.

Sarah was shocked by the waiver as well, as no one had informed her this was the case, but obviously it had been discussed by Anne and the prosecutor. By waiving her legal privilege, Anne had just given her consent for Sarah to disclose everything relating to her case in court when questioned.

"Ms Walters as you now have no issues with legal privilege being claimed over your advice to Ms Shaw, could you please tell the court why Ms Shaw sought your advice and the advice you gave her in her case against the defendant."

"Ms Shaw came to me for legal advice after she and her daughter had been interviewed by the police regarding the sexual abuse of her daughter by the defendant."

The barrister smiled at Sarah with a smug look as though he had somehow caught her out. "Why did she choose to go and see you, Miss Walters? Don't you practise only in the field of family law? Oh yes, and let's not forget you are a very expensive lawyer and one that is very hard to get an urgent appointment with. Yet Ms Shaw managed to get in to see you the next day?"

As the barrister delivered the question, he turned to look at the jury and smiled. He turned back to Sarah and continued the questioning before she could answer. "Why would she be attending the offices of a very well- known family law lawyer at this very stressful time when her daughter had been allegedly sexually assaulted? Odd way of thinking, don't you think?"

The prosecutor objected, "Asking for a psychological opinion, your Honour, is not within the witness's expertise."

Sarah felt the jury's eyes upon her and she was annoyed that the barrister had got their attention with his outrageous line of questioning.

Sarah looked straight at the jury when she replied. "I had previously acted for Anne in her divorce from her former husband. Anne's sister, whom I also knew, called my office to make an appointment for Anne to see me urgently as she needed advice."

The barrister looked bemused, he smiled again at the jury and said to Sarah, "I see. So, it had nothing to do with coming to see you because you're a very successful and high profile family law lawyer, but just because it was a friend in need? Is that what you are trying to say, Ms Walters?"

The jury looked from the barrister to Sarah.

"Anne was a former client who needed legal assistance. It was quite normal for her to consider me in this situation."

The barrister frowned and spread his hands on the bar table. He looked at Sarah and asked in a much sterner voice, "Isn't it the case, Ms Walters, because you knew Ms Shaw and her sister, that you and Ms Shaw colluded in a plan to allege that the defendant sexually abused her daughter so that she could place pressure on him to obtain a multimillion-dollar property settlement, disguised as a divorce property settlement?"

"No, that is not the case, Mr Thomas." Sarah told herself, *Keep the answer short. That's what you always tell your clients to do - just answer the question. Nothing more, nothing less.* Sarah realised just how hard it was.

"Isn't it the case, Ms Walters, that not only Ms Shaw but also her daughter, Jessica, attended your offices?"

"Yes, Jessica came with Anne, as well as Elizabeth, Anne's sister, to the first appointment."

"Could you tell the court why she would have taken her daughter to see you, unless her daughter was also getting, what did you say again? Oh, yes, legal advice?"

Sarah took a deep breath. She looked at the jury. Some stared back at her and others looked down at the pads of paper and pens in their hands poised to note down her response. Sarah looked out into the body of the court room and saw Anne sitting at the back. Her answer to the barrister's overloaded question was clear and deliberate.

"Mr Thomas, Ms Shaw attended my offices once with Jessica. That was Anne's first appointment and it was at a time when Anne didn't want to leave Jessica alone. Jessica didn't sit in the conference room with us but sat outside with my secretary."

The barrister raised his hands dramatically in the air and went on, "That sounds very touching. Now you have set the scene with these two distraught women, could you please tell the court what your advice to Ms Shaw was during this first conference? Could it have been anything to do with how much money she could get out of a property settlement with the defendant if she left him? Did you discuss how much more she could get if she accused him of say... sexually assaulting her daughter?"

The prosecutor stood up and objected, "Your Honour I have given Mr Thomas a lot of leeway here as Ms Walters is a lawyer and an officer of the court; however, this type of questioning is out of line. He needs to put the question to her and allow her to answer it. He must stop trying to answer the question for the witness."

The judge said, "Mr Thomas, I have to agree. Please only ask Ms Walters questions and allow her to answer the question. Ms Walters, please tell the court what advice you gave Ms Shaw."

Sarah turned to the judge, pleased that she could look at her whilst answering the question rather than the creep in front of her. "Your Honour, when Ms Shaw came into my office, she appeared shocked and shaken."

Thomas objected, "I asked what advice she gave her not how she looked, your Honour."

"Let her finish, Mr Thomas. I would like to know how Ms Shaw appeared during the conference with Ms Walters. Go on Ms Walters."

"Anne told me what had happened with Jessica and how Jessica had told the school psychologist what Anthony had done to her. During this time, she sat very still, frozen. She was strangely calm, speaking slowly, looking straight ahead. Clearly, as they could not go home, she said she and Jessica were staying with her sister. The detectives suggested to her that she should obtain urgent family law legal advice to ascertain her position regarding her rights to her home and personal possessions."

The barrister interjected, "So she wanted advice as to how much money she could get from a property settlement. That's the gist of it, isn't it? Not matter how nicely you try to wrap it up, it was all about the money she would get, wasn't it?"

He smiled at the jury, looking very pleased with himself, like he had unravelled the Da Vinci Code.

"No, Mr Thomas. She told me that it hadn't occurred to her to see me until after the detective told her she couldn't go home and recommended to her that she needed to get family law legal advice as to what her options were."

"Ms Walters, how innocently you try to portray this premeditated plan to accuse my client of sexually molesting your client's daughter in order to ransom my client to settle with his wife for far more than she deserved in a property settlement. She knew my client wanted to leave her and that she would no longer be living the life of a millionaire's wife. So, with your help, she devised this plan to get the most she could from the defendant, thinking he would pay it rather than have his reputation destroyed with the most disgusting accusations, and then have to go to trial and spend millions of dollars and years of his life to prove his innocence."

For the first time Sarah looked across at Anthony in the dock. She could see it would be very hard to convince the jury he had committed the abuse on Jessica. He just did not look like a paedophile; in fact, he looked like a shattered man.

Thomas was annoyed at the delay in Sarah's response and brought her to attention with a sharp summons, "Ms Walters!"

Sarah's reply was clinical, "Mr Thomas, I have never been accused of such conduct in my professional career of over twenty-five-years. I have never had a complaint to the Law Society by a client or opposing client or legal team. Your accusations are unwarranted, unfounded and offensive."

It was now Mr Thomas's turn to object to the judge.

"Your Honour, I object to Ms Walters's rant and seek it be struck from the record as unresponsive and that the jury be directed to disregard it."

"Mr Thomas, I must say that although I will request that the comment be struck from the record and direct the jury should dismiss it, I suggest you move on from that line of questioning."

The smile the judge shot Sarah made her feel so much better. "Thank you, your Honour, he said. If the court pleases. Now Ms Walters, what was the advice you gave Ms Shaw, and what advice did you give Jessica when they came together to see you?"

"Firstly, at no time did I give legal advice to Jessica. In that first conference, Mr Thomas, Jessica sat outside my office for most of the time I was speaking to her mother. I wanted to speak to Anne about what happened and what help she was seeking from me. Anne told me how she had received a call from the school psychologist and he had told her that Jessica was very upset, that Jessica had revealed to him the cause of her distress, which was why Anne needed to come to the school straight away."

Sarah looked up and could see the jury's' eyes upon her. She knew she had them now. "Anne told me that Jessica had told her what Anthony had done to her since she was thirteen- years- old." Tears stung Sarah's eyes as she recalled Anne's distress.

"Anne told me that she couldn't give me all the details at the time because she couldn't bring herself to say what Anthony had done, but that the police would be sending me the record of interview and I would see it there. She said that the police had told her she should see a family lawyer now that she couldn't go home, and they didn't think it safe for her and Jessica to approach Anthony now charges were about to be made."

Sarah stopped to draw breath and Thomas cut in, "That was all very touching, Ms Walters, but what was your advice, or didn't you give her any?"

"I asked her to give me the name and numbers of the detectives involved and told her I would get in touch with them and, after they had arrested Anthony, I would speak to Anthony's solicitor regarding making arrangements for her and Jessica. I told her that I would be able to assess quickly whether I could reach a sensible arrangement with Anthony's solicitor and I hoped that would be the case. If not, I would have to think about how we would run her case having regard to the criminal proceedings which were about to ensue."

Sarah noticed Thomas about to stand up, so she said quickly, "I'm not finished Mr Thomas," and he sat down, taken aback.

"I explained to Anne that criminal proceedings always took precedence over civil proceedings, so that her family law case would be adjourned until after the criminal case was heard. What I would have to do was try to get an interim arrangement for her and Jessica for somewhere to live and some maintenance in the meantime, pending the criminal hearing, until the cases were both heard. I told Anne that that could take anywhere from three to five years or even more unless the criminal proceedings could be expedited, which has been the case."

"And how did Anne take the news, Ms Walters, that she would have to wait a couple of years before she got her property settlement? Did she have any idea that she would have to wait for her several millions of dollars to come through from Anthony if she went this way?"

The crown prosecutor stood up and objected. The judge ordered that the comment be struck from the record.

"Mr Thomas, most of my clients wouldn't have expected it, I can confidently say. Anne really didn't seem to be taking much in and she appeared to be, as I said previously, in shock for most of the conference. Her sister decided it was time for them to leave and go home."

Thomas stood up, smirking.

"So, Ms Walters, can you tell us about the conversation with the police and whether Anthony's lawyers were 'reasonable', as you put it, in offering Anne and Jessica with somewhere nice to live and money to enjoy, while they were now accusing him of outrageous behaviour?"

The prosecutor immediately rose to her feet and objected, "That was out of line, Mr Thomas."

The judge then stood up and announced, "I note the time and we shall take the morning tea break now."

Sarah thought she saw the judge flash a sympathetic look in her direction as he was leaving. She was incredibly relieved for the break.

Sarah

Chapter 72

The court officer stood outside the court room and announced loudly that the court was about to recommence sitting. Sarah walked back into the court room and into the witness box, waiting for the judge to walk in. The jury were already seated and as the court officer announced the judge everyone stood up as she entered the room and then sat down. The officer declared the court in session.

Thomas stood up to ask his next question. "Ms Walters, prior to the break, you said that Ms Shaw and her daughter Jessica needed money and housing after Jessica made the allegations against the defendant. Is that correct?"

Sarah hid her exasperation and replied, "What I said was that, after Jessica disclosed to the counsellor what had happened to her, Ms Shaw and her daughter were in the position that they could not go back to their home. They had no funds without the assistance of the defendant, upon whom they financially relied. I said to you that this was an issue the police suggested I could assist them with."

"So, what you're saying is that they needed the defendant to financially support them?"

"Yes, that was the case, Mr Thomas, and he had a duty to do so."

"And isn't it the case, Ms Walters, that you then sought to negotiate a settlement with the defendant on behalf of your client for a family law settlement?"

"Mr Thomas, I commenced negotiations with the defendant and his legal team, on behalf of Ms Shaw, to expedite the criminal matter and the family law matter. My client's application was and still is for a property settlement. It includes a house and a cash amount to my client, which was more than reasonable given the length of the relationship, the contribution made by my client and the net worth of the assets of the marriage."

"That's an interesting way of looking at things isn't it? The net worth of the assets of the marriage. Ms Walters, your client had no assets at the commencement of the marriage, did she? She came into this marriage with her daughter and the clothes on their backs essentially, didn't she? My client had all the assets in his name, my client made all the income and my client provided all the financial security. That was the case, wasn't it?"

Sarah drew a deep breath. She was fuming and needed a moment to calm down as she could see where he was going with this.

Thomas was annoyed by the delay, so he stood up and prompted her, "Ms Walters, are you going to answer my question?"

"I am trying to work out which one to answer first, as there were several questions you asked me at once." Sarah noticed his face starting to flush.

"Ms Walters, you understood my questions, please answer them."

"Yes, Mr Thomas, your client brought most of the assets into the marriage. My client has never denied that, but that doesn't mean that she's not entitled to anything after a ten-year marriage, in which she contributed greatly in both financial and non-financial ways. The Family Court acknowledges that partners contribute in these ways to a relationship."

"Thank you, Ms Walters, but don't you think that her timing was interesting here? She knew that the defendant had told her that he was unhappy and they should separate."

Sarah felt the eyes of the jury piercing into her. It was a typical defence trick to suggest scenarios such as this, that Anthony was going to end the relationship to try and create some doubt in the jury's mind. She looked at the jury and all of them were staring right at her as though they were pleading with her to explain why she would do such a thing. She had been waiting for this moment and she was ready for it.

"To my knowledge there was no such conversation." The jury turned to look at Anthony. He sat in the dock, a handsome man, stylishly dressed, and he had such a gentle, hurt expression on his face. Sarah could see they were finding it difficult to picture him as the monster he was being made out to be.

"Your client thought she would get millions of dollars and she thought that my client would eventually cave in and give it to her. When he didn't, she didn't know what to do. She was stuck with having her daughter proceed with this fictional story and the criminal prosecution with the police."

Sarah shook her head before she said, "Mr Thomas, my family law files were produced on the first day of this hearing to the court. The file contains all my advice in my file notes and correspondence with my client."

Most members of the jury were taking notes. Some of them looked quite confused.

"Ms Walters, your client thought she'd get a quick settlement with a bonus for the sexual abuse allegation and it didn't work out how she wanted. That is the case, isn't it?"

"No, Mr Thomas. Absolutely not", Sarah replied.

"My client would not admit it because it wasn't true. It's that simple." Thomas then sat down and muttered, "No further questions for this witness."

It was the prosecutor's turn to question Sarah. She stood up and the jury looked straight at her, waiting to hear what she would ask Sarah.

"Ms Walters, you said that you advised Ms Shaw to consider a settlement proposal, if it could be achieved with Mr Shaw, that may be less than she would otherwise have achieved in the Family Court. Is that right?"

"Yes, I did."

"And that was because you were concerned that Mr Shaw may get rid of his assets while this criminal case was going on, is that right?"

"Yes, it is."

"I see from your notes that you gave Ms Shaw advice to withdraw all the funds from the parties' joint bank account in your first conference, didn't you?"

"Yes, I did. I was concerned Anthony would withdraw the funds if she didn't."

The prosecutor nodded and then asked, "And did he?"

"Anne could only bring herself to withdraw $10,000.00 of the $50,000.00 balance. The next day, after he was arrested, Anthony withdrew the $40,000.00 balance."

"Did he withdraw anything else from Ms Shaw?"

"Yes," Sarah replied. "Shortly thereafter, he had her car repossessed from her sister's home where she was residing. Anne believed the car was in her name as it was given to her as a birthday present, but she was informed by the man who came to collect it that it was leased by one of Anthony's companies."

"Ms Walters, can you tell the court what Ms Shaw's prospects are in her family law case when it goes to court, after this case is finalised?"

Sarah felt her shoulders slump and realised the answer to this question always depressed her.

"It is very unfortunate, but the reality is that Ms Shaw will not get much, if anything at all. Mr Shaw has either sold or transferred all his assets, except his superannuation, so there is not much the court can award Ms Shaw at this time."

"Fiona looked down at the bar table, found a piece of paper and held it up for the court to see.

"Ms Walters, I am looking at a list of Mr Shaw's assets that I took from your file, which you produced to the court under subpoena from Mr Shaw's lawyers. I can see from that list of assets that at the time Anthony and Anne separated, the asset pool was valued at about $17 million. Is that correct?"

"Yes, it is."

Fiona went on; "And it's all gone?"

"His accountant has said that everything had been sold and used to pay his bills, expenses and legal fees except his superannuation, which they were now trying to access to pay the rest of legal fees and other expenses."

Fiona paused and walked up to the witness box to ask Sarah, "So, what you're saying is that because Jessica and Anne proceeded with this criminal hearing against Mr Shaw, Anne faces the prospect of getting nothing from her property settlement, rather than an order for millions of dollars, had this criminal matter not existed?"

"Yes, that is the case."

"And how did Anne feel about this when she found out?"

"We had discussed this risk from very start, as I stated earlier. Anne said the most important thing was for justice to be done and they were not going to compromise unless Anthony admitted what he had done to Jessica, even if that meant she lost whatever prospect of a financial settlement she might have."

Fiona walked back to the bar table. She and Sarah could both see the jury were now totally focused on what Sarah had said. Fiona stood behind the bar table and looked as though she had finished, but then she picked up another piece of paper on the table and looked up.

"So, Ms Walters you believed the allegations that Jessica made against Mr Shaw were true?"

Thomas stood up and shouted, "I object, your Honour. This witness is not a psychiatrist and her opinion is irrelevant."

The judge turned to Fiona and asked, "Why should we allow Ms Walters' evidence in this regard?"

"Your Honour, Ms Walters has been questioned on her legal ethics by the defence team. This matter relates to Ms Shaw's ethics and why she was conducting the matter. It goes to the heart of the defence team's allegations against Ms Walters."

The judge ruled, "I allow the question, Mr Thomas. Go on Ms Walters and answer the question."

"Yes, I did. I believed Anne and Jessica when they first came in to see me. I have observed both of them over the last few months and I have never had any cause to doubt them. I heard the recording of the phone call between Anthony and Jessica, that was admitted into evidence, where he stated what he had done to her. I also saw that the DNA came back positive for Anthony on the photograph of Jessica that he had said he used to masturbate over. I was convinced by the facts and evidence I had been presented with that he was guilty."

"I have no further questions of this witness, your Honour," Fiona said. She had completed her case.

The judge turned to Sarah and said, "Thank you for attending today, Ms Walters. The court very much appreciates your time. Mr Thomas, are there any further witnesses on behalf of the defence?"

"No, your Honour."

"In that case, we will now break for the day and we will hear closing arguments starting tomorrow morning. Good afternoon."

The judge stood up as did the rest of the court. Fiona collected her files and walked over towards Sarah, who was stepping down from the witness box.

"I just wanted to explain to you what's going to happen now in the trial. I couldn't up until now, as you were yet to give evidence and that was very frustrating. We will both deliver our closing arguments tomorrow to the jury and then the jury will be excused to consider its verdict. We never know how long this will take but having regard to the fact this has been a six- week trial, we would expect that they will take at least three days if not longer to make a decision."

"How did Jessica go in the witness box, Fiona? I know no one could tell me before I gave evidence, but I've been worried as no one has even given any hints. Was she okay? Did you think that the jury believed her?"

"Sarah, Jessica was so brave, she was amazing. She recounted her version of events clearly and accurately and in accordance with the statements she made to the police. When Anthony's barrister tried to attack her sexual experiences and promiscuity, she was resolute in her responses. It was Anthony's jealousy that led to him being so controlling over her going out with other kids and particularly when she was a teenager, because he didn't want her having any experiences with anyone else. It was when Jessica said she needed a date for the school formal that trouble started. Anthony forbade Jessica to go. Anne thought Anthony was being sweetly overprotective and had laughed it all off until she realised that he was serious about not letting Jessica go. It was arguments over the date and the formal that led Jessica's friends to encourage her to speak to the school counsellor, to whom she eventually revealed the source of Anthony's jealousy."

"Tell me", asked Sarah, "Did the phone recording Jessica made on her mobile between her and Anthony get admitted into evidence?"

"Yes, it did. The defence tried as hard as they could to keep it out, but we were determined to press for it to stay in evidence. When Jessica was cross-examined about her motives in getting Anthony on the phone and making the recording of his confession, she was beyond impeachable. I will never forget her face when she replied to the defence barrister when he asked her why she went ahead with it, when it was illegal to do so. Jessica answered, "I knew that I may not be able to use the recording in court, but I needed it for my own sanity. I needed to hear him confess to me that he knew that what he did to me was wrong, when for all those years he had been telling me it was right.' There wasn't a member of the jury who didn't take notes while listening to the recording, which was a very good sign for us."

Sarah suddenly saw that Fiona had become emotional for the first time she had known her. She had tears in her eyes and before Sarah knew it, she had tears in her eyes too.

Anthony

Chapter 73

It had been three days since the jury had gone out to consider their verdict. Each day was becoming more unbearable. Anthony's mind raced with possible reasons for the delay. His lawyers were telling him that it was good news as it meant the jurors were not yet convinced of his guilt. He was not so sure.

Anthony wanted to go and see Peter in hospital as soon as he had found out he had survived the attack, but preparation for the trial had kept him busier than he thought he would be over the last few months. To keep himself sane, he had kept track of Peter's recovery and found out he was currently back in hospital. Peter's over helpful PA always answered Anthony's enquiries when he called, pretending to be a former concerned client. Apparently, Peter was improving with therapy and treatment, but had just gone into hospital for more knee surgery. Anthony wondered if Peter would be touched by his concern when his secretary eventually told him about Anthony's constant enquiries.

Anthony checked with his lawyers, who confirmed that the jury was still out. He decided the timing was right to pay a visit to Peter. He could not wait to see Peter's reaction when he saw him walk into his hospital room; where Anthony had placed him. Arriving at the hospital, Anthony wondered who else might be with Peter. He knew Peter had been transferred into rehabilitation, so getting his room number would not be too difficult. Anthony walked into reception with a large multiple Phalaenopsis orchid arrangement and the nurses were swooning over it.

The head nurse was exclaiming about how gorgeous the plant was, so when Anthony asked to see Peter, she smiled and informed him, "He's doing very well. He's in Room 166."

As he went up in the lift, Anthony felt a mix of excitement and pure revenge. Finally, the tables were turned, and Peter was the one who was suffering. He turned right on Peter's floor and walked along the corridor, the heels of his elegant English brogues clicking smartly on the polished floor. Anthony arrived at the door of Room 166. It was partially open and he peered in. Anthony saw Peter. He was talking to a woman, who was clearly not nursing staff. Anthony knocked and walked in. The woman looked up at him and asked, with a degree of reservation in her voice, "Can I help you?"

Peter turned his head towards Anthony. The light of recognition shone in Peter's eyes. He managed a quiet but audible, "Anthony." "You know him, Peter?" the woman asked him, making sure he was safe.

"Of course, he does!" Anthony said, smiling as he crossed the floor to Peter's bedside. He leaned over Peter and whispered in his ear, "I enjoyed kicking the shit out of you and there is more of it to come." The look in Peter's eyes changed to fear.

Kim was uncertain what was going on. She stood up to intervene and introduce herself. "I'm Kim. Peter's PA."

Anthony was charming, he took her hand and said, "My name's Anthony. Peter and I are old friends. Aren't we, Peter?"

Peter's face was a study in shock and confusion and Anthony could see that Kim was unsettled by Anthony's effect on him. Kim had remained standing and she stepped closer to Peter. She spoke politely to Anthony, "Peter's doing very well, considering what he's been through, but he still has a long way to go before he fully recovers. Look, thank you for coming in, but he really needs to rest now."

Anthony turned his gaze on Peter, who was trying to remain calm. Anthony's presence was making him anxious. His face was flushed, and he was beginning to perspire on his forehead.

"I won't stay then Peter, because Kim says I shouldn't, but I would have liked to."

Anthony brushed Peter's arm as he placed the orchid arrangement on the bedside table. He said in his kindest voice, "I hope I can come back and see you soon. We have so much to catch up on, Peter. You know that our lives have become quite intertwined without us even knowing it. Your ex-wife is not only acting against me for my ex-wife in our divorce, but she has also been called as a witness in my criminal trial for allegations brought by my stepdaughter against me for sexual abuse."

Confusion and exhaustion combined in Peter's eyes at Anthony's words. He suddenly realised that Anthony was the ex-husband of their yoga teacher's sister and the accused paedophile in the court case Sarah had been called as a witness in.

At that moment, Sarah walked into the room. Her timing could not have been more perfect, in Anthony's view.

Sarah was surprised to find Anthony in Peter's hospital room and she said, "What are you doing here, Anthony?"

Anthony answered Sarah, at the same time as giving Peter a light touch on the arm, "Peter and I are old friends, Sarah. We knew each other when I was a kid." Anthony gave a meaningful look at Peter.

Sarah said in a controlled voice, "You need to leave, Anthony, right now."

Anthony was all smiles and manners, as he said, "Of course, Sarah. I was just about to when you walked in, wasn't I, Peter and Kim? I know Peter will fill you in on how we know each other. It goes back a long time, but the impact on my life has lasted forever and Peter will, I'm sure, tell you why."

Peter's eyes searched Sarah's face, trying to read her reaction, then he turned to Anthony, trying to work out what he was intending to do. He looked extremely confused to Anthony, beyond the effects of medication.

Anthony stepped over to the door but stopped to say, as if a mere afterthought, "If you can't remember it all, Peter, don't worry. I'll be able to fill Sarah in because there's nothing I've forgotten. Everything that we ever did together I remember in exact detail." Anthony left the three inhabitants of the hospital room in a state of dismay and uncertainty.

Unsettled by the lightning flashes of an impending storm, Peter asked Kim to draw the blinds. Kim hoped Sarah would not stay too long. It was never easy for her to observe the easy interaction between Sarah and Peter and it was clear for all to see that Peter was still in love with her.

Sarah

Chapter 74

Sarah was shocked to see Anthony in Peter's room and did not quite know what to make of it all. She wondered how he could possibly know Peter and why Peter did not tell her he knew Anthony. Peter called out her name as she continued to stare at the door, deep in her thoughts.

"Sarah! Talk to me!"

Her professional reputation as well as her trust in Peter were on the line. Sarah turned and grilled her ex-husband, "Do you know Anthony? Is it true you have known him since you were kids? You knew about the allegations against him relating to my client's daughter and you didn't tell me you knew him?"

Peter pleaded, "Sarah, I didn't realise it was the same guy that I knew. I hadn't seen Anthony since he was a kid. Like you, I didn't know he was the person that you've been in court against until a minute ago. Of course, I would have told you, had I known."

Sarah continued to search for an explanation. "Peter, why was he here? How did he know you were here?"

"I don't know, Sarah. Like I said, I haven't seen him for thirty years. I don't know why he would even be interested in seeing me."

Sarah was doubtful. "Well, he seems very interested in getting back in touch and for me to know about your past."

At Sarah's last words, the penny dropped for Peter and he realised what Anthony was up to. Peter was worried. Sarah registered the panic on his face and was sharp with him, "What aren't you telling me Peter?"

Peter recalled his habitual advice to his clients, if questioned by the police without him, "Deny, deny, deny, and say you have no recollection," until he arrived. The only problem was that he knew Sarah knew he was buying time right now.

Peter stuttered with nerves, "Sarah, I really can't, I can't recall much now, except I knew him when he was a kid."

Kim, who, unlike her, had been quiet until then, said, "The doctor told me you would feel groggy for a while."

Sarah knew Peter was stalling, and Kim was just trying to help him, but having regard to his condition, she could not press it any further right now. With an audible, impatient sigh, she relented and said, "Okay, Peter. Let's leave this for now. But when you're feeling better, I want to know everything about Anthony."

Peter agreed, "Of course," but the relief in his voice was obvious. Sarah stood up, gathering her bag and coat and said, "I'll get back to the office now. When you're up to it, let me know and I'll bring Chloe in. She has been making a special card for you and is looking forward to seeing you."

Peter's voice was full of emotion as he said, "I can't wait to see her. Please bring in Chloe as soon as it suits you both."

Sarah bent her head to kiss Peter goodbye and in a softer voice, reassured him, "You look pretty good, considering! I'll bring Chloe in on the weekend, so she can spend a couple of hours with you. I know once she sees you she'll want to stay a while. I'll call you tomorrow and see how you're feeling."

Sarah left the room feeling very uneasy. She wondered what Peter could be hiding. He had never been able to lie, and he was clearly lying when he said he could not remember much about Anthony. Her phone rang. It was Kate calling to say that the jury had returned, "I just got the call from Fiona and the jury are back. They've reached a decision. She wanted you to know in case you want to be there when it's handed down. The court is resuming in an hour."

"Thanks Kate. I'll go to the court from here."

Anthony

Chapter 75

The courtroom was full. Not a spare seat in the house and there were rows of people standing at the back. The case had attracted a lot of media interest over the trial. Anthony, had his supporters there, including his sister, who did not believe he was guilty of the accusations.

The court staff and Anthony were now all seated. Anthony looked calm and relaxed, he even smiled in the direction of his family. He had the self-possession of someone who was certain he would be leaving the room a free man. The court officer announced the arrival of the judge and everyone stood. The jury filed into the room and sat down, their faces a picture of controlled inscrutability.

The rest of the people in the court sat down and a strange, eerie silence reigned over the court room until the judge said, "Will the accused please stand up."

The prosecutor read out the charges, her voice resounding around the room. The judge asked the jury foreperson for the verdict. The foreperson rose from her seat, and it was the woman Sarah had guessed it would be. She unfolded the piece of paper in her hands and stared at Anthony as she pronounced the words. "Guilty on all charges."

Anthony stared straight back at the jury as though in disbelief, before turning his gaze towards his legal team.

The judge thanked the jury and dismissed them. The judge then announced to the defence team that she had made her decision in relation to sentencing, so there would be no need for them to apply for bail pending sentencing. She sentenced Anthony to eleven years, nine being non-parole, due mainly to the fact that he had shown no remorse over his actions. The judge found that Anthony was likely to recommit and that his lack of remorse was a contributing factor to that finding.

Anthony retained his composure throughout the ordeal. He sat without moving, as though staring into space, but his eyes were fixated on the judge. The members of Anthony's family were trying to control their emotions, but most were crying. His mother was distraught and was helped from the court.

Sarah could not help but stare at Anthony and wondered what was going on in his head. Had he expected this decision, or had he been overconfident in his defence, that he was just misunderstood? Sarah looked over to Fiona, caught her eye and smiled. She could see the relief on her face and she nodded to her in professional acknowledgment. This had been a hard fought case with high stakes and the verdict must have been a relief. A relief that Jessica's pain had not been in vain and that a victim had been believed and a criminal punished. *It didn't always go that way*, thought Sarah.

The court officers and police surrounded Anthony in the process of leading him out of the courtroom and off to jail. As Anthony stepped out of the box, he looked around the room for the first time since he entered court that day. His eyes locked with the prosecutor. He capitulated and turned away, but then he made eye contact with Sarah. She saw a dark fury in his eyes, then, because she held his gaze, he gestured her with his hand for her to come closer. Unable to control her desire to know what he wanted to say to her, Sarah leaned over to him as he was walked past her towards the exit.

Anthony grabbed her arm and said with a mix of pain and anger, "So did Peter tell you about us, Sarah? Did he tell what he did to me when I was Jessica's age? How he pretended to be my friend and how he gave me drugs so that he could have sex with me?"

Anthony let go of Sarah's arm and moved on towards the exit, being pressed forward by the police, but he turned back for a second before he walked out of the door to look at Sarah, enjoying look of shock on her face.

He continued with his attack, shouting over his shoulder, "That's why I'm like this. Peter did this to me and showed me what it was like. It's his fault I'm here. Tell Peter I will make him pay for it. Now that I know where he is, I will make him pay!"

Anthony's voice trailed off in a muffled screech as he disappeared in a rush of police and court officers. Sarah was left to process what he had just said. She flinched at the slight pressure of a hand placed on her shoulder, but it was the prosecutor, Fiona. "Did you hear what he said?" Sarah sought confirmation from her friend and colleague.

"Yes, I did," Fiona replied. She was dismayed at what she had just witnessed.

"Do you think it's true or is he just trying to get revenge because of my evidence?" Sarah asked, a slight tremor in her voice.

Fiona was unsure but said, "I suppose anything is possible, Sarah, but I can't imagine Peter doing anything like that." She assured Sarah that everything would work out.

They both turned to leave the court room when Sarah felt her phone buzzing in her jacket pocket. She waved Fiona on and took the call, which was from Kate, her secretary, who said she had just heard about the verdict and knew they must all be so relieved.

Kate said she had another reason for the call, "Sarah, a parcel was just delivered to the office marked 'personal and confidential' and 'urgent'. I wasn't expecting anything for you and just wondered if you were?"

"No, I wasn't. I'm just leaving the court and was going to head to dinner with Fiona, Anne and Jessica. Just open it and I'll hold on. I'm exhausted and need a drink. I don't really want to go back into the office, if I don't need to today."

Sarah heard a large intake of breath at the other end of the line. Kate said, "Sarah, you need to look at this. It's from Anthony and it's a long letter with photos. I wouldn't say anything to Anne or Jessica right now, because it mentions them."

Sarah felt a wave of nausea overtake her as she replied, "I am on my way back now."

Sarah

Chapter 76

Sarah's nausea had barely dissipated in the ten minutes it took her to reach the office. Kate had placed the letter and photos on Sarah's desk, with the exception of one photo that she was holding close to her face and studying hard.

She barely acknowledged Sarah's arrival before saying in a flat tone, "It looks like it's Peter to me. There are photos of him with Anthony as kids. You need to read this letter."

Sarah sat down and picked up the photos one by one. They were definitely of Peter and she recognised Anthony as well. They had clearly known each other very well. There was also a girl in a couple of the photos that Sarah did not recognise. She picked up the letter and started to read it.

Sarah,

If you have received this letter, I am on my way to jail. I am sorry to have to tell you my story this way. I would have loved another meeting with you, but you need to know the truth. It affects you as well as Peter, the father of your daughter. If I had not gone to jail I would have done this differently. You need to know what he did to me and the kind of man he really is. I am writing down in this letter, all that I can recall right now but I am sure more memories will come to me in the isolation of my jail cell over the next few years. I will continue to write to you as the memories return. For many years, I buried this in my head and it was only when I bumped into Peter nearly a year ago that my hatred for Peter started to churn in my mind again. When I saw Peter at the hospital, I asked him to tell you everything.

I knew he wouldn't, and I had already started to prepare this letter for you weeks ago. He is a weak and selfish man, Sarah, who ruined my life, which caused me to ruin Jessica's. Peter created the monster that I am. The following pages contain details of as much of my time with Peter that I remember. They detail how Peter and I met through my sister, and how he used her as an excuse to stay over at our house. He gave me alcohol and drugs, sexually abused me at night, while my parents thought he was being a nice boyfriend to my sister and helping to look after her little brother. I have included my sister's phone number, so you can talk to her. I only confided in her after I was charged about what really happened. She thinks I should tell the police, but I see no point to that. Anyway, I have years to think about what I can do about it. I would love to hear your thoughts on this. You will know where to find me if you wish to discuss this further with me.

Regards,
Anthony

Sarah

Chapter 77

After reading Anthony's letter, Sarah knew why he had become the way he was. She knew that Peter had been lying when he had told her at the hospital he had no idea what Anthony was talking about. When she thought of Peter's behaviour over the years, Anthony's letter made more sense to her. She had not seen it that way up until now, but it was beginning to make sense. Sarah realised that Peter's lack of sexual appetite, which she had thought of as gentlemanly and caring, was a lack of female sexual interest. His constant assertions that he was desperate to be "part of a family" were because he needed a front.

How she would deal with this information as far as Chloe was concerned was something that Sarah could not cope with now. She knew how much Chloe loved her father and it would devastate her not to see him. However, the idea of allowing Chloe to be alone with her father, now she had his history, was beyond Sarah's comprehension.

Sarah realised she had to confront Peter with Anthony's accusations. She picked up the phone and called him. Peter sounded pleased to hear from her, "Hi Sarah, nice to hear from you," he said, as though nothing had happened earlier at the hospital.

Sara, ignored Peter's greeting and got straight to the point in a rapid outline of his betrayal. "Peter, you lied to me at the hospital about Anthony. I know what happened between you two.

Anthony has sent me photos, together with a letter. Don't bother denying it. Think about what you have done to Chloe and to me, and then think some more. After you decide to tell me the truth, call me back so we can work out how we handle this, as far as Chloe is concerned."

Peter was non-responsive at the other end, so Sarah continued, "I am going to get the advice of a child psychiatrist, in the interim."

Peter was taken off guard and his brain was still absorbing the fallout from Anthony's letter.

Getting only Peter's continued silence as a response, Sarah said firmly before she hung up, "I will wait for your call, Peter." Kate appeared in Sarah's office with two glasses of wine.

She handed one to Sarah and sat down, taking a large gulp. Confident that the alcohol would have its sedating effect, Kate asked, "Do you have any idea what you're going to do, Sarah?"

Sarah took a deep breath and exhaled loudly, as though expelling the worries of the world, "I can't really explain how I feel or how it's affecting me. I mean, it's all so shocking and I feel as though I can't breathe. But in a strange way, there's a sense of relief, because it explains so much about Peter. It makes sense of a lot of things that had confused me during our marriage."

"I don't even know what to say except I'm so sorry. I keep thinking about Chloe, but I know that you'll protect her."

Sarah stood up and walked to the window; she looked out at the harbour and tried to gather her thoughts.

"Are you worried that Anthony will keep trying to cause trouble for Peter and take this further?" Kate asked.

Sarah walked back to her desk and sat down to answer Kate. "Anthony is looking for revenge against Peter. It's a concern that he's now in jail for a very long time and will have more and more time to dwell on his revenge. I don't think he wants to hurt Chloe. But I don't think that will stand in the way of Anthony hurting Peter. I can't even think where it may end, because then I would have to try and understand the thought processes of a bitter, jailed man and that would send me mad. I think I'll just have to take this as it comes, get as much help and advice as I can and keep Chloe safe."

"I know Peter loves you and Chloe. Despite his mistakes in the past, I know he'll try to do the right thing by both of you."

Sarah smiled and briefly clasped one of Kate's hands across the desk. "I just got off the phone to him, Kate, and he was speechless. He couldn't even respond. I don't really know how he'll deal with this. I keep thinking of how appalling it was that he withheld it all from me, for all this time. Of course, if he had told me, there would never have been Chloe."

A call from Chloe interrupted their conversation, just as her name was mentioned. Her sweet voice piped up, Sarah answered her mobile. "Hi, Mummy, will you be home soon?'

Sarah's heart melted at the sound of Chloe's voice and because of the shock revelations, she could not prevent herself from asking, "Darling, why, is something wrong?"

"No Mum, I just wanted to read you my speech for tomorrow. I had to write it about a book character, so I'm Grumpy Cat, do you remember that book? I've been practising all night and I think it's good, so will you be home before I go to bed for me to read it to you?"

"Of course, I remember Grumpy Cat, darling! I can't wait to hear it, but I won't be home before you go to sleep because I'm going to dinner with a client, tonight. How about I call you back on Facetime and you perform it for me?"

"Mummy, we've never done that before. That's cool!" "I'll hang up and call you straight back."

Sarah called back, and Chloe delivered her speech. Sarah had a tear in her eye watching her beautiful little daughter, speaking so diligently and with such composure.

Chloe's speech came to an end and Chloe looked up and saw Sarah's tears. She cried out in surprise, "Mummy, it wasn't meant to be sad! Why are you crying?"

Sarah laughed and was glad Chloe could see her and not just hear her, "I'm not sad, sweetheart, I'm just so proud of you. That was an amazing speech. I want to hear it again in the morning, okay?"

Chloe jumped up and down, while screaming, "Really, really, really Mummy? You liked it?"

"Yes darling, I loved it. Now Grumpy Cat, I have to go and I want you to know I love you and I'm so proud of you. I'll kiss you when I get home."

"Night, Mummy. Love you too," Chloe said as she hung up the phone.

The phone rang, and Kate said to Sarah, "Your car is here to take you to dinner."

Sarah stood up, grabbed her handbag and turned to Kate, "Thanks for your support Kate. I think dinner is the distraction I need tonight."

Sarah

Chapter 78

The following morning, as Sarah drove up to the front of her office, she noticed that a large delivery truck had double-parked in the street, almost blocking the entrance. Sarah managed to manoeuvre around it, drove down into her parking space and proceeded to get into the lift. The lift stopped at the ground floor and two men stepped in, with trolleys holding several enormous and stunningly beautiful floral arrangements.

"Good morning! They are amazing flowers you have there," Sarah said to the men.

One of the men laughed, shook his head and said, "We have been up and down this lift for half an hour with a truckload of flowers that some guy has sent to one woman in this building. He apparently walked into the florist shop and told the florist that when he was stopped in traffic out the front of their shop, he noticed the magnificent flower arrangements and that he wanted to buy all the arrangements and every single flower in the shop to be delivered immediately. Can you believe how much money he's spent on this? He must be worth a mint."

"Are you serious?," asked Sarah.

"He went in and insisted on buying the entire contents of the florist shop! The girl in the shop said she thought it was the most romantic thing that she has ever seen. Do you reckon it was romantic? I've never heard of such a thing and I reckon my Mrs would have killed me if I had spent that much money sending flowers to her."

Is it romantic or crazy? Sarah asked herself.

Sarah reached to press the lift button for her floor but noticed hers was the only floor selected. Trying to be helpful, she asked, "Which floor are you going to? I'll press it for you."

"The same as you, eleven," the man replied.

The lift stopped at the eleventh floor and they all got out of the lift. Sarah only realised the men were following her when she saw that her reception area looked like a florist shop. There were vases of every sort of flower imaginable; small and large arrangements, posies, even a live rose bush.

Kate stared wide-eyed at the men as they walked in and said, "Is that it? Surely there's no more!" She proceeded to sneeze profusely.

"Good morning, Kate," Sarah said. "Are you okay? What on earth is going on?"

"No, I'm not okay, Sarah," she snapped, which was out of character for the sweet-natured Kate. "I'm having a severe allergy attack to the lilies, thanks to your stalker. What kind of joke is this? Who sends an entire florist shop to someone's office?"

"What? Are they for me?" Sarah asked, quite shocked.

"Who else would attract a lunatic who does this?" Kate replied, regretting the words as soon as they had left her lips.

"Sorry Sarah, that was unfair. I'm just slowly dying from an allergy attack, from the lilies in particular and it's making me quite an unpleasant person."

"Who is this from?" Sarah asked.

Kate replied, between sneezes, "I haven't opened any of the cards attached to the flowers, I thought I'd leave that to you."

Sarah started to sneeze as well, and she could not stop. They both laughed hysterically at the ridiculousness situation.

"It's all those lilies. They're beautiful but full of pollen. Who on earth decided it would be a good idea to send an entire florist shop to a law firm!"

Sarah opened the card attached to the closest flowers. She read aloud, "Thank you for your help, Sarah," with no further message or identification.

I'm too old and busy to play these games, whoever you are, Sarah thought and headed towards her office. She turned to Kate from her office doorway and said, "Kate, please ask the junior clerks to distribute the flowers among all the girls in the office. We need to get them away from you, especially the lilies."

"Will do that right now. Seriously, I'm sure I could have paid off my mortgage with what this would have cost."

"Yes, you probably could have," Sarah agreed, then added, "I'm not quite sure how to take this. It's weird and not normal."

Yes, it was weird and not normal, thought Sarah as she walked towards her office. *Why do I attract men who aren't normal? What is that about me?*

As she walked into her office Sarah's landline started ringing. Kate said, "It's Phil on the phone, Sarah. He said he just needs a minute with you."

"Sure Kate," Sarah replied a little curious as to why Phil was calling. *Surely, he hasn't got another problem already*, she thought as she picked up the call and said, "Hi Phil, how are you?"

Phil was quite surprised at how happy it made him feel when Sarah sounded happy to hear from him. She was making him feel happy in a way he had never felt before.

"I'm really well, Sarah. I just rang to say thanks for your advice about getting some help. In the last couple of months, I have been going to therapy and it's changed my life. I just can't believe it took me so long to realise what I needed to do."

Sarah could not believe what she was hearing. Phil really sounded like a new man. She felt touched that he had called her. "You didn't need to call to thank me, Phil. I did nothing but offer some guidance from my own experience. I'm so glad it helped."

Phil was smiling from ear to ear, Sarah had already opened up to him with saying it was from her own experience. He was sure he had a chance with her and he was not going to blow it.

"I was wondering if you and a few of your staff would like to join me and my PA on a table of ten that I have bought for a fundraiser for the Children's Hospital on Thursday night of next week. I know it's short notice, but I was told they needed a major supporter as one dropped out at the last minute, so I stepped in."

Sarah was almost speechless. The king of selfishness had gone to therapy and was now a major sponsor of an event for the Children's Hospital? She was immediately impressed and responded in an approving voice, "Of course I will come, and I'm sure my staff would love to as well Phil."

"That's great, Sarah. I will have my secretary email through the invitation to you immediately."

"I look forward to it."

Phil was delighted with how this was all falling into place and so he decided to end the call before anything could go wrong, "Me too Sarah, and I hope you enjoy the flowers", he added and hung up before she could reply.

Sarah sat stunned, staring at the phone. She shook her head and laughed to herself before she went out to Kate and said, "It was him. Phil sent the flowers."

Sarah started to laugh so loudly that several people in the front office turned to look at her. Realising this was not her normal behaviour in front of her staff, Sarah quietened down before she asked Kate, "How many relationships has Phil had in the last ten years we've acted for him?"

Kate rolled her eyes and said, "There've been six girlfriends he's settled with and he's been divorced twice, so you could say he is highly experienced."

"Oh my goodness Kate, I have been rejecting Phil for as long as he's been retaining me to act for him. After all these failed relationships, he realised something wasn't working and so he's even gone into therapy, which is something that men like Phil don't do. He is doing everything he can to convince me to be with him."

Kate looked at Sarah and it seemed that a softness had suddenly enveloped her body. She looked calm and gentle, almost glowing as she was smiling and she looked at the flowers surrounding her.

Kate replied, "By the look of things, Phil may have finally got your attention Sarah."

"It's my Achilles' heel Kate. I have always given people the benefit of the doubt that they can change. I think it came from being bullied at school. The only way I could cope with it was feeling sorry for the person bullying me and calling me names and believing that they would one day see the light and change."

Kate nodded and said, "You do tend to help a lot of people who don't deserve your help. In fact, I've never seen anyone being taken advantage of as much as you have. For an intelligent woman when it comes to men, you are sometimes very naive."

As Sarah started to rearrange the Peonies in their vase, she noticed a small envelope pinned to the ribbon wrapped around them. She opened it and saw the card had been written by hand. "Without you, everything is nothing." This was a side of Phil she had not seen before, or had she?

Sarah sat down at her desk wondering what she had gotten herself into. She had spent years with a psychologist to try and deal with her anxiety and insecurities, and yet she seemed to be falling into old habits of giving the unforgivable another chance. She could hear her therapist saying to her, "It was all those years you spent as a child feeling you were never good enough, or never entitled to love, that keeps you trying to find it in the wrong places."

"You know he won't give up?" Kate said, breaking the silence between them.

Sarah realised Kate was right, "I'm not quite sure what else to do but continue to reject his advances."

"Sack him as a client, Sarah. Can't you see the guy is so low that he is using a children's charity function to further his cause of impressing you. There's a side to you that is so naïve, and it's a shocking contrast to the extremely intelligent and worldly side. I am becoming very worried about you."

Sarah smiled as she said, "Kate, as the saying goes, if you do the same thing over and over again, expecting a different result, then its madness. I may not be totally cured of trying to see the nice side of people - even if they are clearly monsters. But I'm aware that I have a blindside and because of that, I won't make the same mistake again. Anyway, he's taking his PA to the ball and I'm dying to meet her - aren't you? Surely it's worth going just to see her in person?"

Kate laughed, "Okay you have me there. We have to meet her! I need to know what a fixer of all things good and bad looks like." Kate was relieved Sarah had changed the subject from Phil.

Sarah brought herself back to her clients and matters, "I think we should get on with our day. I'm going to make a couple of quick calls before I head off to meet Rupert for a quick coffee before I head to the Family Court at 10 a.m."

"Rupert?" Kate asked.

"You do want me to get an update on Geoffrey and Jane's cases, don't you?" Sarah replied.

"Jane's case I do. I think the funeral is this week. I couldn't care less about Geoffrey quite frankly."

Sarah started on her first call and called Hilary's mobile. Sarah was emotional as she said, "Hilary, I just wanted to thank you for all you have done for me. Without you I would probably be still under my bed, hiding from the world."

"Thank you darling, but what happened that has made you feel reflective?"

Sarah had been thinking about this call for a few weeks now and was certain it was something she wanted to do. Hilary sounded tired and Sarah was becoming alarmed at how ill she had become recently. Sarah went on to ask, "I'm just on my way to the Family Court and I wanted to run something by you before I put it to my client this morning."

"What is it Sarah?"

"I would like to offer my client's daughter one of your scholarships, but of course I want to fund it. I would like the scholarship to continue paying for the school she is currently attending. She's a lovely fifteen year old girl and her step-father has just been convicted of sexually abusing her from when she was thirteen years old. He's now in jail and I'm about to go to the Family Court to start her mother's property case, but I already know that most of the matrimonial assets have been moved or disposed of and her prospects of keeping Jessica in school for much longer are slim. I have made initial contact with the school and they are happy to help me with this."

Hilary said, "Of course you can, and we have a place for another girl to receive a scholarship for next year, but if you want to pay for her fees why don't you just do it directly?"

"I have realised life is a series of sliding doors, some by chance and some by the decisions you make. Because of you, because you cared, I got a chance and I know now how to choose the right door. I want to be able to give another girl who is having a tough time, like I was, that chance. I want this to be anonymous and the fund is the perfect way to do that. Anne is a very proud woman and she wouldn't accept this from me should I offer it. If, however, Jessica wins a scholarship that would be different."

Until this call Hilary had been feeling down and unwell, but she now her spirits lifted. Sarah was not only going to continue her legacy, but she would grow it. Hilary knew that not only would many young women benefit from this, but that Sarah would enjoy the rewards, as she herself had done, in ways that she could not yet imagine. Hilary remembered how much joy it had given her over the last thirty years to watch all her girls develop through their school years, with the assistance of her scholarship, especially Sarah. These moments had made the loss of her only child bearable, as it had given it a purpose.

Sarah wondered if Hilary was upset by her request as there was a long silence at the other end of the phone. She asked softly, "Hilary are you still there?"

"Yes, I am Sarah", Hilary assured her." "I'm sorry for pausing. I was touched by your generosity to this family and how you, like me, know the importance of helping people anonymously. Of course, you can do this through the scholarship fund. I am delighted."

The joy Sarah felt surprised her, and she told Hilary how grateful she was. "Thank you, Hilary. I really wanted to be able to give this lady some good news today. I know the only thing that matters to her is her daughter and that she can continue her education."

"How are they coping financially?"

"She's lucky to have a very supportive and financially secure sister with no children. This is her biggest problem right now and I'm sure if I can take this issue away, she will manage with her sister's help to move on with the rest of her life."

"I am so happy we can help her Sarah," Hilary replied. She wondered if Sarah could tell that she had a lump in her throat.

"Without you I wouldn't be helping anyone Hilary and I know that. Thank you for letting me do this, Hilary.

"My pleasure, Sarah. Now you had better head off to court," Hilary replied and they said their goodbyes to each other.

Hilary walked to her bedroom window and looked out onto her beautiful gardens, which were in full bloom. She knew that Sarah and Chloe would love living here as much as she had and that gave her great consolation during these dark remaining days. She wondered what Sarah's life would have been if her parents had not died in the car accident and she wondered how different her life would have been if her own daughter had survived; an event which led to the end of her marriage. Knowing her days were numbered, and knowing she wanted to share all she had with Sarah, she sat at her desk to continue writing her memoir, "To Be Continued".

Love Bites is the first novel by Julie Singleton. Julie lives in Sydney, Australia and is the mother of four children. Julie was admitted to practice as a lawyer in NSW in 1990, working mainly in the area of Family Law.

www.juliesingleton.com

www.ingramcontent.com/pod-product-compliance
Lightning Source LLC
Chambersburg PA
CBHW030958260626
47169CB00002B/591